COMPETITIVE ADVANTAGE THROUGH PEOPLE

COMPETITIVE ADVANTAGE THROUGH PEOPLE

Unleashing the Power of the Work Force

JEFFREY PFEFFER
Stanford University
Graduate School of Business

HARVARD BUSINESS SCHOOL PRESS
Boston, Massachusetts

First published in the United States by the Harvard Business School
Press in hard cover, 1994; in paperback, 1995
Copyright © 1994 by Jeffrey Pfeffer
All rights reserved
Printed in the United States of America

99   5   (pbk.)

LIBRARY OF CONGRESS CATALOGING-IN-PUBLICATION DATA
Pfeffer, Jeffrey.
    Competitive advantage through people: unleashing the power
of the work force / Jeffrey Pfeffer.
      p. cm.
    Includes bibliographical references and index.
    ISBN 0-87584-413-8 (hc)
    ISBN 0-87584-717-X (pbk)
    1. Personnel management—United States. 2. Organizational
behavior—United States. 3. Competition—United States.
I. Title.
HF5549.2.U5P5 1994
658.3'14—dc20   93-26599
                                                  CIP

The paper used in this publication meets the requirements of the
American National Standard for Permanence of Paper for Printed
Library Materials Z39.49-1984.

Contents

105338

PART **III**

Prospects for Change

Acknowledgments

This book has only one author, but many people have provided tremendous encouragement and assistance in its development.
When Jim Baron joined the Stanford faculty in 1982, in addition to
teaching our core course in organizational behavior, he wanted to develop an elective. "Why not do something that incorporates your research in organizations and labor markets?" I said. The elective he first
taught, which I subsequently taught and which he now teaches again,
will soon be part of our core curriculum. The absence of a good text for
the course prompted me to write this book. Over the years, he and I
have spent numerous hours talking about issues in the management of
a firm's human resources. Not only has he been a great colleague, but he
took a first draft of this manuscript on a trip to Singapore and provided
detailed comments on his return. He, and the students I have taught in
the course, have helped me clarify my thinking enormously.

A number of friends provided useful commentary on early drafts of
the manuscript. Beth Benjamin once again took time away from her

doctoral dissertation and Stan Winvick stole time from his busy schedule at Advanced Micro Devices to provide very important guidance.

Much of what I know about achieving competitive advantage through the work force I have learned from some truly remarkable individuals in interesting firms. Dave Spence and Jay Duhon of Boise Cascade, Vit Eckersdorf of Bofors, and Peter Thigpen of Levi Strauss were kind enough to share their wisdom and experience with both me and my students. Robert Mountain, Bill Izabal, and numerous managers gave freely of their time to describe the process of changing human resource practices at ESL. Stan Winvick and his colleagues at AMD arranged opportunities to learn about what that firm was doing, how, and why.

Special thanks go to two people. Rick Seaman, a student of mine at Stanford is now with the Solectron Corporation. He, Walt Wilson, manager of the Milpitas site, Ko Nishimura, the CEO, and many other Solectron employees provided important information and perspective. Rick read a first draft of the manuscript. Working in a Baldrige-award-winning company, he was used to measures. So he gave me a chart showing the proportion of each of those chapters he had highlighted. I hope I did better with this version. And Charles O'Reilly, who moved from Berkeley to Stanford as the book was being written, read the manuscript *twice*, providing examples, insights, and most of all, encouragement and enthusiasm. As I revised the manuscript, Rick's and Charles' questions and comments were foremost in my mind.

This is my sixth book and the second with the Harvard Business School Press. My friends at the Press, particularly Carol Franco, my editor, and Natalie Greenberg, an editor who can both devastate your work and help it at the same time, as well as the people who market the books, have earned my undying gratitude. They all exemplify the idea of quality people and a quality organization. I appreciate all their efforts on my behalf.

The Stanford Graduate School of Business supports me generously. I particularly appreciate our dean, Mike Spence, and my colleagues in organizational behavior who almost always understand that my primary job is research and teaching and give me the time and freedom to do it—and don't complain about my missing meetings, when I do, too loudly.

This book would never have been finished on time, or perhaps at all, without the gracious, friendly, and extraordinarily competent help of my assistant, Joni Podolsky. Joni provided comments, questions, and editing. Working with her on this project has been a pleasure.

This book is dedicated to the amazing Kathleen, the keeper of my spirit, my best friend, and a person of beauty, grace, and above all, courage and determination.

PERFORMANCE THROUGH PEOPLE

I

Sources of Sustained Success

1

Suppose that in 1972, someone asked you to pick the five companies that would provide the greatest return to stockholders over the next 20 years. And suppose that you had access to books on competitive success that were not even written. How would you approach your assignment? In order to earn tremendous economic returns, the companies you picked should have some sustainable competitive advantage, something that 1) distinguishes them from their competitors, 2) provides positive economic benefits, and 3) is not readily duplicated.

Conventional wisdom then (and even now) would have you begin by selecting the right industries. After all, "not all industries offer equal opportunity for sustained profitability, and the inherent profitability of its industry is one essential ingredient in determining the profitability of a firm."[1] According to Michael Porter's now famous framework, the five fundamental competitive forces that determine the ability of firms in an industry to earn above-normal returns are "the entry of new competitors, the threat of substitutes, the bargaining power of buyers, the bargaining power of suppliers, and the rivalry among existing competitors."[2] You should find industries with barriers to entry, low supplier and buyer bargaining power, few ready substitutes, and a limited threat of new entrants to compete away economic returns. Within such industries, other conventional analyses would urge you to select firms with the largest market share, which can realize the cost benefits of economies of scale. In short, you would probably look to industries in which patent protection of important product or service technology could be achieved and select the dominant firms in those industries.

You would have been very successful in selecting the five top-performing firms from 1972 to 1992 if you took this conventional wisdom and turned it on its head. The top five stocks, and their percentage returns, were (in reverse order): Plenum Publishing (with a return of 15,689%), Circuit City (a video and appliance retailer; 16,410%), Tyson Foods (a poultry producer; 18,118%), Wal-Mart (a discount chain; 19,807%), and Southwest Airlines (21,775%).[3] Yet during this period, these industries (retailing, airlines, publishing, and food processing) were characterized by massive competition and horrendous losses, widespread bankruptcy, virtually no barriers to entry (for airlines after 1978), little unique or proprietary technology, and many substitute products or services. And in 1972, none of these firms was (and some still are not) the market-share leader, enjoying economies of scale from moving down the learning curve.

The point here is not to throw out conventional strategic analysis based on industrial economics but simply to note that the source of competitive advantage has always shifted over time. What these five successful firms tend to have in common is that for their sustained advantage, they rely not on technology, patents, or strategic position, but on how they manage their work force. Our first task is to explore how and why some sources of competitive success that were important in the past are less so now and why the work force, and how it is organized and managed, is an increasingly important source of competitive advantage. This is the topic of this chapter. The chapter also considers how achieving competitive advantage through the work force affects the development of some human resource policies and practices.

Remember, to provide extraordinary returns over time, any source of competitive advantage must be difficult to imitate. So after Chapter 2 describes some of the critical elements of a system for effectively managing the work force, and Chapter 3 provides evidence for the success of these practices, it is time to consider in some detail the barriers, both internal and external, that make doing the right thing with respect to managing the work force so difficult. If we are, either as individual organizations or as a society, to move to more effective ways of managing the work force and to implementing what we know with a shorter time lag, it is imperative that we fully understand the factors that stand in our way. Chapter 4 argues that some of the barriers are the business heroes, the implicit theories of behavior, and the language used in managing people. Chapter 5 considers the legacy of a history of adversarial relations and how that history can and must be overcome to have much chance of becoming more effective. Chapter 6 treats the U.S. legal system and shows how it provides neither justice nor a framework for effective management practice. Chapter 7 considers the potentially positive role of labor organizations in overcoming some of these barriers as well as why this potential is so seldom exploited. Chapter 8 describes various sources of internal corporate resistance, and some ways of overcoming that resistance. Having considered the various barriers to doing the right thing, I treat the issue of change in the last section of the book. Chapters 9 and 10 provide some evidence for the positive effects of the quality movement in reforming the management of the work force and review a framework for considering work force practices that some companies have used with encouraging results.

The very factors that made Southwest Airlines, Wal-Mart, Plenum, and other organizations such as Nordstrom, Lincoln Electric, and the New United Motor plant of the Toyota–GM joint venture so successful are things that are difficult to imitate. That is what provides such competitive leverage, the ability to almost literally make gold out of lead— exceptional economic returns in highly competitive, almost mundane industries. The paradox of this book, and of courses and seminars in how to manage the work force, is that even if we succeed in changing what we do, the basis of sustained competitive success will alter again.

At the moment, however, we are a long way from having to worry about that problem.

THE CHANGING BASIS OF COMPETITIVE SUCCESS

People and how we manage them are becoming more important because many other sources of competitive success are less powerful than they once were. Recognizing that the basis for competitive advantage has changed is essential to develop a different frame of reference for considering issues of management and strategy. Traditional sources of success—product and process technology, protected or regulated markets, access to financial resources, and economies of scale—can still provide competitive leverage, but to a lesser degree now than in the past, leaving organizational culture and capabilities, derived from how people are managed, as comparatively more vital.

Product and Process Technology

One important source of competitive advantage was product technology, protected by patents or other proprietary know-how. In 1959, Xerox developed and prepared to introduce its first plain-paper copier. Some 13 years later, in 1972, it enjoyed a market share of more than 90% with machines that, although improved, still relied, fundamentally, on the same technological foundation. How many companies, industries, or products today could retain more than 90% of the market on the basis of 13-year-old technology? A quote from the annual report of Sun Microsystems, a computer workstation manufacturer, makes the point: "Sun's avowed intention [is] doubling the performance of its high-end workstations about every 18 months, on average."[4]

Since product life cycles are shortening and new-product introductions are coming much more rapidly, relying on a static product technology for success is increasingly problematic:

> Research has shown that new product introductions are vital to most manufacturing firms' growth and prosperity. A Booz, Allen and Hamilton

study of over 700 *Fortune* 1000 companies estimated that new products would provide over 30 percent of these firms' profits during a five-year period from 1981–1986. . . . The same study suggested that the number of new products introduced by these firms was expected to double compared to the previous five-year period.[5]

The rapid development of computer-aided design (CAD), computer-aided manufacture (CAM), the linking of design and manufacture in CAD/CAM systems, and a myriad of other innovations that facilitate product design and introduction all erode how long one can achieve competitive success solely through proprietary product or service technology. George Stalk and Thomas Hout argue that the growing rate of product obsolescence makes the ability to rapidly innovate increasingly important.[6] They found that market share, profits, and costs are all related to the speed with which companies can accomplish things. Peter Thigpen, former senior vice president of manufacturing at Levi Strauss, noted that, assuming a 20% annual growth rate in the market, a 12% annual price erosion, and a five-year product life, a 50% development cost overrun results in a 3.5% reduction in after-tax profits; production costs that are 9% too high result in a 22% reduction in profits; but being just six months late in shipping the product costs a full one-third of the after-tax profit potential.[7]

The increasing pace of product change means that a technical edge, even once achieved, will erode quickly and must be renewed. The need for continuous innovation and rapid response to market and technological changes virtually requires a work force that delivers superior performance.

Not only is the length of product life cycles diminishing, there is an erosion in the protection provided by patents because of competitors' ability to imitate product innovations. One of the most comprehensive studies of this question examined 48 product innovations of firms in the chemical, drug, electronics, and machinery industries.[8] The study found that, on average, the imitation cost to innovation cost ratio was approximately .65, and the ratio of imitation time to innovation time was about .70.[9] Although patents provided some protection, particularly in pharmaceuticals, the protection was less than one might think. "Contrary to popular opinion, patent protection does not make entry impossible, or even unlikely. Within 4 years of their introduction, 60% of the patented successful innovations . . . were imitated."[10]

Firms sought competitive advantage not only in their product technology but also in the process technology used to produce the product or service. General Motors was perhaps the archetype of this approach, investing heavily in technology to automate its factories in the 1980s. The company spent some $40 billion for modernization and new facilities, in the process substituting fixed costs for variable costs.[11] In fact, GM spent enough money on capital equipment to have purchased both Honda and Nissan.[12] Unfortunately, it did not get much for that investment.

There are several problems with seeking competitive advantage through investments in process technology. First, little of that technology is proprietary—the people who sell you robots or point-of-sale terminals or software to analyze production or service delivery will sell the robots, terminals, and software to your competitors. Your ability to obtain the benefits of, let alone get any advantage from, this technology—which is often widely available and readily understood—depends on your ability to implement it more rapidly and more effectively. This almost inevitably involves the skill and motivation of the work force.

Second, investment in specialized technology is not a substitute for skill in managing the work force; it actually makes the work force even more crucial for success. This is because more skill may be required to operate the more sophisticated and advanced equipment, and with a higher level of investment per employee, interruptions in the process are increasingly expensive. This means that the ability to effectively operate, maintain, and repair equipment—tasks all done by first-line employees—becomes even more critical.

Paul Adler noted that "in banks, a fully on-line system integrating numerous branches meant that people at the extremities . . . would have to be absolutely reliable, since any data they entered . . . would be fed instantaneously into all the bank's accounts and corresponding funds transferred instantaneously."[13] He also noted that in the case of numerically controlled machine tools, in spite of manufacturers' promises, the skill requirements of machinists have remained constant or increased. They often required expanded training and higher levels of responsibility, even with the more technologically sophisticated machines.

When the Shenandoah Life Insurance Company spent some $2 million to computerize its processing and claims operations in the early 1980s, it found that it got almost nothing for its expenditure—it still required 27 working days and 32 clerks in three departments to handle a policy conversion.[14] Only after the company changed how it organized and managed its work force—relying on semiautonomous teams of 5 to 7 people, upgrading training and skills, and paying more for the more responsible and more skilled workers—did case-handling time drop and service complaints virtually disappear. "By 1986, Shenandoah was processing 50% more applications and queries with 10% fewer employees than it did in 1980."[15]

Finally, investments in process technology provide only limited competitive advantage because, as the senior manufacturing executive in the paper-making division of a large forest products company said, "Machines don't make things, people do." Commenting on the tremendous investment in advanced computer technology to automate factory processes, one writer perceptively noted: "[I]t is rather ironic that the application of artificial intelligence to manufacturing is becoming a popular topic. If intelligence is so helpful to manufacturing in its artificial form, then why have the benefits of the real intelligence been overlooked so far."[16]

Protected and Regulated Markets

Another way in which firms achieved competitive success was by avoiding competition through protected or regulated domestic markets. Some years ago while visiting Italy, I noticed that there were many Fiats and almost no Japanese cars—indeed, only about 2,000 Japanese cars per year were sold in Italy during the mid-1980s. This sales level did not reflect the relative prices and product qualities or consumer tastes, but resulted from a limit on the imports of Japanese cars. Fearful of the power and success of Fiat after World War II, Japan struck a bargain in which the Japanese automobile market would be protected from Fiat while the Italian market would be protected from Japanese automakers.

With the growing importance of free-trade areas in Europe, North America, and elsewhere, and with the increasing investment in manufacturing facilities all over the world (e.g., the building of Japanese automobile plants in the United States and Europe), the ability to sustain competitive success by foreclosing markets is disappearing. The changing role of foreign trade in the United States and the world economies over the past few decades has been truly remarkable—and the growth of both exports and imports means that firms are now competing not only domestically but globally: "In 1950 real exports and imports of goods and services were under 5 percent of real GNP. . . . [B]y 1980 real exports and imports were 12.2 percent and 10.4 percent of real GNP, respectively. In 1988 exports were 13.1 percent and imports 15 percent of GNP."[17] Thus, between 1950 and 1990, foreign trade grew from less than 5% to almost 30% of the U.S. gross national product.

The automobile industry nicely illustrates the move toward the internationalization of markets and its consequences. The share of imports in the U.S. passenger car market soared from 7.3% in 1966 to 14.8% 10 years later and to 29.3% by 1982.[18] Similar increases were occurring elsewhere as well—from 1966 to 1982, imports of passenger cars in France rose from 13.9% to 21.7%; in Germany from 13.7% to 24.9%; and in the United Kingdom from just 5% to 57.7%. As markets opened to foreign competition, production of motor vehicles shifted. In 1950, companies in the United States produced some 75.4% of the total world output of motor vehicles (trucks, buses, and automobiles), with Europe producing 19.8% and Japan essentially none.[19] Thirty years later, motor vehicle production located in Europe was 37.6%, 28.6% in Japan, and only 20.8% in the United States. The globalization of competition has occurred in telecommunications equipment and financial services as well. For instance, 31% of the business loans, 21% of the assets, and 14% of the total deposits in the United States are now controlled by foreign or foreign-owned banks.[20]

Regulation can limit competition by setting prices and by restricting entry.[21] In the United States, for many years entry into transportation industries such as airlines and trucking was strictly controlled. MCI's success as a provider of long-distance telephone service came only after the company won a protracted struggle to even be permitted to operate. The wave of deregulation sweeping the United States and the rest of the world, however, has eliminated many protected markets. Moreover, there is some evidence that once deregulated and opened to competition, markets are difficult to close or reregulate. Thus, these trends seem to be irreversible.

Access to Financial Resources

Another traditional source of competitive advantage was access to financial resources. With less efficient capital markets, a firm's ability to finance itself through substantial financial resources afforded protection from competitors less able to acquire the resources necessary to mount a serious challenge. This source of competitive advantage has eroded in the face of increasingly efficient financial markets in which capital moves worldwide on an unprecedented scale. The venture capital industry is now international, so that if U.S. investors, for instance, are unwilling to bear the risk of financing leading-edge technologies in pharmaceuticals, semiconductors, and equipment, foreign investors will pick up the slack. Table 1-1 is a partial listing of the extent of direct foreign investment in important California leading-edge companies and technologies in the 1980s.

As one author noted:

> The growth of international direct investment by multinational corporations has outpaced the growth of the world economy and world trade in the 1980s. . . . Not only do United States multinational corporations face stronger competition from foreign multinationals in international markets, but affiliates of foreign firms—often with new production technologies and different management techniques—have become more active in the United States.[22]

Between 1967 and 1987, worldwide outward direct investment increased from $112 billion to $1.023 trillion, an average annual growth rate of 12.4%. The U.S. share of this outward direct investment declined from 50% to 31%. Meanwhile, direct foreign investment in the United States grew dramatically, from $9.9 billion in 1967 to $272 billion in

Table 1-1   Selected Examples of Direct Foreign Investment in California, 1981–1990

Firm	Investor	Country	Percentage Holding
Biotechnology			
Genentech	Roche	Switzerland	60
Mycogen	Kubota	Japan	9.6
Chiron	CIBA-Geigy	Switzerland	6.2
Genencor	Cultor Oy/Kodak	Finland/U.S.	100
Cetus	Roche	Switzerland	3.5
Cytel	Sandoz	Switzerland	100
Semiconductors and Equipment			
Zymos	Daewoo	South Korea	35
Siltec	Mitsubishi	Japan	33
Varian's Tube Division	Thorn EMI	United Kingdom	100
Siscan Systems	Mitsubishi	Japan	11.5
Computer Hardware and Peripherals			
NeXT	Canon	Japan	17
Poquet Computer	Fujitsu	Japan	38
MIPS Computer	Kubota	Japan	25
Ardent Computer	Kubota	Japan	44
Wyse	Private investors	Taiwan	100
System Integrators	Birmingham	United Kingdom	100
Fortune Systems	French government	France	100

Source: David J. Teece, "Foreign Investment and Technological Development in Silicon Valley," Copyright 1992 by The Regents of the University of California. Reprinted from the *California Management Review*, Vol. 34, No. 2. By permission of The Regents.

1987, a growth rate of some 17.8% per year.[23] Capital is now less important as a source of competitive advantage because the money to finance a good idea, or strong management, is increasingly available to all attractive projects.

Economies of Scale

Yet another source of competitive advantage that is now less significant than it used to be is economies of scale. The famous Boston Consulting

Group experience curve postulated that a firm that entered a market early and achieved large production volumes would face significantly lower costs as it achieved the benefits of learning as well as more traditional scale economies. Although there is some evidence for the economic benefits of large market share,[24] there is much evidence that this source of competitive advantage is diminishing in importance. The trend toward more fragmented markets, with the need to cater to the specialized tastes of particular subsegments of the population, has been described in detail by Piore and Sabel in their book about flexible specialization.[25] In general, the same computer-aided design and manufacturing technologies that make imitation easier also make it possible to more economically design and manufacture a more differentiated product line.

Several examples help make the point. Consider first so-called natural monopolies, such as telecommunications and electric power generation. Even here, evolving technology makes it possible for smaller competitors to effectively exploit market segments. In downtown Chicago, an independent company laid its own fiber-optic cable and provides telephone service to a set of commercial clients in that densely populated area. Stanford University has its own telephone system to handle both data and voice communications on the campus. Electric utilities compete with industrial clients that now dispose of their wastes in co-generation facilities, which produce power from the heat. In the steel industry, the so-called minimills are a well-known phenomenon, in many instances more profitable and cost-competitive than their larger competitors. The ability of the Japanese to make car models profitably, even when they sell fewer than 100,000 units per year, has given firms with that capability a tremendous competitive advantage. And finally, the textile industry, particularly suppliers of men's clothing, traditionally competed on the basis of price and did so by making large lots of standard products. With major retailers now wanting to stock leaner inventories and be more responsive to shifting customer tastes and what actually sells, the basis of success has shifted to the ability to deliver the product quickly. "Rather than allowing order response times of one month or more, the lean retailer currently requires 13 days for order fulfillment. In two years, the response time will decrease to 6 days."[26]

Without debating whether scale economies and market share ever provided the advantages that some claimed, it is clear that whatever those advantages, they are smaller now than they once were and will probably be even smaller in the future.

The Importance of the Work Force and How It Is Managed

As other sources of competitive success have become less important, what remains as a crucial, differentiating factor is the organization, its employees, and how they work. Consider, for instance, Southwest Airlines, whose stock had the best return from 1972 to 1992. It certainly did not achieve that success from economies of scale. In 1992, Southwest had revenues of $1.31 billion and a mere 2.6% of the U.S. passenger market.[27] People Express, by contrast, achieved $1 billion in revenues after only 3 years of operation, not the almost 20 it took Southwest. Southwest exists not because of regulated or protected markets but in spite of them. "During the first three years of its history, no Southwest planes were flown."[28] Southwest waged a battle for its very existence with competitors that sought to keep it from flying at all and, failing that, made sure it did not fly out of the newly constructed Dallas–Fort Worth international airport. Instead, it was restricted to operating out of the close-in Love Field, and thus was born its first advertising slogan, "Make Love, Not War." Southwest became the "love" airline out of necessity, not choice.

In 1978, competitors sought to bar flights from Love Field to anywhere outside of Texas. The compromise Southwest wrangled permitted it to fly from Love to the four states contiguous to Texas.[29] Its competitive strategy of short-haul, point-to-point flights to close-in airports (it now flies into Chicago's Midway and Houston's Hobby airports) was more a product of its need to adapt to what it was being permitted to do than a conscious, planned move—although, in retrospect, the strategy has succeeded brilliantly. Nor has Southwest succeeded because it has had more access to lower-cost capital—indeed, it is one of the least leveraged airlines in the United States. Southwest's planes, Boeing

737s, are obviously available to all its competitors. It isn't a member of any of the big computerized reservation systems; it uses no unique process technology and sells essentially a commodity product—low-cost, low-frills airline service at prices its competitors have difficulty matching.

Much of its cost advantage comes from its very productive, very motivated, and by the way, unionized work force. Compared to the U.S. airline industry, according to 1991 statistics, Southwest has fewer employees per aircraft (79 versus 131), flies more passengers per employee (2,318 versus 848), and has more available seat miles per employee (1,891,082 versus 1,339,995).[30] It turns around some 80% of its flights in 15 minutes or less, while other airlines on average need 45 minutes, giving it an enormous productivity advantage in terms of equipment utilization.[31] It also provides an exceptional level of passenger service. Southwest has won the airlines' so-called triple crown (best on-time performance, fewest lost bags, and fewest passenger complaints—in the same month) *nine* times. No competitor has achieved that even once.[32]

I will give numerous examples of achieving competitive success through people in this book. What is important to recognize now is why success, such as that achieved at Southwest, can be sustained and can not readily be imitated by competitors. There are two fundamental reasons. First, the success that comes from managing people effectively is often not as visible or transparent as to its source. We can see a computerized information system, a particular semiconductor, a numerically controlled machine tool. The culture and practices that enable Southwest to achieve its success are less obvious. Even when they are described, as they have been in numerous newspaper articles and even a segment on "60 Minutes," they are difficult to really understand. Culture, how people are managed, and the effects of this on their behavior and skills are sometimes seen as the "soft" side of business, occasionally dismissed. Even when they are not dismissed, it is often hard to comprehend the dynamics of a particular company and how it operates because the way people are managed often fits together in a system. It is easy to copy one thing but much more difficult to copy numerous things. This is because the change needs to be more comprehensive and also because the ability to understand the system of management practices is hindered by its very extensiveness.

Thus, for example, Nordstrom, the department store chain, has enjoyed substantial success both in customer service and in sales and profitability growth over the years. Nordstrom compensates its employees in part with commissions. Not surprisingly, many of its competitors, after finally acknowledging Nordstrom's success, and the fact that it was attributable to the behaviors of its employees, instituted commission systems. By itself, changing the compensation system did not fully capture what Nordstrom had done, nor did it provide many benefits to the competition. Indeed, in some cases, changing the compensation system produced employee grievances and attempts to unionize when the new system was viewed as unfair or arbitrary.

Achieving competitive success through people involves fundamentally altering how we think about the work force and the employment relationship. It means achieving success by working *with* people, not by replacing them or limiting the scope of their activities. It entails seeing the work force as a source of strategic advantage, not just as a cost to be minimized or avoided. Firms that take this different perspective are often able to successfully outmaneuver and outperform their rivals. In the remainder of this chapter, I address two issues—training and the use of contingent work force—to show how viewing people as a source of success changes the formulation of both public policy and managerial strategy.

TRAINING AND SKILL DEVELOPMENT

If competitive success is achieved through people, then the skills of those people are critical. Consequently, one of the most obvious implications of the changing basis of competitive success is the growing importance of having a work force with adequate skills. Historical studies show that between 1929 and 1982, education prior to work accounted for 26% of the growth in the productive capacity of the United States, with learning on the job contributing to an additional 55%. It seems clear that "learning in school and learning on the job are by far the most important factors behind American economic growth and productivity in this century, and will determine the nation's economic prospects in the next."[33] The evidence, however, is that skill problems in the U.S. work force are widespread and growing. Moreover, there is little evidence that U.S. employers, for the most part, are doing what is required to address this problem.

Regarding the first point, the skill problem, an overview of training and preparation for work concluded, "As we approach the end of this century, it becomes ever more apparent that the demand for more skilled workers is on a collision course with the quantity and quality of the labor supply."[34] In an article reporting the declining position of the United States in world trade in telecommunications equipment, the New York Telephone Company reported that "it tested 57,000 job applicants in 1987 and found that 54,900, or 96.3%, lacked basic skills in math, reading, and reasoning."[35] A human resource planning document prepared at the Bank of America in 1990 reported that "Chemical Bank in New York must interview 40 applicants to find one who can be successfully trained as a teller";[36] "at Pacific Bell in Los Angeles, 95% of the 3,500 people who recently took a competency test for entry-level jobs not requiring a high school education failed"; and "at Motorola, 80% of its applicants cannot pass a simple 7th grade English comprehension or 5th grade math test. At Bell South in Atlanta, fewer than 1 in 10 applicants meet all qualification standards."[37]

A U.S. Department of Education report covering document, prose, and quantitative literacy summarized the findings of a study mandated by Congress because of its concern about skill deficiencies in the work place and came to equally grim conclusions.[38] For instance, in 1986, only about 50% of all high school graduates achieved literacy at a level that would enable them to follow directions to travel from one location to another using a map, and only 10% of the graduates could use a bus schedule to select the appropriate bus for given departures and arrivals.[39] Only 3% of high school graduates could orally interpret distinctions between types of employee benefits, and just 4.5% could estimate cost using grocery unit-price labels.[40] Assessments of mathematical proficiency are also distressing.[41] Almost one-quarter of high school seniors could not accurately determine the cost of a simple meal from a short menu of items and prices,[42] and fewer than half "demonstrated a consistent grasp of decimals, percents, fractions, and simple algebra."[43]

The response to the skills deficit, and to the growing recognition that competitive success will depend on a firm's employees, has been less than overwhelming. For instance, "though 73% of employers polled by placement consultant Right Associates expect a skilled-labor shortage, three fourths don't have a plan to keep most-needed workers."[44] A follow-up to the famous Workforce 2000 report undertaken by the Hudson Institute and the consulting firm Towers Perrin

> reports pressing shortages of technical, professional and secretarial workers at many companies. . . . But managers aren't responding to the changes quickly enough, the study suggests. It cites a lack of "leading-edge" recruitment and training strategies. . . . Companies . . . have been slow to make a strong commitment to training the workers they do hire. Two-thirds of the surveyed firms spend less than $2,000 for classroom and other on-the-job education for first-year workers.[45]

Training tends to go to those already fairly well trained, most often in the management or professional ranks. Much less is done to upgrade the skills of front-line employees. The Bank of America's human resource planning document noted that "nation-wide companies are three to four times more likely to offer workshops on stress-management or how to run meetings than to train laborers seeking to upgrade their positions."[46] Another study reported that while 17% of executive, administrative, and managerial personnel received training provided by their employers in a given year, the comparable figure for machine operators was 4%.[47]

There are several reasons why many organizations provide less training than is optimal. First, unlike many other countries, the United States presently has no specific public policy designed to encourage training. Although such expenditures are obviously tax-deductible, in many countries there is a requirement that 1% or so of payroll (wages) be spent on training. If less than the prescribed amount is spent, the difference goes to the government as a tax. Also, unlike many other countries, there is little coordination from the government, industry associations, or other collective organizations to formulate training policy and standards and to facilitate the training enterprise. For instance, in New Zealand, legislation has established coordinating bodies for training in various industries, and these bodies tend to be active in setting standards, developing curricula, implementing certification, and so forth.

Second, the costs of training funded by the company are clear and immediate, but the benefits are often long term and may, in fact, accrue to other organizations. If I train someone and the person leaves to work for another employer, then the other organization obtains the benefits of my organization's expenditures. Economic theory, consequently, suggests that general training, of use in numerous jobs, be funded by the trainee, who, after all, stands to reap the benefits. Firm-specific training, for skills that are of use primarily to a particular organization, should be funded by that organization. Of course, what constitutes general or firm-specific training is likely to be very much open to question, and firms will therefore have a tendency to underinvest in skill development.

Third, training's benefits are inherently long term. Under the pressure of short-term budget or profit pressure, training, particularly in the United States, is often the first thing to be cut. Every dollar saved on skill building this year flows immediately to pretax profit, and the loss of competitive position that may be caused is less clearly visible and, in any event, will probably occur only sometime in the future.

This, however, does mean that organizations that choose to do so can use training, and the skills developed thereby, as a competitive weapon. As one example, consider the New United Motor automobile assembly plant in Fremont, California, a joint venture of Toyota and General Motors. Under the agreement establishing the joint venture, a certain proportion of the production was to go to Toyota and a portion to GM. When the Nova was being produced for GM at the plant, and sales weren't sufficient to keep the plant busy, rather than laying off workers, the company gave them other tasks such as painting and repair, and trained them extensively in statistical process control (SPC), how to work in groups, how to analyze jobs and the work process, and so forth. The plant manager at the time remarked that in the 1990s, having a skilled and committed work force would be the key to success in the automobile industry and wanted to ensure that this facility would be competitive with the best in the world. Indeed, many of the Japanese transplant automobile assembly facilities surprised people with the extensive training they provided workers. Often, selected workers were sent to Japan prior to the start-up, and workers were routinely given as much as four times the amount of initial training that was customary in the U.S. automobile industry. This training obviously costs money, but the Japanese believed that it would produce a work force with the skills to provide a competitive advantage in an industry facing excess manufacturing capacity.

Using training to gain a competitive edge is diffusing to U.S. auto-makers as well. When General Motors opened a new truck plant in Fort Wayne, Indiana, that relied not only on new technology but also on team-based production, both workers and management went through intensive training in group problem solving and interpersonal dynamics.[48] The 3,000 employees at the factory received 1.9 million hours of training, or about 633 hours per worker, to learn the new technology and develop skills in working in teams.

At Advanced Micro Devices' submicron development center, a state-of-the-art development and manufacturing facility producing wafers with circuits of less than 1 micron in width, the company spends over 40,000 hours and $1 million per year on training for its approximately 400 employees in the facility. The firm believes that this training, and other innovative practices, are the only way to benefit from a capital investment in plant and advanced manufacturing equipment in excess of $300 million.

In a world in which your competitors treat training as a luxury, don't know how to organize and deliver it, and don't link it tightly to the strategic objectives of the business, your organization's ability to maintain appropriate training can produce real competitive advantage.

Moreover, public policies that facilitate, encourage, or enable training enhance the competitiveness of those who are subject to those policies.

THE "EXTERNALIZATION" OF EMPLOYMENT

If competitive success is achieved through people—if the work force is, indeed, an increasingly important source of competitive advantage—then it is important to build a work force that has the ability to achieve competitive success and that cannot be readily duplicated by others. Somewhat ironically, the recent trend toward using temporary help, part-time employees, and contract workers, particularly when such people are used in core activities, flies in the face of the changing basis of competitive success. This raises the questions of why these practices seem to be growing, what effects they have on the ability to achieve advantage through people, and what the implications are for organizations that might follow a different strategy.

At the most fundamental level, it is obvious that, at the limit, if all employees are temps or contract workers, or even if they are part-timers, they cannot serve as a basis of distinction. As is the case with technological equipment, the temporary agencies will furnish staff to all customers. Outside contractors will work for anyone, and part-timers, many of whom are in that status involuntarily, have insufficient attachment or commitment to a particular organization to provide it with some comparative advantage. Consider the case of professional services, such as law, accounting, or management consulting. Why use McKinsey, the consulting firm, or Jones, Day, the large law firm, or KPMG Peat Marwick, the accounting firm, and pay a premium price to do so, if these companies simply hired contract or temporary workers? The distinctive competence of a professional services firm is the skill of its staff and if those people can be obtained just as readily elsewhere, and if they have no attachment to a particular firm, then the competitive position of the organization is diminished. This is why many well-managed professional services firms emphasize recruitment, selection, and building strong cultures to retain the skilled employees who constitute the basis for their success. To the extent that people are a source of competitive success for firms other than those in professional services, the same logic applies.

Nevertheless, taking employees out of the organization or diminishing their attachment to it is a growing trend.[49] For instance, between 1970 and 1984, the temp industry outgrew the GNP by almost 2 to 1 and grew 21% faster than even the computing equipment industry over that same time period. A study of flexible employment in California reported that the number of temps grew 800% from 1972 to 1985, more than seven times the rate of employment growth in nonagricultural industries.[50] Contracting for services has made business services industry growth outstrip even the growth of services provided to consumers—with employment doubling between 1974 and 1984.[51] Part-time work has also increased in prominence. As the nonagricultural work force grew 54% between 1970 and 1990, the number of people involuntarily employed part time increased more than 120%,[52] so that by 1985, part-time work constituted almost a quarter of total employment in the state of California.[53]

The reasons behind this growth are many. It is often much quicker to staff using these sources of labor. Hiring a so-called permanent employee requires possibly posting the job, collecting applications, screening, and making a final selection. Getting a temporary requires a phone call, and the person can often be there within an hour. Speed in filling the position is a mixed blessing, however. On the one hand, you get someone quickly. On the other hand, the absence of the formal process may mean you have people who would not meet the regular requirements. In a study at Apple Computer, managers were asked whether they would be willing to hire the contingent employees on a regular basis. In about 80% of the cases, the response was that the person did not meet Apple's hiring standards. These same people, however, performed almost 25% of the corporation's jobs in the mid-1980s, working on everything from hardware to software development and quality control.

A second reason for using contract or temporary workers is that the unit may not have authorization to hire. Many organizations manage head count much more stringently than they manage monetary budgets. This permits them to trumpet figures like sales per employee or, in the case of government, for political leaders to announce that they have reduced the size of government. However, if all one has done is replace regular employees with outsiders or temporaries, the presumed savings may be illusory or worse. For example, during the Reagan administration's drive to cut the size of government, the Department of Energy went from 21,208 employees in 1980 to 16,103 in 1989. But outside contracts increased 56% just between 1986 and 1990, and a study by the General Accounting Office "found that most of the department's $522 million in support service contracts in the fiscal year 1990 were . . . signed because the agency 'lacked sufficient resources' to properly perform the activities."[54]

Third, the use of contingent employees is a buffer to absorb fluctuations in demand while avoiding the morale problems that layoffs engender. The traumatic 1985 layoffs at Apple, an organization with a strong culture, caused many managers to want to avoid a repeat of the situation. One way was to use very lean staffing levels and contingent workers to do the additional work. A study of 442 private firms observed that both the seasonality and cyclicality of demand affected the use of temporaries. However, neither factor affected the extent of contracting out.[55] The use of contingent employment to buffer a set of critical, core employees is one that is compatible with achieving competitive advantage through the work force.

Finally, one of the most important reasons why organizations use contingent employees is that they cost less. The issue of cost is complex, as there are many costs (and possibly offsetting benefits) that need to be accounted for. In many organizations, as at Apple, a facilities charge is levied for permanent employees, since they need work space, but not for contingent workers. Of course, this cost saving is illusory if one has temporary workers who actually occupy space continuously.

Temporary and contract employees may also cost less because they are paid less and do not receive the benefits—particularly health insurance, retirement, and vacation—of regular employees. Katherine Abraham reported that "the average wages for less-skilled workers . . . employed in the business service sector are from 15 to 30% lower than average wages for workers holding similar jobs in manufacturing,"[56] and a study of contract workers in petrochemical facilities found that such workers earned less even after numerous characteristics were statistically controlled.[57] Wages, however, are often the same or even higher for contingent workers in high-skilled occupations. The evidence is that benefits are not offered on a pro rata basis to part-time employees[58] and are less likely to be offered to low-skilled workers in business services compared to the same jobs in manufacturing.[59] The desire to save on benefits costs is so strong that "Federal civil service regulations were changed in June 1985 to permit the federal Office of Personnel Management to hire temporary workers for up to 4 years without providing fringe benefits."[60]

Many of the benefits of using contingent employees are immediate and measurable. The disadvantages or costs are more likely to accrue over time and occur in ways that make them less readily captured by traditional accounting systems. Consequently, there is a tendency for organizations, particularly those under immediate financial pressure, to overuse these arrangements and thereby lose the opportunity to achieve some market advantage through their work force.

The biggest disadvantage of contingent employment arrangements is the difficulty in obtaining loyalty, dedication, or willingness to expend extra effort on behalf of the organization. One Hewlett-Packard executive commented, "They don't tend to be dedicated to the corporate ideal. . . . They're here to make money, not to fulfill the corporate vision."[61] Sometimes it is even difficult to get them to do their jobs:

> Shortly after Carroon & Black Corp. hired a temporary worker to stuff 80,000 insurance certificates into envelopes . . . the company found thousands of documents dumped in a freight elevator. The "temp" had become bored working alone and thought nobody would notice if she cut her work load.[62]

The costs of reduced productivity, diminished motivation, and less commitment to the organization can be "large and sometimes subtle."[63]

The use of contingent workers also affects the likelihood of the organization's obtaining strategic advantage through training and the development of a skilled work force. Contingent work arrangements preclude the organization's capturing the benefits of any firm-specific knowledge or capabilities that the employees may develop. More important, the work arrangements themselves discourage training and development—hiring temporaries or outside contractors is, after all, sometimes done to enable the organization to change its skill set or avoid taking the time and incurring the cost to develop its own people.

A contingent, poorly trained work force can be a dangerous one in the wrong setting. In the chemical industry, maintenance and repair tasks are often contracted out, with contract employees performing about a third of that work during regular operations and half of the work in upgrading or repairing equipment.[64] These less educated, experienced, and trained workers are associated with the growing number of serious accidents in petrochemicals. From January to June 1991, "of the 11 work place accidents known to involve explosions, fires, and spills in the United States petrochemical industry . . . nine were reported to involve contract employees."[65] In nursing, the use of temporary agencies to solve staffing shortages had two adverse effects. With a short-term palliative, the organizations seldom addressed their fundamental problems. Quality control was a major problem. Temp nurses were used in positions for which they were not qualified; they worked excessive hours for several different clients; and the poor performers were simply reassigned to a different hospital until the performance deficiencies were again noticed.[66]

The appropriate use of a contingent work force involves first understanding the real sources of success in one's business and then ensuring that key activities are performed by people with enough connection to the organization that they are likely to do a good job and to receive the necessary training and skill development, either through on-the-job learning or through more formal programs. Wal-Mart, although a discount chain, uses fewer part-timers and temporary-help employees than virtually any of its competitors. Wal-Mart sees an important component of its success coming from customer service and from the ability to tap into localized knowledge of customer wants and needs. Seeking advantage in part through its work force, the company staffs itself to have the opportunity to obtain a more dedicated and skilled set of employees.

By contrast, People Express, a low-cost airline begun in the first wave of deregulation, staffed its reservation agent positions with temporary workers. Travel agents tended not to sell People's tickets, so for most customers, the first point of contact was the reservation agent. Feeling left out of the company culture, with no career mobility prospects, these individuals did not provide an initial point of customer contact that was consistent with the service the airline sought to offer.

The allure of the immediate cost and benefit savings may be seductive, but the costs of contingent employees can be high. The critical decision involves determining whether people will be a source of distinct competitive advantage and, if so, in what activities they are the most critical. Contingent employees should be used with great caution in such activities.

Considering the issues of training and contracting out provides two concrete illustrations of how thinking about the extent to which sustainable competitive advantage originates from the work force helps us make sound decisions about policies and practices related to managing the work force. It is by making the right choices about managing people that firms such as Nordstrom, New United Motor, Wal-Mart, Lincoln Electric, and Southwest Airlines achieved their well-known success.

What Effective Firms Do with People 2

Contrary to some academic writing and to popular belief, there is little evidence that effective management practices are 1) particularly faddish (although their implementation may well be), 2) difficult to understand or to comprehend why they work, or 3) necessarily contingent on an organization's particular competitive strategy. There are interrelated practices—I enumerate 16 in this chapter, but the exact number and how they are defined are somewhat arbitrary—that seem to characterize companies that are effective in achieving competitive success through how they manage people. This chapter describes these practices, explains how and why they are interrelated, and provides some evidence that these practices are neither as new or faddish, nor as contingent on a particular approach to the market, as some might think. The next chapter reviews some evidence regarding their effectiveness and their comparatively slow pace of adoption and diffusion. Combined, the two chapters obviously raise the question of why these practices aren't implemented more readily. Understanding this and some ways of remedying the problem are a major focus of this book.

Before I enumerate these practices, some cautionary words are in order. It would be difficult to find a single organization that does all of these things or that does them all equally well. Some successful firms have tended to do a higher percentage, and it is useful to grade one's own organization against the overall list. Nevertheless, the reader should not expect to find many organizations that do everything. Which practice is most critical does depend in part on the organization's particular technology and market strategy.

A second important caution is to recognize that it is possible for an organization to do all of these things and be unprofitable and unsuccessful, or to do few or none of them and be quite successful. How? These factors are almost certainly related to an organization's ability to achieve competitive success through its work force. But although that may be an important basis of success, and one that is even increasing in importance, it is clearly not the *only* basis of success. IBM, for instance, has done many of these things and has built a skilled and dedicated work force. That in and of itself, however, could not overcome a product strategy that overemphasized large, mainframe computers. People Express, now defunct, also built a strong culture, selectively recruited, and used innovative compensation and work organization strategies to build flexibility and productivity in its operations. Indeed, it was one of the lowest-cost providers of airline services. But this cost advantage could not overcome other problems, such as the founder's edifice complex, which resulted in too-rapid expansion, acquisition of Frontier Airlines and becoming seriously financially overleveraged, and a growth rate that was not sustainable given the firm's fundamental human resource policies. In focusing on managing the work force, I highlight only *one* dimension of the several that determine organizational performance.

By the same token, it is possible to be successful, particularly for a while, doing none of these things or even their opposite. Frank Lorenzo took over Continental Airlines and put it into bankruptcy in 1983 to break its union contracts. To say he played hardball with his employees was an understatement. Lorenzo's strategy was founded on financial and negotiating skills, not on his work force. For a while, these strategies worked—although Continental lost $161 million in 1983, by 1985 it earned about $60 million, a very rapid turnaround. Similarly, Carl Icahn at Trans World Airlines made money, for a while, taking strikes and fighting with his work force, seeking success through financial strategies. Neither airline succeeded in the long run, but in the short run, cutting wages and benefits, cutting employment levels, and managing through fear can produce temporary results. Today these strategies are in use in a couple of the major California banks, whose key to success seems to have been to acquire other large banks; close down redundant branches; lay off employees, literally by the thousands; adjust work hours to make a higher proportion of the work force part-time and therefore not eligible for benefits; and use these cost reductions on a large asset and revenue base to increase profits.

There are two problems with the strategy employed in airlines and banking. First, these are both service industries, and it is incredibly difficult to get high performance and give good service over a long period with disgruntled employees. Second, and perhaps more fundamental, cutting wages, benefits, and employment levels can scarcely be a basis for sustained success over time because there is nothing particularly innovative or unique about these strategies—they can be readily imitated by others. It is important to keep in mind that this discussion focuses on *long-term* success, and clearly in the short term, one can do a number of other things to provide quick financial returns.

Managing the work force effectively is not always equally essential to competitive success. Moreover, whether one needs the performance of all employees or only the contributions of a few, talented individuals also varies according to the nature of the technology involved. Masahiko Aoki noted:

> [T]here are industries in which wide differences in productivity across countries do not seem to be attributable to a mere difference in managerial abilities. For example . . . it appears indisputable that Japanese auto producers have a systematic productivity advantage over U.S. producers. . . . One possible explanation lies in the exceptional diligence of Japanese workers and their loyalty to the employing firm. . . . But if this is so, how can we explain the fact that Japanese labor productivities are considerably lower than American productivities in certain industries—

such as petrochemical, food processing, and pharmaceutical—despite the lifetime employment of equally diligent workers?[1]

Aoki's answer is that the Japanese style of managing the work force stimulates a system of shop-floor entrepreneurship. Some industries and technologies require the effective performance of everyone in the organization in order to be successful and rely on incremental adjustments made at localized work sites, while other industries rely primarily on discontinuous, unique breakthroughs in products or processes by one or a few individuals. Seen in this light, it is understandable that the United States excels in pharmaceuticals, where product development (rather than manufacture or service) is critical; in petrochemicals and food processing, in which highly automated equipment is essential; and in entertainment, where the good script or musical score is the key. It is also not surprising that a system that does not produce the best results from everyone in the work place has difficulty in industries such as machine tools, assembly, or service, in which success is more a function of the insights and activities of many employees at all stages and levels.

A third word of caution is that these practices have potential downsides as well as benefits and are not necessarily easy to implement, particularly in a one-at-a-time fashion. One obvious problem is that they all necessarily entail more involvement and responsibility on the part of the work force. There are many employees who would rather work only with their bodies and check their minds at the door—particularly if that is what they have become accustomed to—and instituting work practices that entail more effort and involvement may force turnover. These practices may be resisted by others in the organization as well, for reasons I cover later.

The reader is cautioned that implementation issues loom large, regardless of how sensible the practices may be.

SIXTEEN PRACTICES FOR MANAGING PEOPLE

The following policies and practices emerge from extensive reading of both the popular and academic literature, talking to numerous people in firms in a variety of industries, and the application of some simple common sense. The particular way of subdividing the terrain is less important than considering the entire landscape, so the reader should realize that the division into categories is somewhat arbitrary. The themes, however, recur repeatedly in studies of organizations. It is important to recognize that the practices are interrelated—it is difficult to do one thing by itself with much positive result. Although I illustrate some of the more prominent interconnections, some of the effects of the practices on each other I leave to the reader to assess.

Employment Security

The Lincoln Electric Company "is the largest manufacturer of arc welding products in the world, operating twenty plants in fifteen countries"[2] with sales of close to $1 billion. During its history, it has driven a number of larger competitors (such as General Electric) out of the market, has consistently earned between 10% and 15% after-tax return on equity, and has been the leading U.S. manufacturer of arc welding equipment since World War II.[3] One of its fundamental policies is that of employment security:

> Our guarantee of employment states that no employee with three years or more of service will be laid off for lack of work. . . . [N]ot once in more than thirty years has a Lincoln employee . . . been terminated for lack of work. . . . [T]he policy does *not* protect any employee who fails to perform his or her job properly, it *does* emphasize that management is responsible for maintaining a level of business that will keep every employee working productively. The institution of guaranteed employment sprang from our belief that fear is an ineffective motivator. If an employee lives in fear of being laid off, the natural tendency will be to make a job last as long as possible. Relief from such anxiety frees people to do their best work.[4]

Security of employment signals a long-standing commitment by the organization to its work force. Norms of reciprocity tend to guarantee that this commitment is repaid, but conversely, an employer that signals through word and deed that its employees are dispensable is not likely to generate much loyalty, commitment, or willingness to expend extra effort for the organization's benefit. New United Motor Manufacturing (NUMMI), the Toyota–GM joint venture in California, guaranteed workers' jobs as part of the formal labor contract in return for a reduction in the number of job classifications and an agreement not to strike over work standards. This commitment was met even in the face of temporarily slow demand, and many observers believe that as a result, trust between employees and the organization increased substantially. Employment security is not only for larger organizations such as Lincoln and NUMMI. Digital Pictures, Inc., a young and small software company in the interactive video business, grants job security because the founder and president believes that it helps attract and keep talent.[5]

Taking on people not readily eliminated exerts pressure to be careful and selective in hiring. Moreover, "employment security enhances employee involvement because employees are more willing to contribute to the work process when they need not fear losing their own or their coworkers' jobs. Employment security contributes to training as both employer and employee have greater incentives to invest in training,"[6] because there is some assurance that the employment relationship will be of sufficient duration to earn a return on the time and resources expended in skill development.

Although employment security is an exception in the United States, it is the norm in Western Europe and many industrialized countries. For instance, laws in Belgium, France, Germany, the Netherlands, Luxembourg, and the United Kingdom all require some degree of advance notice to workers in the case of layoffs, some minimum level of severance pay, and in all instances require consultations with a local works council, employee representatives, and/or any union in the organization.[7] Employers' ability to get around employment security protections by using contract or temporary workers is limited in Europe, as use of these employment arrangements is also regulated.[8]

Employment security provisions, voluntarily adopted by individual firms, are presumptively rational responses designed to achieve a more effective work force. However, there is no evidence that even government-mandated employment security has had adverse effects on either firms or the labor market. In a comprehensive review of existing empirical evidence, as well as new data on the operation of the West German labor market, Christopher Buechtemann concluded:

> Judging by the available empirical evidence, the theoretically derived assumption that legal employment protection regulations have put a severe restraint on firms' manpower policies preventing them from carrying out necessary workforce adjustments seems to be largely unfounded. . . . Likewise the experience of the German Employment Promotion Act has so far disproved expectations that a relaxation or partial abolition of institutional lay-off and dismissal restraints would have a significant impact on firms' hiring decisions and thereby stimulate job creation.[9]

Another study comparing production employment and shipments in the United States and Germany for the period 1974–1984 reached the same conclusion.[10]

One concern managers sometimes express is that guaranteed employment will foster a "civil service" mentality and a lack of emphasis on performance. This is probably less of a problem than is sometimes thought but, in any case, is not likely to be an issue if employment security is coupled with financial incentives for excellent performance and with work organization practices that motivate employee effort and capture the benefits of know-how and skill. Particularly if work is organized in teams so that there is a degree of peer monitoring and pressure, and there are rewards for performance, employment security will probably have more positive than adverse motivational consequences.

Selectivity in Recruiting

Security in employment and reliance on the work force for competitive success mean that one must be careful to choose the right people, in the right way. Studies covering populations ranging from machine operators, typists, welders, and assembly workers to foundry workers, weavers, and lathe operators—all in self-paced jobs so that individual differences mattered—indicate that, on average, the standard deviation in performance is about 20% of the mean. Furthermore, the mean ratio of output for employees performing at the ninety-fifth percentile compared to those performing at the fifth percentile was 2; or the most productive employees were about twice as good as the least productive.[11] Southwest Airlines worries a lot about hiring the right people. In fact, it flies some of its best customers to Dallas and involves them in the flight attendant hiring process, believing that those who are in contact with the front-line employees probably know best what makes a good employee. At Lincoln Electric, hiring is done very carefully because employees are expected to make a lifetime commitment to the company. Lincoln selects for both the desire to succeed and the capacity for growth.[12]

When General Mills set up a new cereal-manufacturing line at its Lodi, California, plant that intended to follow innovative management practices, existing workers volunteered for the assignment, and these volunteers were carefully screened. One of the practices of many of the Japanese automobile-manufacturing plants opened in the United States that proved especially newsworthy (at least judging by the number of articles generated) was their extensive screening of employees. Some of this was undoubtedly done to weed out those who were likely to be prounion, but much of the screening was to find those people who could work best in the new environment, could learn and develop, and needed less supervision. There was little screening for particular skills, under the assumption that these could be readily learned. At Nordstrom, the very effective specialty retailer whose sales per square foot are about double the industry average, salespeople are hired carefully. Often, they are recruited from competitors. The Nordstrom environment is competitive, fast-paced, and high-pressure, so Nordstrom tends to recruit sales clerks who are young and college-educated, seeking a career in retailing.[13]

Besides getting the right people in the door, recruiting has an important symbolic aspect. If someone goes through a rigorous selection process, the person feels that he or she is joining an elite organization. High expectations for performance are created, and the message sent is that people matter.

High Wages

In labor markets, as in other markets, there is a tendency to get what you pay for. If you want to recruit outstanding people, and want them to stay with the organization, paying more is helpful, although not absolutely necessary. High wages tend to attract more applicants, permitting the organization to be more selective in its hiring. This selectivity is important in finding people who are going to be trainable and who will be committed to the organization. Paying more makes turnover less likely, as there is less chance that someone will be able to increase his or her income by moving. Perhaps most important, higher wages send a message that the organization values its people. Particularly if these wages are higher than required by the market, employees can perceive the extra income as a gift and work more diligently as a result.[14] Nordstrom typically pays its people an hourly wage higher than the prevailing rate for retail clerks at comparable stores. Coupled with incentive pay for outstanding work, Nordstrom salespeople often earn twice the average retail income.

Organizations often try to economize by paying lower wages under the mistaken assumption that lower wages equal lower labor costs. However, this is not inevitably the case, for labor costs are importantly affected not only by what people are paid but also by how productive they are. New United Motor pays among the highest wages in the automobile industry, but its labor costs are substantially lower than average because it takes about half as many labor hours to assemble a car in the plant. People Express paid its front-line workers quite well compared to the industry average, yet had lower labor costs than its competitors. At Lincoln Electric, some pieceworkers earn more than $100,000 per year, and more than 100 earned in excess of $60,000 in 1991. Nevertheless, because of the tremendous productivity, Lincoln's costs are low, and indeed, the company regularly lowers the prices of its products to pass along these efficiency gains to its customers.

David Levine found that workers whose wages were higher than might be predicted based on standard demographic and human capital factors expressed higher levels of job satisfaction, were less likely to quit, and indicated that they would work harder.[15] In another study of business units of major U.S. companies, he discovered a positive relation between changes in wages and changes in productivity. Moreover, "the increase in productivity from an increase in wages was approximately large enough to pay for itself."[16] Thus, there is systematic evidence, as well as case examples, that support the efficiency effects of paying more.

In addition to confusing labor costs with labor rates, companies sometimes believe that lowering labor costs is essential for competitive success. This is not invariably the case, even in cost-competitive businesses, because in many organizations, labor costs are a small fraction of the total costs. Furthermore, even if labor costs (let alone labor rates) are higher, it may be that enhanced service, skill, and innovation more than compensate by increasing the level of overall profit. For instance, the discount retail store industry is furiously competitive, and costs are an obsession. One of the more successful retailing chains has been Costco Wholesaling Corporation: "[D]espite its attention to expenses, Costco does not skimp on employee salaries, Mr. Sinegal [the president] maintains. 'We pay $1 more an hour to our employees than Sam's or Price. . . . We start our people at $8 an hour and boost them in three to four years to $14 an hour. It works for us. If you pay good wages, you get better productivity.'"[17]

Another example of increasing wages as a way of *increasing* profits comes from Wendy's, a company in the highly competitive and cost-conscious fast-food industry. The CEO of Wendy's, facing declining company profitability, decided that the best way to become the customer's restaurant of choice was to become the employer of choice.[18] This entailed improving both benefits and base compensation, instituting a quarterly bonus, and creating an employee stock option plan. The results were dramatic: "Our turnover rate for general managers fell to 20% in 1991 from 39% in 1989, while turnover among co- and assistant managers dropped to 37% from 60%—among the lowest in the business. With a stable—and able—work force, sales began to pick up as well."[19]

Incentive Pay

People are motivated by more than money—things like recognition, security, and fair treatment matter a great deal. It is certainly true that particularly in the United States, there has been a tendency to overuse money in an effort to solve myriad organizational problems. However, it is also true that fairness and justice virtually dictate that if people are responsible for enhanced levels of performance and profitability, they will want to share in the benefits. Consider the alternative—if all the gains from extra ingenuity and effort go just to top management or to shareholders (unless these are also employees), people will soon view the situation as unfair, become discouraged, and abandon their efforts. Thus, many organizations seek to reward performance with some form of contingent compensation.

Lincoln Electric is deservedly famous for its piecework and incentive bonus plan. Contrary to first impressions, the plan does much more than merely reward individual productivity. Although the factory work force is paid on a piecework basis, it is paid only for good pieces—workers correct quality problems on their own time. Moreover, defects can be traced to the individual who produced them. Quality is emphasized as well as productivity. Additionally, piecework is only a part of the employee's compensation. Bonuses, which often constitute 100% of regular salary, are based on the company's profitability—encouraging employees to identify with the whole firm. They are also based on the individual's merit rating, and that rating is, in turn, based on four equally important aspects of performance: dependability, quality, output, and ideas and cooperation.[20] This broader evaluation mitigates the pernicious tendencies of simplistic incentive systems to go awry.

Merit pay made on an individual basis is controversial, with some people believing it actually harms performance. The former director of human resources at Mars candy company noted that "companies spend all this time and energy on merit programs and all they do is make employees angry."[21] The quality expert W. E. Deming believes that "the merit rating nourishes short-term performance, annihilates long-term planning, builds fear, demolishes teamwork, and nourishes rivalry and politics."[22] However, regardless of one's position on merit pay for individuals, it is possible and indeed desirable to reward performance, if not on an individual level, then on the basis of performance by groups, subunits, or even the entire organization.

Gain sharing, profit sharing, and similar plans reward organizational members for improvements in overall performance. One particular gain-sharing program, IMPROSHARE, "rewards all covered employees equally whenever the actual number of labor hours used to produce output in the current week or month is less than the estimated number it would have taken to produce the current level of output in the base period."[23] Results from a survey sent to all known users of the program revealed a median productivity increase of 8% in the first year and a cumulative productivity gain of 17.5% after three years.[24] A comprehensive review of the literature on profit sharing, which includes gain sharing, concluded that "profit sharing and productivity are positively related. . . . [M]ost case studies show improved performance when there is profit sharing or gain sharing."[25] Sharing the gains of increased performance may motivate greater work effort, but at a minimum, it fulfills employees' expectations for deriving some benefits from outstanding work.

Employee Ownership

Employee ownership offers two advantages. Employees who have ownership interests in the organizations for which they work have less conflict between capital and labor—to some degree they are both capital and labor. Employee ownership, effectively implemented, can align the interests of employees with those of shareholders by making employees shareholders, too. Second, employee ownership puts stock in the hands of people, employees, who are more inclined to take a long-term view of the organization, its strategy, and its investment policies and less likely to support hostile takeovers, leveraged buyouts, and other financial maneuvers. Of course, to the extent that one believes this reduced risk of capital market discipline inhibits efficiency, significant employee shareholding is a disadvantage. However, the existing evidence largely contradicts this negative view.

If one looks at a typical income statement for Lincoln Electric, for example, in 1974, one observes that the year-end incentive bonus amount is 72.2% of income before tax, or put another way, if the bonus were eliminated, pretax income available to shareholders would be some 72% larger. The company that year—and that year is quite typical—paid out more than 40% of its pretax income as incentive bonuses to its employees.[26] How can Lincoln do that? Particularly as it pays line workers exceptionally high salaries, why don't shareholders demand a larger share of the firm's profits? It can do this, and other things that also take a very long-term view, largely because almost 50% of the employees at that time (now about 80%) owned stock in the company, and the company's shares are closely held by employees, the Lincoln family, and foundations.[27] In the absence of such overlap between employees and shareholders, there certainly would be great temptation to capture more of the income for one group or the other, probably the shareholders. These bonuses are paid after piece-rate earnings, which are set so that Lincoln employees' base wages are at an already competitive level.

It is probably no coincidence that all five of the companies mentioned in Chapter 1 as providing the best shareholder returns from 1972 to 1992 appear on The Employee Ownership 1000, a listing of "1000 companies in which employees own more than 4% of the stock of a corporation" traded on the New York or American stock exchanges or the over-the-counter market.[28] Although employee ownership is no panacea, and its effects depend largely on how it is implemented, the existing evidence is consistent with the view that employee ownership has positive effects on various dimensions of firm performance.[29] Nor are these positive effects confined to the United States. In 1988, of the firms listed on the eight Japanese stock exchange markets, 91% had employee stock ownership plans, and in firms with such plans, almost 50% of the work force participated.[30] A study of the incidence and effects of employee stock ownership concluded that these plans "have favorable effects on employee incentives and enterprise productivity" and cited other studies showing that, in Japan, ESOPs reduced both employee quit rates and the cost of capital.[31] Employee share ownership is an important part of the Japanese employment relations system and, although de-emphasized compared to other arrangements, such as internal labor markets and lifetime employment, is apparently an important part of the reason for the persistent success of many Japanese firms.

Information Sharing

The adoption of some form of gain sharing requires information sharing. It also encourages more disclosure of information to people in the enterprise because, as owners, employees have more power and expect to be treated as owners. Bofors is a successful employee-owned printing company located in the San Francisco area. It has excellent productivity, modern capital equipment, and employees dedicated to avoiding waste in either materials or labor. One of its senior managers, explaining what it was like to manage in such a firm, noted that because the employees were also owners, they both demanded and received more consultation about operations and much more information about productivity and profitability. Such information sharing is essential to ensure the success of profit sharing and of efforts to achieve competitive advantage through the work force:

> [D]isclosure is integral to profit sharing because employees need at the very least to be informed as to what profit is. Moreover, if greater employee identification with the employing enterprise is to be elicited, then disclosure of information would seem essential to make clear the relationships between cost and profit, and between performance and prospects, and thus provide an informed basis for employees to appreciate how their own interests and those of the company are related.[32]

Some have argued that the very fact that incentive programs require more information sharing, coupled with many managements' reluctance to disclose information because they fear the loss of control, are reasons why such schemes diffuse less than they might.

At Lincoln Electric, "information is shared with all employees regarding the financial and market position of the organization," using both oral and written media.[33] Levi Strauss installed a quality enhancement program accompanied by gain sharing at its manufacturing plant in Blue Ridge, Georgia, with excellent results. In a six-month evaluation of the program, surveyed employees responded overwhelmingly that they understood the concept and the measures, and thought that they were fair and could affect them.[34] This was essential for the program to work. Moreover, one of the obstacles to implementing the program, there and at other Levi plants, was the reluctance of some departments to share information as required.

If people are to be a source of competitive advantage, clearly they must have the information necessary to do what is required to be successful. At the Advanced Micro Devices submicron development center, there are computer terminals throughout the plant that every employee has been trained to use in order to obtain information about product yields, development progress, production rates, or any other aspect of the operation. One reason sometimes given for not disclosing information to large numbers of employees is that it may leak to competitors. When Robert Beck was head of human resources for the Bank of America, he perceptively told the management committee, reluctant to disclose the bank's strategy and other information to its employees, that the competitors almost certainly knew the information already; typically, the only people in the dark are the firm's own employees.

Participation and Empowerment

Sharing information is a necessary precondition to another important feature found in many successful work systems: encouraging the decentralization of decision making and broader worker participation and empowerment in controlling their own work process. At NUMMI, employees are taught how to break down jobs into their component parts, analyze them, and search for efficiencies. At Nordstrom, the written philosophy states:

> We also encourage you to present your own ideas. Your buyers have a great deal of autonomy, and are encouraged to seek out and promote new fashion directions at all times. . . . Nordstrom has a strong open-

door policy and we encourage you to share your concerns, suggestions and ideas. . . .

Nordstrom Rules:

Rule #1: Use your good judgment in all situations. There will be no additional rules.[35]

At Lincoln Electric, "every worker must be a manager, and every manager must be a worker. . . . In self-management is found the true meaning of efficiency, because nothing increases overhead as quickly and non-productively as extra layers of management."[36] The organization has a flat structure; for instance, the vice president of sales has more than 35 regional sales executives reporting to him. The company also has an advisory board composed of people elected by their fellow workers who meet with senior management biweekly. They have the right to question anything the company does. In one instance, the CEO and chairman was interrogated as to why he thought it necessary to fly to Europe on the Concorde. He was able to provide a satisfactory answer, and had he not done so, it is unlikely that he would have flown that way again. Although the board has no decision-making power, its questions and suggestions are, by company norms and culture, expected to receive prompt attention, with reports on the matter due back most often by the next meeting.

The evidence is that participation increases both satisfaction and employee productivity.[37] Autonomy is one of the most important dimensions of jobs and was the focus of many job-redesign efforts undertaken as part of the quality of working life movement in the 1960s and 1970s.[38] The fundamental change involves moving from a system of hierarchical control and coordination of activity to one in which lower-level employees, who may have more or better information, are permitted to do things to enhance performance. At Levi Strauss's jeans factory, when it was time to purchase new forklift trucks, the drivers themselves got involved. They determined specifications, negotiated with suppliers, and made the final purchase decision, in the process saving the company money as well as obtaining equipment more appropriate for that plant. At Eaton, a unionized manufacturer, workers tired of fixing equipment that broke down and suggested that they build two new automated machines themselves. They did it for less than a third of what outside vendors would have charged and doubled the output of the department in the first year.[39]

Autonomy works best when it is coupled—as it is in many, although not all, of these cases—with rewards for the increased performance that autonomy can bring as well as training in the skills necessary to take true responsibility for one's own work process. And assurance of job security helps ensure that the increased productivity doesn't result in job loss.

Teams and Job Redesign

The traditional organizational hierarchy serves at least two functions: it provides monitoring and supervision, to ensure that employees don't shirk their duties or otherwise take advantage of their employer, and it provides coordination across interdependent tasks. Even with more empowered workers, the need for coordination remains, as does the need for some discipline and monitoring. Organizations are, after all, interdependent systems, and autonomy cannot mean that people do whatever they decide to do whenever they decide to do it.

Fortunately, there is an alternative to the traditional organizational hierarchy that preserves much of the sense of autonomy even as it provides some level of monitoring and the requisite coordination. This alternative is the use of teams. Because most people are inherently social creatures, deriving pleasure from social interaction, groups exert a powerful influence on individuals. Groups enforce conformity pressures, and these include norms about appropriate work quantity and quality. Also, groups provide social information and certainty about how to evaluate the conditions of the work setting and what the critical dimensions of work really are. Both conformity pressures and informational social influence mean that groups have enormous effects on individual behaviors.

Management has typically seen these influences as perverse, leading to restrictions in output, formation of unions, and resistance to management control. Indeed, group pressures can at times have precisely these results. However, positive results from group influences are more likely when there are rewards for group efforts, when groups have some autonomy and control over the work environment, and when groups are taken seriously and become the fabric of the organization.

Organizations that have tapped the power of teams have often experienced excellent results. Monsanto, a large chemical company, implemented work organization based on self-managed teams at its chemical and nylon complex near Pensacola, Florida. Teams of workers were responsible for hiring, purchasing, job assignments, and production.[40] Management was reduced from seven levels to four, and the plant experienced increases in both profitability and safety. At a 318-person submarine systems plant owned by AT&T, costs were reduced more than 30% through the use of teams.[41] Federal Express uses teams in its back-office operation with great success—service problems fell 13% in 1989 after the company's 1,000 clerical workers were organized in teams and given additional training and authority.[42] One of the more dramatic examples of the benefits of using teams occurred at Johnsonville Sausage. In 1986, a manufacturer asked Johnsonville to produce private-label sausage. The president was about to decline the new business, because he believed that the plant was already at capacity and could not handle the additional workload. However,

> before deciding, he assembled his 200 production workers, who are organized in teams of five to 20, and asked them to decide. . . . After . . . ten days, they came back with an answer: "We can do it." . . . The teams decided how much new machinery they would need and how many new people; they also made a schedule of how much to produce per day. Since Johnsonville took on the new project, productivity has risen over 50% in the factory.[43]

Much of the success of the NUMMI automobile assembly plant in California is attributed to teams, and indeed, there is some evidence that the entire plant functions as one superteam.

Teams work because of the peer monitoring and expectations of co-workers that are brought to bear to both coordinate and monitor work.

Indeed, even critics of the team concept often argue that the problem with teams as a substitute for hierarchy is not that this approach doesn't work but that it works too well. Thus, a dissident union leader in the NUMMI plant noted: "[W]hen the team's under pressure, people try to meet the team's expectations and under peer pressure, they end up pushing themselves too hard. . . . The team concept is a nice idea, but when you put the teams under pressure, it becomes a damn effective way to divide workers."[44]

Training and Skill Development

Worker autonomy, self-managed teams, and even a high-wage strategy depend on having people who not only are empowered to make changes and improvements in products and processes but also have the necessary skills to do so. Consequently, an integral part of most new work systems is a greater commitment to training and skill development. Note, however, that this training will produce positive returns only if the trained workers are then permitted to employ their skills. One mistake many organizations make is to upgrade the skills of both managers and workers but not change the structure of work in ways that permit people to do anything different. Under such circumstances, it is little wonder that training has no apparent effect.

At Advanced Micro Devices' submicron development facility, some 70% of the technicians came from older facilities at AMD. In keeping with AMD's emphasis on employment stability, as old facilities were closed, people were evaluated with respect to their basic skills. If accepted, they were put through a seven-month program at Mission College—at full pay and at company expense—and then went to work in the new facility. This training not only demonstrated the firm's commitment to its employees, which was then reciprocated, but also ensured that the facility would be staffed with highly qualified people who had been specifically trained for their new jobs.

At a Collins and Aikman carpet plant in Georgia, more than a third of the employees were high school dropouts, and some could neither read nor write. When the firm introduced computers to increase productive efficiency, however, it chose not to replace its existing work force but to upgrade its skills. After spending about $1,200 per employee on training, including lost job time, the company found that the amount of carpet stitched increased 10%. Moreover, quality problems declined by half. The employees, with more skills and better morale, submitted some 1,230 suggestions, and absenteeism fell almost by half.[45] At Hampden Papers, a paper mill, the organization began spending 1.97% of the total payroll on education and training. Although productivity benefits were difficult to quantify, the president of the firm noted that "workers who take part in classes have lower rates of absenteeism and job turnover. They also tend to get higher performance ratings from their supervisors."[46]

If people are to be given more information about operations, they need skills in employing that information to diagnose problems and suggest improvements. That is why training is such an important part of virtually all quality improvement programs.

Cross-Utilization and Cross-Training

Having people do multiple jobs has a number of potential benefits. The most obvious is that doing more things can make work more interesting—variety is one of the core job dimensions that affect how people respond to their work. Variety in jobs permits a change in pace, a change in activity, and potentially even a change in the people with whom one comes in contact, and each of these forms of variety can make work life more challenging. Beyond its motivational effects, having people do multiple jobs has other important benefits. One is keeping the work process both transparent and as simple as possible. At People Express, for instance, one of the avowed motivations for having people do several tasks was to ensure that those tasks did not become too complicated. If people are expected to shift to new tasks readily, the design of those tasks has to be straightforward enough so they can be learned quickly. A second, somewhat related benefit is the potential for newcomers to a job to see things that can be improved that experienced people don't see, simply because they have come to take the work process so much for granted.

Multiskilling is also a useful adjunct to policies that promise employment security. After all, it is easier to keep people at work if they have multiple skills and can do different things. By the same token, maintaining employment levels sometimes compels organizations to find new tasks for people, often with surprising results. When Mazda, the Japanese automobile manufacturer, suffered a decline in business in the 1980s, rather than laying off factory workers, it put them to work selling cars, which, in Japan, are often sold door to door. At the end of the year, when awards were presented to the best salespeople, the company discovered that the top ten were all former factory workers. They could explain the product effectively, and of course, when business picked up, the fact that factory workers had experience talking to customers yielded useful ideas about product characteristics.

A similar thing occurred at Lincoln Electric. When domestic business declined 40% year to year in the early 1980s, one way Lincoln avoided layoffs was by sending pieceworkers into the field to sell—to small garages, machine shops, and other places that were not large enough to have been regularly serviced by Lincoln's normal channels of distribution. Not only did these people sell arc welding equipment in new places to new users, but since much of the profit from this equipment comes from the sale of replacement parts, Lincoln subsequently enjoyed greater market penetration and greater sales as a consequence.

At Lechmere, a retail chain owned by Dayton-Hudson, the company experimented with cross-training and utilization of employees at a new store in Sarasota, Florida. The store offered the workers raises based on the number of jobs they learned to perform, a variant of a pay-for-skill plan. The work force, composed of 60% full-time employees rather than the 30% typical for the chain, was substantially more productive than in other stores. "Cashiers are encouraged to sell records and tapes. Sporting goods salesmen get tutoring in forklifts. That way Lechmere can quickly adjust to changes in staffing needs simply by redeploying existing workers. The pay incentives, along with the prospect of a more varied and interesting workday, proved valuable lures in recruiting."[47]

At AMD's new submicron development facility, the organization uses skill-based pay to encourage people to learn many jobs. Moreover, it uses cross-functional teams to do development, solve problems, transfer design to manufacturing—in short, almost everything. Managers at the facility believe that cross-training and cross-utilization of people, organized in teams, facilitate the development of seamless organizational boundaries. These seamless boundaries, in turn, enhance productivity by making integration among the various parts of the semiconductor design and manufacturing process easier and faster.

At NUMMI, "workers in each team were cross-trained on each others' tasks and rotated between tasks."[48] As one worker noted:

> Rotating jobs means that everyone in the team is contributing as much as everyone else. In the traditional plant, older workers with more seniority would get the easier jobs. . . . Now we've eliminated those easy jobs by rotation, and if someone has a harder time on one job because they're older or their hands aren't big enough, the team helps out by rotating faster.[49]

Symbolic Egalitarianism

One important barrier to decentralizing decision making, using self-managed teams, and eliciting employee commitment and cooperation is symbols that separate people from each other. Consequently, it is not surprising that many of the firms that are known for achieving competitive advantage through people have various forms of symbolic egalitarianism—ways of signaling to both insiders and outsiders that there is comparative equality and it is not the case that some think and others do. At New United Motor Manufacturing, the executive dining room was eliminated, and everyone eats in the same cafeteria. Everyone wears a blue smock. There are no reserved places in the employee parking lot.

Communication across levels is greatly enhanced by the opportunity to interact and meet in less formal settings. This means that senior management is more likely to know what is actually going on and be able to communicate its ideas more directly to everyone in the facility. The reduction in the number of social categories tends to decrease the salience of various subdivisions in the organization, diminishes "us" versus "them" thinking, and provides more of a sense of everyone working toward a common goal. This egalitarianism makes cross-movement easier because there are fewer status distinctions to be overcome. At AMD's submicron development center, there is no "direct labor," no hourly employees—everyone is salaried. There are no process or equipment engineers, no maintenance organization, no quality control technicians. There are two job classifications—master technician and manufacturing engineer. Similarly at NUMMI, there is only 1 classification for Division 1 personnel compared to more than 80 previously. The number of skilled trades classifications shrank from 18 under the old General Motors system to 2.[50]

Egalitarian symbols come in many forms. In some organizations, it is dress—few who have worked in a manufacturing facility have not heard the phrase "the suits are coming" when people from headquarters, typically more formally dressed, arrive. Japanese organizations almost invariably have pins with the organization's insignia or logo that virtually everyone wears, reminding each of his or her identification with the organization. Physical space is another way in which common fate can be signaled, or not. The CEO of Solectron, a contract manufacturer that won the Malcolm Baldrige award, does not have a private office, and neither does the chairman. Contrast this with the situation at a major paper and forest products company in which access to the CEO's floor is controlled by a locked door. John DeLorean's graphic description of the fourteenth-floor headquarters for General Motors is one of hushed, quiet offices reached by a private elevator that was secured—in other words, executives cut off from the rest of the organization.[51] Open office arrangements have their own problems, including an absence of acoustical privacy at times, but they do signify more equality. Reserved parking spaces, private dining rooms, and other symbols of rank are inconsistent with an egalitarian culture.

Although symbolic egalitarianism would seem easy to implement, the elimination of status symbols is often one of the most difficult things for an organization to do. A friend bemoaned the fact that just as he had reached a managerial level that entitled him to use a private dining room, have preferential parking, and occupy a larger office, his employer embarked on a total quality movement and eliminated all of these perquisites. At Eaton's plant in Lincoln, Illinois, a move toward self-managed teams and productivity bonuses met resistance when it involved altering the office arrangement: "When engineers at Lincoln were evicted from their office enclave and the department was moved out onto the shop floor, the department chief and a colleague quit in protest."[52]

Wage Compression

Teamwork is fostered by common fate, and common fate is enhanced to the extent that people in an organization fare comparably in terms of the rewards received. Although issues of wage compression are most often considered in terms of hierarchical compression, and particularly CEO pay relative to that of others, there is a horizontal aspect to wage compression as well. It can have a number of efficiency-enhancing properties for organizations.

It is important to remember that wage compression is distinct from incentive pay. Incentive pay simply means that people are rewarded, either individually or in groups, for their performance. These rewards can be large, producing wide variation in salaries, or small, producing substantially less variation. It is also important to recognize that incentive pay—particularly when applied to larger units such as work groups, departments, or the entire organization—can either reduce or increase the wage dispersion that would otherwise exist. Most gain-sharing and profit-sharing programs actually reduce pay dispersion, although they need not do so.

When tasks are somewhat interdependent and cooperation is helpful for accomplishing work, pay compression, by reducing interpersonal competition and enhancing cooperation, can lead to efficiency gains.[53] Furthermore, large differences in the allocation of organizational rewards can motivate people to achieve these rewards. Although increased motivation can produce greater efforts, large differences in rewards can as readily result in excessive time and energy spent on ingratiating oneself with one's supervisor or trying to affect the criteria for reward alloca-tion.[54] By this reasoning, a more compressed distribution of salaries can actually produce higher overall performance, as there is less incentive for individuals to waste their time on gaming the system.

To the extent that wages are compressed, pay is likely to be de-emphasized in the reward system and in the organization's culture. This has some obvious economic benefits—people are not constantly wor-rying about whether they are compensated appropriately and at-tempting to rebargain their salaries. A de-emphasis on pay can also fo-cus attention on the other advantages of organizational membership such as good colleagues and work that is interesting and meaningful. There is a literature in psychology that suggests we attempt to figure out why we are doing what we are by looking at ourselves as an outside observer would.[55] If we see we are very well paid, perhaps on a contin-gent basis, for what we do, we are likely to attribute our behavior to the economic rewards. If, however, we are not particularly well paid, or if pay is less salient, and if it is distributed on a less contingent basis (which will make it less salient), then we are likely to attribute our be-havior to other, more intrinsic factors such as the inherent enjoyment of the work. In other words, being paid in a contingent fashion for what we do can actually undermine our intrinsic interest in and satisfaction with that activity.[56] Thus, pay compression, by helping to de-emphasize pay, can enhance other bases of satisfaction with work and build a cul-ture that is less calculative in nature.

Table 2-1 shows the relative compensation of top executives for vari-ous functions in the United States, Germany, and Japan, with the pay of the top manufacturing executive being set to 1.00 in each country. The table reveals not only the relative importance of different functions in the different countries but also differences in the degree of horizontal pay dispersion. In the United States, the top-paid functional executive, in finance, earned on average some 58% more than the senior personnel executive, the lowest paid. In Germany, the head of the highest-paid function, research and development, earned 31% more than the lowest-paid executive, in personnel. In Japan, however, the head of the highest-paid function earned only 13% more than the head of the lowest-paid

Table 2-1   Relative Compensation of the Top Executive of Various Functions in the United States, Germany, and Japan

	United States	Germany	Japan
Finance	1.31	.94	1.00
Manufacturing	1.00	1.00	1.00
Research and Development	.90	1.06	1.05
Sales and Marketing	.91	1.04	.93
Personnel/Human Resources	.83	.81	1.02
Percentage by which highest salary exceeds lowest	58%	31%	13%

Source: Developed from data in Dana Milbank, "Dying Breed: No Glamour, No Glory, Being a Manufacturer Today Can Take Guts," *The Wall Street Journal*, June 3, 1991, A1, A5.

function, on average. In Japan, careers are often multifunctional within a single organization, while in the United States, at the other extreme, there is much more functional specialization and a tendency for mobility to be within a particular specialty and across firms. If one wants to move people across units or functions, it is easier to do so if their standard of living is not drastically altered by each move. Thus, to the extent that cross-functional movement is desired, to enhance information flows and the development of a broader skill set, reduced wage differences horizontally make it easier for such movement to occur.

Vertical pay dispersion sends a signal that the lower-paid, lower-level people matter comparatively less. This may be fine in some technologies and under some strategies, but it is quite inconsistent with attempting to achieve high levels of commitment and output from *all* employees. Herman Miller, the highly successful office furniture manufacturer, ties the chief executive's salary to that of the workers—the CEO receives 20 times the average worker's pay in salary and bonus. "'People have to think about the common good,' says Max DePre, a member of Herman Miller's founding family and now the company's chairman."[57] Ben & Jerry's, the financially very successful producer of premium ice cream, limits pay so that no one can earn more than seven times what the average worker receives. In a strong-culture organization, one will tend to find, and will indeed want to have, more compressed pay because pay dispersion lessens the sense of community and common fate that strong-culture organizations seek to build as a source of competitive success.

Promotion from Within

Promotion from within is a useful adjunct to many of the practices described. It encourages training and skill development because the availability of promotion opportunities within the firm binds workers to employers and vice versa. It facilitates decentralization, participation, and delegation because it helps promote trust across hierarchical levels; promotion from within means that supervisors are responsible for coordinating the efforts of people whom they probably know quite well. By the same token, those being coordinated personally know managers in higher positions. This contact provides social bases of influence so that formal position can loom less important. Promotion from within also offers an incentive for performing well, and although tied to monetary rewards, promotion is a reward that also has a status-based, nonmonetary component. Perhaps most important, it provides a sense of fairness and justice in the work place. If people do an outstanding job but outsiders are being brought in over them, there will be a sense of alienation from the organization.

One other advantage of promotion from within is that it tends to ensure that people in management positions actually know something about the business, the technology, and the operations they are managing. There are numerous tales of firms managed by those with little understanding of the basic operations, often with miserable results. David Halberstam's history of Ford Motor tells how finance took control of the company. Not only were these people not "car men," they knew little about automobiles, technology, production processes, or the market—anything that could not be conveyed via statistics—and had little interest in learning.[58] The problem with managing only through statistics is that without some understanding of the underlying processes that produce the measures, it is likely that managers will either focus on inappropriate measures or fail to fully comprehend what they mean.

By contrast, at Lincoln Electric, almost everyone who joins the company learns to weld—Lincoln's main product is, after all, arc welding equipment. Graduation from the welding program requires coming up with some innovation to the product. At Nordstrom, even those with advanced degrees start on the sales floor. Promotion is strictly from within, and when Nordstrom opens a new store, its key people are recruited from other stores around the country. This helps perpetuate the Nordstrom culture and values but also provides assurance that those running the store know what they are doing and have experience doing it the Nordstrom way.

Long-Term Perspective

The bad news about achieving competitive advantage through the work force is that it inevitably takes time to accomplish. By contrast, a new piece of equipment can be quickly installed; a new product technology can be acquired through a licensing agreement in the time it takes to negotiate the agreement; and acquiring capital only requires the successful conclusion of negotiations. The good news, however, is that once achieved, competitive advantage obtained through employment practices is likely to be substantially more enduring and more difficult to duplicate. Nevertheless, the time required to implement these practices and start seeing results means that a long-term perspective is needed. It also takes a long time horizon to execute many of these approaches. In the short term, laying off people is probably more profitable compared to trying to maintain employment security; cutting training is a quick way to maintain short-term profits; and cross-training and cross-utilization may provide insights and innovation in time, but initially, the organization foregoes the advantages of more narrow specialization and the immediate proficiency achieved thereby.

What determines an organization's time horizon is an important issue, but one outside the scope of this book. In general, however, there is some evidence that family ownership, employee ownership, or other forms of organization that lessen the immediate pressures for quick earnings to please the securities market are probably helpful. Lincoln Electric is closely held, and the Nordstrom family retains a substantial fraction of the ownership of that retailer. NUMMI has Toyota as one of the joint venture partners, and Toyota's own plans for the facility virtually dictate that it take a long-term view, which is consistent with its culture and tradition. Again, the Walton family's ownership position in Wal-Mart helps ensure that the organization takes a long view of its business processes.

It is almost inconceivable that a firm facing immediate short-term pressure would embark on activities that are apparently necessary to achieve some competitive advantage through people. This is one of the reasons for the limited diffusion of these practices. If the organization is doing well, it may feel no need to worry about its competitive position. By the same token, if the organization is in financial distress, the immediate pressures may be too severe to embark on activities that provide productivity and profit advantages, but only after a longer, and unknown, period of time.

Measurement of the Practices

Measurement is a critical component in any management process, and this is true for the process of managing the organization's work force. Measurement serves several functions. First, it provides feedback as to how well the organization is implementing various policies. For example, many organizations espouse a promotion from within policy but don't fulfill this objective. Often, this is because there is no systematic collection and reporting of information such as what percentage of the positions at given levels have been filled internally. A commitment to a high-wage policy obviously requires information as to where in the relevant labor market the organization's wages fall. A commitment to training is more likely to be fulfilled if data are collected, not only on the total amount spent on training but also on what types of employees have received training and what sorts of training are being delivered.

Second, measurement ensures that what is measured will be noticed.

Out of sight, out of mind is a principle that applies to organizational goals and practices as well as to people. One of the most consistent findings in the organizational literature is that measures affect behavior.[59] Most people will try to succeed on the measures even if there are no direct, immediate consequences. Things that are measured get talked about, and things that are not, don't. For three years, I served as a consultant to the commander of the Army and Air Force Exchange Service, the organization that runs the post exchanges (as well as many other similar activities). I and three other outsiders were charged with the responsibility of attending board of directors meetings and bringing to management's attention things that would improve the organization's level of customer service and its financial performance. My focus, the organization's human resource policies and practices, faced a severe problem—at each board meeting, detailed financial information was presented on sales and profits compared to last year as well as sales and profits by region, by category of merchandise, by line of business, and so forth. The only information regularly presented about people was their cost (where the assumption was that less was better) and their productivity, expressed as dollars of sales per employee. Although, partly at my urging, many nice things were typically said about the importance of people, especially in retailing, to the delivery of customer service and to enhancing the performance of the organization, such good intentions would and could do little in the absence of concrete measures to implement them.

It is, therefore, not by accident that organizations seriously committed to achieving competitive advantage through people make measurement of their efforts a critical component of the overall process. Thus, for example, at Advanced Micro Devices' submicron development facility, management made how people were managed a priority and measured employee attitudes regularly to see whether they were "achieving the vision." One survey asked questions such as: How many teams are you on in your own department and with members of other departments? How many hours per week do you spend receiving training and training others? The survey also asked the extent to which people agreed or disagreed with statements such as: There is problem solving at all levels in my work group; people in my work group are encouraged to take the initiative; a spirit of teamwork exists in our work group; my work group is service-oriented; there is open and honest communication among people in my work group. Such a survey permits the organization to see the extent to which it is actually doing what it thinks it wants to.

In a similar fashion, when Levi Strauss installed gain sharing at its plant in Blue Ridge, Georgia, it followed up with a survey assessing how well people understood the quality enhancement process, the gain-sharing program, each person's individual role, individuals' understanding of the measures, and how much improvement each perceived in teamwork, communications, quality, productivity, and cost-effectiveness. The company also measured cost per unit of production, absenteeism in the plant, and workers' compensation claim experience before and after the program was introduced.

In a world in which financial results are measured, a failure to measure human resource policy and practice implementation dooms this to second-class status, oversight, neglect, and potential failure. The feedback from the measurements is essential to refine and further develop implementation ideas as well as to learn how well the practices are actually achieving their intended results.

Overarching Philosophy

Last, and possibly most important, is having an overarching philosophy or view of management. It provides a way of connecting the various individual practices into a coherent whole and also enables people in the organization to persist and experiment when things don't work out immediately. Moreover, such a philosophy makes it easier to explain what the organization is doing, justify it, and mobilize support from internal and external constituencies. Most simply put, it is hard to get somewhere if you don't know where you are going. In a similar fashion, practices adopted without a deeper understanding of what they represent and why they are important to the organization may not add up to much, may be unable to survive internal or external problems, and are likely to produce less than stellar results.

Table 2-2   New versus Old Paradigms at Levi Strauss

Old Paradigm	New Paradigm
Economy of *scale* as basis for improvement logic	Economy of *time* as basis for improvement logic
Quality involves trade-offs	Quality is a "religion." No compromise.
Doers are separate from thinkers	Doers must also be thinkers
Assets are things	Assets are people
Profit is the primary business goal	Customer satisfaction is the primary business goal
Hierarchical organization. Goal is to please the boss.	Problem-solving network organization. Goal is to please the internal or external customer.
Measure to judge operational results	Measure to help people make operational improvements

Source: Presentation by Peter Thigpen at the Stanford School of Business, February 26, 1991.

Many companies that seek competitive success through their people and practice a number of the approaches listed really began with some underlying principles or else developed them early in the process. Levi Strauss's quality enhancement process began with the understanding that "manufacturing for quality and speed meant breaking the old paradigms," turning the culture upside down and completely reorienting the parameters of the business.[60] The company, and its manufacturing senior vice president, explicitly articulated the underlying assumptions of the old way of thinking and the new, as illustrated in Table 2-2.

At Lincoln Electric, a strong moral foundation buttresses the management practices: "The sons of a minister, John C. and James F. Lincoln had been raised with the words, 'Do unto others as you would have them do unto you' ringing in their ears. It was not difficult for them to adopt the golden rule as a basic operating premise of their company."[61] As James Lincoln noted: "If those crying loudest about the inefficiencies of labor were put in the position of the wage earner, they would react as he does. The worker is not a man apart. He has the same needs, aspirations, and reactions as the industrialist. A worker will not cooperate on any program that will penalize him. Does any manager?"[62] Lincoln went so far as to actually write a book on his views and the incentive management program.[63]

Writing about Nordstrom's incredible success, Richard Pascale noted, "Nordstrom's underlying culture (or organizational paradigm) is at the heart of things. It is more important than its product/market strategy, organizational structure or compensation system."[64] Advanced Micro Devices began in the submicron development facility by creating a vision. It was one of the first groups in the company to go through this exercise, but it has now diffused to other parts of the firm. Its particular vision embodied the following principles: continuous rapid improvement; empowerment; seamless organizational boundaries—no functional silos; customer centeredness; high expectations; and technical excellence.

Developing a coherent view of the employment relation is not invariably part of the manager's tool kit. Taking the time, as AMD did, to develop a vision of how the facility was to operate may strike some as inefficient. Yet it seems clear that the survival of the separate practices that appear to generate success is somewhat dependent on there being glue to knit things together—this glue is a system of values or beliefs about the basis of success and how to manage people.

TRENDS AND FADS OR ENDURING TRUTHS?

It is easy to sense that what passes for the current managerial wisdom is quite faddish. Such a view, of course, helps justify doing nothing. I have, on occasion, heard managers, if a proposed change is inconsistent with their own practices and values, say: "I don't really need to do this or even take it very seriously because, after all, some other idea will come along in a while." There probably is a great deal of faddishness in terminology ("total quality" is currently in) and possibly even in what some organizations do. But it is important to recognize that fads in the adoption of practices may not be related to actual changes in either the knowledge base of management or the effectiveness of various policies.

An illustration should make the point clear. One of the oldest and most reliable findings in psychology is the principle of reinforcement. As developed by B. F. Skinner and others,[65] it states simply that the probability of a behavior's recurring is higher if it has been reinforced in the past and diminishes if, when the behavior occurs, nothing happens or something aversive occurs. I know of no studies that have demonstrated that the idea of reinforcement is period-dependent. What is reinforced, of course, varies over time and across cultures, but the idea that behavior, if reinforced, is more likely to recur appears to be a universal law—given the current evidence. By contrast, the use of incentives in organizations is clearly something that follows fads and fashion. Pay for performance is in at the moment, but it may be out after a while. Organizations experiment endlessly with various forms of incentive schemes. This instability in reward practices is not related to instability in underlying principles of human behavior; more likely, it is caused by an inadequate theoretical model of behavior and incomplete knowledge of basic social science as well as a tendency to do whatever is recommended at the moment, regardless of whether it makes sense in terms of what we know about behavior.

Similarly, people are almost always willing to trade security (diminished risk) for lower economic returns (lower salaries). Obviously, people vary in terms of the risk-return deal they are willing to make, but other things being equal, certainty is customarily preferable to uncertainty. Nevertheless, policies of employment stability come and go, as does the use of contingent work arrangements that diminish both the certainty and the strength of attachments between employees and their employers.

Many management practices seem like fads because they are adopted without much understanding or because they are implemented without an underlying philosophy or set of values. Founded on neither knowledge nor substantive belief, they are prone to be adopted or abandoned according to the taste of the time. This trendiness does not mean that the value of the underlying practices or the ideas on which they are based are themselves fluctuating.

What is striking, in fact, is the enormous consistency over time—

not in every small detail, but in the basic foundations of practices that have made some organizations successful on the basis of how they manage people. The seeds of Lincoln Electric's incentive management program were sown in 1914 when James F. Lincoln became vice president and general manager and established an advisory board of elected representatives from each department of the company.[66] Much of the Lincoln system evolved more than 40 years ago and has been remarkably unchanged over that period. Similarly, Nordstrom's philosophy and management practices have existed for decades. Southwest Airlines has obviously evolved its management systems as it has grown, but the underlying philosophy—which emphasizes the importance of people, having fun, and recognition of employees—is largely unchanged since the company was founded.

Indeed, what is so striking is how stable basic ideas of how to manage people have been over time. For instance, Douglas McGregor published his famous treatise on Theory X and Theory Y management more than 30 years ago. He argued "that a central assumption of organization theory was that authority is the central, indispensable means of managerial control."[67] Theory X, which dominated managerial thinking and provided the foundation for much management practice (then and now), assumed that the average person has an inherent dislike of work and will avoid it if possible. Because of this effort aversion (to use modern economic terminology), people needed to be induced and controlled to exert adequate effort; and furthermore, the average person likes to be directed, prefers to avoid responsibility, and seeks security.[68] Theory Y assumptions, by contrast, include: the expenditure of both physical and mental effort is natural; people will exercise self-direction in the service of objectives to which they are committed; under the proper conditions, people seek responsibility; the ability to exercise imagination, creativity, and ingenuity is widely distributed in organizations; but under current management practices, much human potential is wasted or underutilized.[69]

McGregor recognized the self-fulfilling nature of management practice—people will behave in a way consistent with how they are treated, thereby validating the underlying assumptions. He also recognized the inherent limitations of formal authority and power for getting things done in work organizations:

> An agent of the Textile Workers Union of America likes to tell the story of the occasion when a new manager appeared in the mill where he was working. The manager came into the weave room the day he arrived. He walked directly over to the agent and said. . . . "I am the new manager here. When I manage a mill, I run it. Do you understand?" The agent nodded, and then waved his hand. The workers, intently watching this encounter, shut down every loom in the room immediately. The agent turned to the manager and said, "All right, go ahead and run it."[70]

Describing Levi's gain-sharing program at Blue Ridge, Peter Thigpen, the corporation's senior manufacturing executive, noted that "the program is not terribly different than the first Scanlon plan devised by a local union leader at Empire Steel and Tinplate in Ohio in 1935."[71] The Scanlon principles include: 1) sharing the economic gains from improvements in organizational performance, with all organizational members except top managers participating; 2) a formal method for having all organizational members contribute ingenuity and brainpower to the improvement of organizational performance, often accomplished by means of committees that operate like quality circles, receiving, evaluating, and distributing ideas for improvement; and 3) the consequent improvement of relations across functional groups and levels of the organizational hierarchy.[72] A system of management that is now almost 60 years old but encompasses many practices that are being rediscovered and reapplied today belies the assertion that these ideas are in some sense either new or trendy.

Someone seeking to explain the limited diffusion of effective practices for managing the work force will have to look to something other than novelty or faddishness. The first case about Lincoln Electric's success came out of Harvard Business School in 1947, and writings about incentives and gain sharing, participative management, and quality improvement teams are more than 40 years old. Reflecting on the literature on effective management practices over the years, one is struck not by its change but rather by the tremendous continuity in ideas.

ARE EFFECTIVE MANAGEMENT PRACTICES CONTINGENT ON STRATEGY?

A second challenge to implementing these 16 practices that successful firms employ in managing people is the idea that how one manages people is contingent on the organization's competitive strategy. One variant of this argument suggests that if Nordstrom, for example, is succeeding through a unique organizational culture that provides outstanding service, then one would want to compete with Nordstrom not by doing the same thing—perhaps better—but by doing something completely different. It is important to recognize that competing on the basis of human resources is *not* the only source of success, so that one might compete with Nordstrom or any other organization using other competitive weapons such as information technology and systems, product differentiation, and so forth. This does not mean that these practices are not almost invariably effective ways to achieve competitive success through people, only that there may be other bases of competition that a firm can use.

A second argument for the contingency of these practices is based on the observation that the adoption of so-called flexible forms of work organization (which include many of the practices enumerated in this chapter) "is correlated with being in a competitive product market, having a technology which requires high levels of skill, engaging in customized production, and following what can be termed a 'high road' strategy which emphasizes variety and quality in contrast to low cost."[73] Jeffrey Arthur, studying U.S. steel minimills, argued that a cost-leadership market strategy reduces management's need and incentive to engage in commitment-enhancing practices, compared to firms following a differentiation strategy dependent on flexibility, quality, and variety.[74] The argument, then, takes two forms: 1) because we observe that the use of high-commitment work practices varies systematically, the effectiveness of these practices or their appropriateness also varies in a similar fashion; and 2) in particular, cost-based strategies can use traditional management approaches, whereas strategies based on product differentiation, quality, and customer responsiveness require the use of high-commitment strategies to a greater extent.

The logic is compelling but not entirely consistent with the evidence. Although it may be true that certain types of strategies virtually necessitate the use of high-commitment work practices, there is little evidence that such work practices don't also help firms following other strategies such as cost minimization. Of course, Lincoln Electric has for years followed a cost-based competitive strategy, consistently lowering both its costs and its prices—which is how it has built market share, driven out many competitors, and deterred entry on the part of potential competitors. But Lincoln uses many of the practices enumerated. Similarly, Southwest Airlines and People Express were both low-cost carriers, competing on the basis of price, and yet both employed many of these practices as well. Arthur's study of the connection between market strategy and industrial relations practices in the American minimill industry revealed that although the vast majority of mills following a low-cost business strategy adopted cost-reducing industrial relations practices (minimizing skill levels, wages, training, and participation), some 10% following the cost-reduction strategy used commitment-maximizing practices.[75] Furthermore, some 40% of the mills following a differentiation strategy used a strategically inappropriate (cost-reducing) industrial relations system. Thus, there was a significant connection between strategy and industrial relations practices, but the connection was far from perfect. Some firms pursued cost-minimizing strategies even when they were seeking advantage through quality and flexibility, and others pursuing a low-cost strategy nevertheless used high-commitment work practices. The latter result is quite consistent with the fact that retailing firms such as Costco and Wal-Mart, competing on the basis of price, nevertheless use many high-commitment work practices with their employees.

Obviously, how one would implement these practices will vary significantly, based on a given organization's strategy and its particular technology and market environment. What teams and incentive compensation might look like in retailing would probably differ from what one would observe in a manufacturer of arc welding equipment. In this sense, one would want to think systematically about the particular skills and behaviors one needs to execute the particular strategy in a specific market environment and obviously adjust the implementation of these practices to fit those requirements. However, there is an important distinction between the contingent nature of the *implementation* of these practices, which everyone would agree is necessary, and the idea that the practices themselves do not provide benefit in many, if not most, situations.

If one wants to achieve competitive advantage through people, there is little evidence that one should not use the practices enumerated. The specific implementation of the practices, and the form they may take, are obviously contingent not only on strategy but also on other contextual factors such as location, nature and interdependence of the work, and so forth. Of course, one can achieve competitive success on the basis of things other than people. However, particularly because many of the other bases of success are more readily imitated (e.g., it is easier for someone to copy a low-wage, low-skill, low-commitment work system), only at one's potential peril should one refuse to at least consider using these practices.

The Evidence for Slow Learning and Unrealized Potential

3

In Chapter 2, I asserted that there are practices for managing the employment relation that often produce excellent outcomes and implied that they are not very widely adopted. This chapter presents evidence on both these points. While there is evidence for the effectiveness of these ways of managing the work force, and that they are not particularly new or trendy, the data indicate that it is quite problematic to diffuse and sustain these practices. This raises the fundamental question of what the problems are. There are many, but before considering them, we first need to be fully convinced that these practices are at once effective and undiffused.

THE EVIDENCE FOR EFFECTIVENESS

Many, although certainly not all, organizations that have installed a system of high-commitment work practices or alternative work arrangements have attempted to measure their effects. In other instances, researchers have done the assessment. Thus, for example, at Advanced Micro Devices, the success of the new way of organizing and managing work at the submicron development center is evidenced by the following outcomes: 1) the very first wafer worked; 2) in 30 weeks, the facility went to production status, compared to the normal 18 months; 3) 1 million EPROMs (erasable *programmable read-only* memories) were produced in a year; 4) the facility experienced much faster time from development to production; 5) in 27 weeks, it was able to achieve a 70% yield on production; and 6) it achieved six unique process flows.[1] At Levi Strauss's Blue Ridge plant, the cost per unit in the three quarters after it installed its gain-sharing and quality enhancement process averaged 5.5% less than in the prior three quarters; absenteeism decreased 13%; and workers' compensation claim experience improved.[2] Between 1935 and 1974, the productivity of Lincoln Electric's production workers increased at more than twice the rate for all manufacturing industries.[3] During the 1980s, a time when many retailers went bankrupt, Nordstrom grew at a rate of 20% per year and tripled its sales while merely doubling its space; its sales per square foot of $380 were almost double the industry average of $194.[4]

There are literally hundreds of cases like these. However, many of these examples make drawing inferences about the effects of work arrangements difficult; for instance:

- Things other than work practices change at the same time, which makes attributing the improvements to a particular cause problematic.
- In many, if not most, instances, one or very few things were changed; because of the interconnections among the elements of managing work, evaluating the change of only one thing is troublesome, even if that change proves effective.
- In many instances, the outcome measures are not proximately related to the fundamental business processes.

What I have chosen to do in this chapter is to review an exemplary case study—the Toyota–General Motors joint venture—and then consider more systematic evidence from the automobile and textile industries and other settings that speak to the potential of the work practices described previously. This is not intended to be a comprehensive review but one that illustrates the broad outlines of what has been learned and how that learning has occurred.

New United Motor Manufacturing (NUMMI)

Although there are literally hundreds of cases attesting to the performance improvements possible from adopting more effective ways of managing people, the case of the Fremont, California, plant of General Motors has attracted a disproportionate amount of attention. This is probably because it was one of the earliest case studies to collect systematic, quantitative data on performance, both before and after the change, and because productivity in automobile assembly can be fairly clearly assessed. Perhaps its greatest attention-getting property was this: although little changed—the plant didn't move, new workers weren't hired, there was not much new technology—a new system of management increased productivity approximately 100%. This dramatic improvement, carefully documented, makes the NUMMI case noteworthy.

The joint venture between Toyota and General Motors occupied the Fremont plant of GM, which had been closed in 1982. The plant was organized by the United Auto Workers union, both while it was owned by General Motors and after it reopened under the governance of the joint venture. The facility had developed a reputation for having high levels of absenteeism, alcohol and drug abuse, and poor productivity and quality.

When the plant reopened in late 1984, it did so with a work force overwhelmingly comprised of workers who had presented such problems in the past:

> Of 5300 applications sent to former GM-Fremont employees, 3200 were returned. Over the next 20 months, 2,200 hourly team members were hired, approximately 85% of them from the old GM-Fremont plant, including the entire union hierarchy. . . . NUMMI's work force was unusu-

ally old compared to other assembly plants, the average age being 41. . . . Some 26% were Hispanic, 20% black, and 15% female.[5]

The applicants for hourly jobs were evaluated jointly by management and union officials. The "union had insisted that the company offer compelling reasons for rejecting a candidate and that an arbitration procedure be established to handle disputes over selection."[6] The participation of the union in the rehiring process makes it implausible that the group that returned was particularly malleable or docile.

The NUMMI system had many of the elements associated with achieving competitive success through people:

- Employees were carefully screened and selected in a three-day assessment process that included individual and group interviews, written tests, and production simulations.[7]
- There was extensive training of new hires, including a "four-day orientation program that explained the team concept, production system, quality principles, attendance rules, safety policies, labor-management relations, and so forth."[8]
- Job security was formally written into the labor contract.
- Everyone in the production function wore the same blue smock, and management cafeterias and reserved parking were eliminated, providing a sense of equality in the facility.[9]
- The plant employed teams and the team concept. The president of NUMMI at the time commented: "The team concept is not just the small groups on the shop floor. It also applies to the plant as a whole. . . . This way, the workers see that the company isn't the property of management, but of everyone together. And the key to this team concept is trust and respect."[10]
- There was a suggestion system to encourage employee involvement and participation; moreover, efforts were made to accept, in some form, 95% of the suggestions made.[11]
- There were considerably fewer job classifications, and most important, tasks were integrated as appropriate. Thus, for instance, "NUMMI is the only stamping plant in the world in which every-

body is allowed to do repairs. . . . We don't have inspectors on the production line. . . . [W]e want to build a culture where inspection is everybody's job."[12]

- There were monetary rewards for accepted suggestions, but the principal reward was recognition, highly valued by the employees.[13]
- There was significant wage compression, with hourly workers making the same rate regardless of their job and team leaders earning only 40 cents an hour more than team members.[14]
- Hourly workers were comparatively well paid, not only by the standards of the local labor market but also by comparison with other GM plants. For instance, in 1991, NUMMI workers earned $17.85 per hour and typically were paid some 10 to 30 cents per hour more than workers in other GM plants.[15]
- There was extensive sharing of information about plant performance, sales of products produced by the plant, quality, and safety.[16]
- There was an overarching philosophy—in this instance, the idea of a production system.[17] One NUMMI employee noted:

GM had no real production system . . . at least nothing that people on the floor ever saw. . . . At NUMMI, we've got a comprehensive system that ties together in a defined and disciplined way standardized work, just-in-time inventory, preventive maintenance, quality control—a system that everyone on that shop-floor understands and respects.[18]

The results of the NUMMI system were truly extraordinary. Absenteeism fell from 20% to 25% to between 3% and 4%. Grievances fell from a rate of 5,000–7,000 in a three-year contract period to just 100 in an 18-month period. Participation in the suggestion system went almost immediately to 50% and, by 1991, had increased to more than 85%.[19] The increases in both productivity and quality were dramatic. Table 3-1 presents the results of a study done by John Krafcik, a quality control engineer at NUMMI from 1984 to 1986. This study compares productivity and quality at NUMMI with previous levels when the plant was managed by General Motors as well as with a comparable GM plant in

Table 3-1   Productivity and Quality Comparisons among Four
Automobile Plants

Productivity	Framingham 1986	GM-Fremont 1978	NUMMI 1986	Takaoka 1986
Overall Productivity				
Hourly (hours/unit)	36.1	38.2	17.5	15.5
Salaried	4.6	4.9	3.3	2.5
Total	40.7	43.1	20.8	18.0
Corrected (adjusted) Productivity				
Hourly	26.2	24.2	16.3	15.5
Salaried	4.6	4.9	3.3	2.5
Total	30.8	29.1	19.6	18.0
NUMMI's Advantage	57.1%	48.5%	—	−8.2%
Quality Indicators				
GM Audit	125–130	120–125	135–140	135–140
Owner Survey	85–88	NA	91–94	92–94
Consumer Reports (Reliability Index)	2.1–3.0	2.6–3.0	3.6–3.8	3.8–4.0

Source: John Krafcik, "Learning from NUMMI," unpublished International Motor Vehicle Program Working Paper (Cambridge, MA: Sloan School of Management, MIT, 1986).

Framingham, Massachusetts (now closed), and a sister plant operated by Toyota in Takaoka. Krafcik's corrected productivity data take into account factors such as relief time, differences in product size, differences in option content, and an adjustment for different welding requirements. Three different quality measures were used—one from *Consumer Reports*, one from an internal GM audit, and one from an owners' survey. Table 3-1 illustrates that NUMMI produced higher-quality products with significantly fewer labor hours than at the other GM plants and was almost as productive as the Toyota plant in Japan. Not only were productivity and quality good, but so, too, was the quality of working life. By 1991, internal surveys "showed that the overall proportion of people describing themselves as satisfied or very satisfied with work at NUMMI" was 90%.[20]

The Automobile Industry

The case study of NUMMI is just one example of a number of studies that have examined work arrangements and their effects on productivity and quality in the automobile industry. A study of 18 General Motors plants over the 1970–1979 period concluded that "industrial relations performance affects economic performance."[21] The study revealed that there was greater improvement in industrial relations and economic performance in plants that developed a high level of quality of work life activity.

A cross-sectional study of 25 plants in a U.S. automobile company investigated the relationship between various measures of plant-level industrial relations and quality of work life programs and measures of both efficiency and quality. Efficiency was "an index that compared actual hours of direct labor input to standardized hours calculated by the company's industrial engineers,"[22] and quality was an index "derived from a count of the number of faults and demerits that appeared in inspections of the product."[23] The study found that high levels of involvement in quality of work life programs were correlated with "relatively good attitudes among salaried employees, high levels of participation in suggestion programs, and low grievance and discipline rates."[24] Table 3-2 displays the relationships between various dimensions of the industrial relations climate in each plant and quality and productivity. The conclusion is clear: efficiency is positively related to workers' attitudes, participation in suggestion programs, and involvement in quality of work life programs and negatively related to the rates of grievances, disciplinary actions, and absenteeism.

The most comprehensive study on the world automobile assembly industry was conducted by MIT researchers. It demonstrated in large scale what NUMMI and John Krafcik's earlier work had shown on a more limited basis—that there were enormous differences in productivity and quality across automobile assembly plants, even in the same country, and even under similar ownership. Table 3-3 presents data from that study on quality and productivity for the *volume* (as opposed to

Table 3-2 Correlations between Economic Performance and Industrial Relations System Measures in 25 Manufacturing Plants

	Direct Labor Efficiency	Product Quality
Grievance rate	−.48***	−.18***
Absenteeism rate	−.25**	.05
Disciplinary actions rate	−.25***	−.21**
Participation in suggestion programs	.38***	.73***
Quality of work life program involvement	.17*	.26**
Salaried workers' attitudes	.40***	.48***

Source: Harry C. Katz, Thomas A. Kochan, and Mark R. Weber, "Assessing the Effects of Industrial Relations Systems and Efforts to Improve the Quality of Working Life on Organizational Effectiveness," *Academy of Management Journal* 28 (1985), 519.
 *p < .10
 **p < .05
 ***p < .01

exclusive, such as Rolls-Royce) car manufacturers, including Ford, Chrysler, and General Motors in the United States; Fiat, Volkswagen, and Renault in Europe; and all the automobile companies in Japan. The data show an almost 2 to 1 difference in productivity within categories between the most and least efficient plant and almost 3 to 1 differences in quality.

To what are these differences in productivity and quality attributable? Some of the differences are related to variation in automation: "We estimate that on average automation accounts for about one-third of the total difference in productivity between plants."[25] However, "at any level of automation the difference between the most and least efficient plant is enormous."[26] Some of the differences are also related to the extent to which automobiles are designed to be easily manufactured. However, the MIT study found that in general, it was the organizational features of the plant that accounted for up to half the performance differences.[27] The study referred to the most effective and efficient production system as a "lean" system. The principal elements

Table 3-3   Automobile Assembly Plant Productivity and Quality

| | PRODUCTIVITY (HOURS/VEHICLE) | | |
	Best	Weighted Average	Worst
Japanese-owned plants in Japan	13.2	16.8	25.9
Japanese-owned plants in North America	18.8	20.9	25.5
U.S.-owned plants in North America	18.6	24.9	30.7
U.S. & Japanese-owned plants in Europe	22.8	35.3	57.6
European-owned plants in Europe	22.8	35.5	55.7
Plants in newly industrializing countries	25.7	41.0	78.7
	QUALITY (DEFECTS/100 CARS)		
Japanese-owned plants in Japan	37.6	52.1	88.4
Japanese-owned plants in North America	36.4	54.7	59.8
U.S.-owned plants in North America	35.1	78.4	168.6
European-owned plants in Europe	63.9	76.4	123.8
Plants in newly industrializing countries	27.6	72.3	190.5

Source: James P. Womack, Daniel T. Jones, and Daniel Roos, *The Machine That Changed the World* (New York: Rawson Associates, 1990), 89, 90.

of a lean or flexible production system are listed in Table 3-4. The MIT study noted that such a system

> transfers the maximum number of tasks and responsibilities to those workers actually adding value to the car on the line. . . . This, in turn, means teamwork among line workers and a simple but comprehensive information display system that makes it possible for everyone in the plant to respond quickly to problems and to understand the plant's over-all situation. . . . [W]orkers respond only when there exists some sense of reciprocal obligation, a sense that management actually values skilled workers, will make sacrifices to retain them, and is willing to delegate responsibility to the team.[28]

John Paul MacDuffie, using these data, statistically evaluated the relationship between attributes of work organizations and productivity

Table 3-4   Elements of Lean or Flexible Production

Elimination of buffers or inventory, including extra workers

Quality and efficiency are seen as positively related, with quality preeminent

Emphasis on ability to change from one product to another quickly

Multiskilled workers with a good understanding of the production process

Higher level of training

Commitment to retain highly trained workers

Compensation that is partly contingent on corporate, plant, and/or individual performance

Reduction of status barriers

High-commitment work practices

---

and quality.[29] He found a positive correlation of .36 between productivity and quality, indicating that there was no trade-off between the two. His production organization index contained three components: 1) the use of buffers; 2) work systems, which include the percentage of employees in work teams, the number of production-related suggestions per employee, extent of job rotation, and so forth; and 3) human resource management policies, including selection and hiring criteria, degree of status differentiation, and extent of training. Overall, the production organization index explained some 36% of the variation in both productivity and quality for this large sample of automobile assembly plants.[30]

The Textile Industry

The automobile industry study sparked other attempts to see to what extent work organization practices affected productivity and quality in other industries. One of the first is an ongoing examination of the textile industry. This industry shares with automobiles a number of characteristics, including intense foreign competition, the fact that it is primarily an assembly business, that costs are important, and a tradition in which workers, paid by the piece, tended to have little skill, training, or say in their own work process. The example from Levi Strauss previously described provides one illustration of how changing these elements of the employment relationship can be beneficial.

The textile industry also illustrates vividly how it requires a fundamental shift in ways of thinking to remain competitive. In the first place, it is not clear that there should be a U.S. textile industry at all. The apparel industry has traditionally competed on the basis of price and has, consequently, relentlessly sought to drive down costs.[31] At Levi Strauss, re-engineering jobs and increased mechanization have halved the labor time of making a pair of blue jeans in the past 20 years. The pressure on wages has been intense. Textile industry workers in 1991 earned, on average, only 61% of the average hourly wage paid to all manufacturing workers.[32] Even at that, however, U.S. wage levels are many times more than those of workers in other parts of the world. For instance, hourly earnings in Korea, Singapore, Hong Kong, and Taiwan are a third or slightly less of average U.S. wages.[33] Ironically, the very success in holding down wages and increasing productivity has resulted in direct labor costs being a small fraction of the final product's cost. For instance, direct labor accounts for less than 15% of the cost of a pair of stone washed jeans. Even though 1) labor costs are typically a small fraction of the cost of the final product, and 2) the U.S. textile manufacturers could scarcely compete simply on the basis of labor rates, given wages in other countries, U.S. manufacturers have traditionally been obsessed with reducing unit labor costs and have sought to compete on the basis of cost.

Of course, other bases of competition are available. Quality and product variety are obvious ones, but so, too, is customer service. The new retailers—stores such as Wal-Mart and Dillard's—want to minimize both their inventory and the possibility that they will be out of stock of an important item. Consequently, the ability to deliver the needed merchandise rapidly is another, increasingly important, potential basis of competitive success.

In their pursuit of the holy grail of labor cost reduction, textile manufacturers developed the so-called bundle method of production. This system relies on centralized cutting and an assembly process that "entails breaking assembly of the various cut pieces into a long series of distinct operations. Each operation is done by a single worker operating at a stationary sewing machine."[34] The system requires buffer inventory between the individual work stations "to minimize the downtime of workers given uneven assembly time requirements for different operations. Standard practice is a one-day buffer between operations."[35] Thus, the time required to move a given piece of clothing from initial to final stages of production depends on the number of different assembly steps. It takes 40 days under the bundle system for a pair of pants with approximately 40 separate operations to move from cut pieces to final product.[36] Note, by the way, that most of the time, nothing is happening to the particular garment—its pieces are waiting to be worked on. The head of manufacturing for Levi Strauss estimated that under this system of production, the proportion of time that a given garment (or its constituent pieces) was being worked on was less than 10%—more than 90% of the time, it was sitting in an in-process inventory.

This system of production, with its sequential interdependence, has made it difficult to introduce new technology to any one operation because line balancing is important. Further, the monotonous, repetitive, and increasingly low-skilled work has caused labor turnover and a high rate of occupational injury—for example, in 1990, the incidence of repeated trauma (repetitive motion) injury was 8 times as high for apparel workers making suits and coats as it was for the work force as a whole and was more than 20 times higher for workers making trousers and slacks.[37]

An alternative system of production, called modular production, originated in the 1980s but has diffused very slowly. Under modular production, tasks are grouped and assigned to members of a module, or a work team. "Rather than dividing work among separate operators, a group works together to produce a major portion of the final garment product, or in some cases the entire garment."[38] Modular production either requires or facilitates multiskilling of workers and job rotation; the use of group rather than individual piece-rate incentives and pay based on the acquisition of additional skills; much more training; fewer supervisors; and more mobility based on skill acquisition.[39] Modular production, where it has been introduced, has been almost as efficient as the bundle system but has reduced the throughput time anywhere from 80% to 90%.[40] Additionally, turnover has decreased substantially, and workers' compensation experience has improved. There is also some indication that quality and the ability to shift from one product to the other can be enhanced under a modular system.

The textile industry presents its own version of lean or flexible production—modular production—and illustrates the advantages that can be obtained under this system. However, the industry also illustrates how difficult it is to change firms' understanding of the basis for competitive success, even when present strategies are clearly not very feasible given the economic characteristics of the industry.

Other Industry Examples

The evidence from other industries and from the few cross-industry studies available confirms what we have seen in automobiles and textiles: there are invariably competing ways of managing the work force, and those that are consistent with the practices described in Chapter 2, producing a better employee relations environment, tend to be associated with improved performance on a number of dimensions. One example comes from the shipping industry.

Richard Walton examined the evolution of the shipping industry over decades in eight countries. Although, from 1960 to 1973, tonnage grew every year, after 1973, growth first slowed and then seaborne trade actually decreased.[41] In this increasingly competitive environment, labor costs loomed large. For instance, in 1980, crew costs on a U.K. vessel "were almost one-fourth of total costs and over 40% of operating costs. In a comparable vessel in the Third World, crew costs would be one-third the United Kingdom's; in the United States, they would be more than double the United Kingdom's."[42] As in textiles, and to a lesser extent automobiles, shipping firms would have to become substantially more productive in high-wage countries to survive under increasingly adverse economic conditions (or alternatively, obtain legislative protection for some of their markets—another strategy that has worked fairly well in this industry).

Traditional work organization on board ship bore little resemblance to the practices that bring competitive success through people:

> The officers and crew were always cordoned off into separate classes. . . . The schedule of work activities—who would do what and when—was drawn up by the officers and adhered to by the crew. . . . [T]here were no suggestion boxes. There was little or no flexibility in work assignments. . . . No one was expected to work in the engine room one day and on the bridge the next.[43]

However, between 1966 and 1983, four major types of change occurred, to a greater extent in some countries and on some ships than in other countries and on other ships:

1. From a strict hierarchical, departmental structure with narrow, fixed roles to one in which roles are more broadly defined and assignment patterns more flexible
2. From rotary hiring halls . . . to ongoing employment relationships between seafarers and ship owners, and from a high turnover of onboard personnel to a pattern in which more individuals return to the same ship after shore leave
3. From a pattern of central authority to more delegated authority and participative decision making
4. From a rigid, caste-like social structure to one that is more flexible, with a deemphasis of status symbols[44]

Shippers in Norway, Holland, and Japan were the most likely to adopt the new ways of organizing work; the United Kingdom, Sweden, and West Germany adopted innovative work arrangements to a moderate degree; shipping industries in Denmark and the United States were the least innovative over this period.[45] This is unfortunate for the United States since "the innovations were increasingly regarded by ship owners not only as desirable but also as . . . necessary for high wage countries to compete."[46] The evidence was that these innovations provided numerous benefits: 1) flexibility in staffing and increased decentralization permitted smaller crews; 2) symbolic egalitarianism saved space by eliminating separate dining and lounge areas and separate galleys; 3) decentralization and multiskilling led to better-quality decisions and faster implementation; and 4) more competent, flexible, and cohesive crews produced improved safety records.[47] The United States, a laggard in adopting the new ways of organizing work, also lagged in its ability to reduce its crew size. Walton reported that for newer, advanced ships, U.S. crews were occasionally as much as twice as large as European and Japanese crews for container ships and roll-on/roll-off cargo vessels and about 10% larger for tankers.[48]

In the paper industry, a study of nine unionized mills over the 1976–1982 period discovered a relationship between employee relations practices and productivity—specifically, the more grievances filed in the mill, the lower the mill's productivity.[49]

In the United States, with few exceptions (Southwest and Delta being two), most airlines have followed practices with respect to their employees that are, for the most part, diametrically opposite of what would be required to achieve competitive advantage through people—and this in a service industry. The legacy of the "tough" posture with respect to the work force includes the disappearance of Eastern and the bankruptcy of TWA and Continental (the latter twice). However, "the tough tactics that airline managers used to gain huge cost savings from labor . . . in the last decade will haunt the industry in the future, a study of airline labor relations concludes."[50]

The future problems are many. First, the easy gains from downsizing crews and cutting wages have largely been accomplished. During the 1980s, airlines went from being the third highest-paying industry to the seventeenth. Additional gains will have to come from a more productive labor force. Second, the growth in size and increased financial leverage of air carriers render them less able to take a strike or job action, as "they could not quickly replace the thousands of pilots, flight attendants and mechanics who would be needed to keep a carrier operating."[51] Third, the increasing internationalization of both air service and competition means that U.S. airlines confront these challenges after waging a war on the unions that the unions survived, so "the industry is facing at times hostile and increasingly determined union leaders across the bargaining table just when it needs to cut costs further."[52] It is little wonder that Southwest Airlines, pursuing a different course, sells for 31 times earnings in a cyclical, competitive industry.

While reviewing the existing data on employee involvement and quality of work life programs, one writer concluded:

> Research data show that established ... programs typically increase worker satisfaction with the job and the organizational context across a wide variety of organizational types. ... [O]rganizational productivity improvements ... have been present in less than half of most large-scale studies. ... [I]t is rare for EI/QWL programs to be associated with any diminishing in organizational performance.[53]

Although there is virtually no evidence that changing employment relationships as described diminishes organizational outcomes, and much evidence demonstrating positive effects, and even though many of these ideas have been in existence literally for decades, there is scant evidence that such work place reforms have been adopted with either alacrity or enthusiasm. Examining the extent of diffusion of work place reform reinforces the conclusion that change in practice comes only with difficulty.

THE EVIDENCE FOR DIFFUSION AND PERSISTENCE OF CHANGES IN THE EMPLOYMENT RELATIONSHIP

The evidence seems clear: in instituting new practices to achieve competitive advantage through people, change comes slowly and backsliding is frequent. The textile industry study concluded: "In a world where much of the competitive strategy ... depends on time, workers ... are critical."[54] The existing bundle system of production—characterized by low wages, little career mobility, and high levels of occupational injuries—is explicitly favored by very few interests in the industry. Some industry observers note that the alternative, modular production system can solve labor shortage, absenteeism, and turnover problems.[55] Another group, "including major textile-fiber suppliers and the Amalgamated Clothing and Textile Union, have cited the system as key to the long run survival of U.S. apparel firms."[56] Nevertheless, diffusion has been minuscule. In 1985, 97% of all manufacturers used the bundle system, according to industry surveys. Although this figure decreased to 90% by 1988 and to 82% by 1992, given the economic pressures and the fact that industry publications were filled with articles advocating the new system, one might have expected more change.[57] The components of the bundle system, such as individual (rather than group) piece rates and narrow (as opposed to broad) training, also maintained their dominance in the industry.

General Motors entered the joint venture with Toyota, NUMMI, explicitly to learn about Japanese manufacturing practices. Nevertheless, the firm did many things to discourage learning and transfer of experience. It permitted other GM executives to spend just one day in the plant, and that day was mostly spent listening to presentations on technology (not the crucial element in the organization's success); the firm took GM executives rotating out of assignments in NUMMI and moved them individually (as opposed to in groups) to primarily staff or consultant roles in dispersed locations; many observers believed that the company did not push the car, the Nova, that was originally manufactured for GM at the plant, so when its sales were low, GM could point to the failure of its participation in NUMMI; in short, GM seemed to almost actively resist learning from the NUMMI experience.[58]

There have been a number of surveys of work force management practices whose results, taken as a whole, are consistent with respect to several points: 1) there has clearly been some increase in the use of commitment-building practices in the 1980s; 2) nevertheless, diffusion and adoption remain comparatively limited, confined to a minority of firms; and 3) there is almost no relationship between the reported success of a practice and its adoption. Rather, practices that are easier to adopt, in the sense of altering less fundamental power relationships in the firm, are the ones most likely to be adopted.

In 1982, the New York Stock Exchange conducted a comprehensive survey designed to answer the question: "What is American management currently doing to achieve more labor cooperation, to reduce costly adversarial tactics, to enhance the quality of production, and to

Table 3-5   Occurrence and Evaluation of Various Employment
Relation Practices, 1982

Activity	Percentage of Companies with Activity	Percentage Rating Activity as	
		Very Successful	Somewhat Successful
Job enlargement	7	25	42
Job rotation	6	24	43
Job design/redesign	15	26	48
Formal training	25	37	40
Personalized work hours	9	44	32
Suggestion systems	13	13	49
Quality circles	14	28	29
Salarying blue-collar workers	2	67	15
Surveys of employee attitudes	15	22	47
Production teams	5	32	36
Labor/management committees	8	16	55
Group productivity financial incentives	2	18	58
Profit-sharing incentives	8	26	47
Stock purchase plan	7	14	47

Source: Compiled from data in William C. Freund and Eugene Epstein, *People and Productivity*
(Homewood, IL: Dow Jones–Irwin, 1984), 119, 160.

raise the quality of work life?"[59] Table 3-5 displays the results from two
portions of that survey: the proportion of the total sample who reported
doing the activities and the proportion who assessed these activities as
being either very or somewhat successful. The data in the table indicate
that although many of these practices were rated overwhelmingly as
successful, only one of them, formal training, was in use at even a quarter of the surveyed firms. In fact, on average, these activities were employed in fewer than one in ten companies. Second, the data in the
table show little relationship between the rated success of the practices

and the frequency of their adoption. For instance, the most successful practice was salarying blue-collar employees, used in only 2% of the surveyed firms. Production teams were employed by only 5%. New ways of organizing and compensating work were adopted by few companies, regardless of their success ratings. By contrast, activities that were less disruptive to the underlying structure of the employment relationship—such as conducting attitude surveys, instituting quality circles, and implementing suggestion systems—occurred with greater frequency.

A 1987 survey sent by the General Accounting Office to 934 companies listed in the 1986 *Fortune* 1000 (the 500 largest service companies and the 500 largest industrial firms) and a follow-up 1990 survey sent to 987 of the *Fortune* 1000 companies provide evidence for somewhat more widespread adoption of innovative practices by the late 1980s, but also little increase in most practices between the time of the two surveys and, overall, a fairly low level of implementation.[60] Table 3-6 presents data on practices that examine the extent to which they were adopted in 1987 and 1990, as well as the percentage of firms reporting that they evaluated the practices as successful or very successful. The percentage reporting at least some substantial activity in this area appears to be much larger than in the earlier stock exchange survey—with the exception of self-managed teams and gain sharing, all the other practices were being implemented with more than 20% of the firm's work force in well over 20% of the organizations, in almost every case. Some practices— such as all-salaried pay, profit sharing, and survey feedback—were being employed, at least to some extent, in about half of all the firms.

These data also suggest a somewhat stronger relationship between the rated success of these practices and the extent to which they have been adopted. Data on information and training, from the same surveys, are also instructive. In 1990, barely more than half the firms reported providing 60% or more of their employees with information on their own unit's operating results, while only a quarter informed a majority of employees about new technologies that could affect them; less than one-fifth provided information on competitors' relative positions, and less than half shared business plans and goals with a majority of

Table 3-6   Extent of Diffusion and the Evaluation of Various
Employment Practices in 1987 and 1990

Practice	Percentage of Firms Reporting Either No or Fewer Than 20% of Employees Covered		Percentage of Firms Evaluating the Practice as Either Successful or Very Successful
	1987	1990	1990
Self-managing teams	92	90	60
Quality circles	71	70	52
Job enrichment or redesign	78	68	53
Survey feedback	54	49	70
Participation groups other than QCs	63	49	73
All-salaried pay	44	54	76
Profit sharing	55	56	71
Gain sharing	93	89	54
Knowledge/skill-based pay	85	83	60
Employee stock ownership	47	45	72
Work group or team incentives	—	79	61

Source: Compiled from data in Edward E. Lawler III, Susan Albers Mohrman, and Gerald E. Ledford, Jr., *Employee Involvement and Total Quality Management* (San Francisco: Jossey-Bass, 1992), 27, 28, 55, 57.

employees. Although more than three-quarters shared overall company operating results, this is not surprising, nor does it represent much information disclosure, since the majority of these very large companies are publicly traded and so the information is generally available. These figures suggest that sharing of information is quite limited, and there is little evidence of any change between 1987 and 1990.

In 1990, two-thirds of the firms offered no form of employment security as part of their personnel policies.[61] Moreover, few firms reported that they had trained a majority (more than 60%) of their employees in the past three years in group decision making (only 6% reported having done so); leadership skills (3%); skills in understanding the business (2%); quality control and statistical analysis (9%); and team-building skills (8%). But 35% had furnished job-skills training to a majority of their employees in the past three years.[62] Thus, although firms were, on the whole, offering skills training, they were not affording many employees the broader training necessary to play a more active role in the business, nor were they offering a sense of security that would induce employees to take a more active, committed role.

A broader 1991 survey of firms with more than 50 employees, drawn from Dun & Bradstreet's establishment file, provides a somewhat more optimistic picture. That study concluded that "about 35% of private sector firms with fifty or more employees have achieved substantial use of flexible work organization,"[63] a term referring to the use of four practices: self-directed work teams, job rotation, employee problem-solving groups or quality circles, and the implementation of a total quality management program.[64]

It is, by the way, far from a trivial task to assess the extent to which work practices are in use. For in few firms do any practices cover 100% of the employees, and thus, the question becomes, what fraction of a firm's employees must be covered before we are willing to say that the firm has "adopted" some practice or set of practices that can positively affect the performance of its work force? A second issue is who responds to the questions about the implementation of various practices. Virtually without exception, the surveys are answered by a corporate official, often in human resources. Therefore, the surveys may be more of a measure of intentions than of what is actually implemented or felt in the work place, and the responses may be subject to some social desirability bias—given the generally positive nature of many of these work place practices, respondents will likely tend to err on the side of reporting something as existing. Plans or practices may exist on paper but not be fully or adequately implemented. Consequently, it seems likely that the reported estimates of the diffusion of work force management practices are generous rather than conservative.

In addition to these comprehensive surveys, other evidence suggests that the spread of new practices for managing the employment relation has been slow. For instance, a survey of 584 companies in the United States, Canada, Japan, and Germany conducted by Ernst & Young for the American Quality Foundation reported that U.S. firms were laggards in the use of employee suggestion programs. The study found that "computer companies involve only 12% of their employees in idea-suggestion programs," while automobile manufacturers, rating the highest in this area, "involve just 28% of their workers."[65] By contrast, 34% of Canadian bank workers and 78% of Japanese car makers had functioning employee suggestion programs. The Commission on the Skills of the American Workplace, a spin-off from the Carnegie Corporation, noted that

> "the vast majority" of U.S. employers aren't moving to "high performance" work organizations, which requires educated workers, nor investing to train employees. Fully $27 billion of the $30 billion in annual training outlays is spent by . . . only 0.5% of all U.S. companies, and fewer than 200 of these employers . . . spend more than 2% of their payroll on formal training.[66]

Furthermore, even when high-performance work practices are adopted, they may not last very long, another caution to be exercised in interpreting the surveys previously discussed. For example, one review of the evidence on the persistence of quality of working life programs concluded that such programs have "high mortality rates."[67] A study of plants operating during the 1970s found that after five years, 75% of the quality of working life programs had ceased to exist.[68] Research by the University of Michigan's Survey Research Center on eight plans begun between 1973 and 1978 found that by 1984, all had been terminated.[69] Another study estimated that about 40% of employee involvement or quality of working life plans failed within the first two or three years.[70]

These data have some important implications for both managers and policy makers. They speak, first, to the difficulty of implementation. One should not presume that just because some practices are efficient or provide substantial competitive benefits they will be readily or easily adopted. Moreover, the data speak to the need for vigilance. Just starting a program or instituting some practice does not guarantee it will survive very long. This latter finding speaks to the need to be systematic and systemic in one's approach and to have some overriding vision or plan that supports implementation. The mortality risks to these innovations, even when they are potentially quite beneficial, are both real and high. However, the data also speak to changes taking place in the management and structuring of the employment relationship—trends that are consistent with what we know about the effective management of people at work. Under competitive pressure and with much encouragement from the business and academic press, change is occurring. The question of why so slowly, particularly in the United States, and why with such great difficulty, leads us to consider the institutional, legal, and ideological context within which U.S. firms operate as the beginning of an explanation of the structure of work in America.

BARRIERS TO DOING THE RIGHT THING

II

Wrong Heroes, Wrong Theories, Wrong Language

4

WRONG HEROES

It is May 12, 1989, and a chief executive officer from a major U.S. corporation is coming to speak to the students of Stanford's Graduate School of Business. Although executives often address the student body, this talk will be unusual—being reported on the front page in the local newspapers and featured on local television news programs. The talk will be newsworthy, not for its content, but for the demonstrations and disruptions that accompany it. For Frank Lorenzo, the CEO of Texas Air—which owns Eastern Airlines, Continental Airlines, People Express, and what was formerly Frontier Airlines—the head of the largest airline company in the world, is the speaker. Outside the auditorium in which he is speaking, 300 or so union workers and their allies are protesting, throwing eggs, pounding long poles, forming a picket line, and creating a disturbance requiring the presence of numerous police. However, while the reception outside may be hostile, inside Lorenzo is welcomed as a hero. Introduced to the packed auditorium by the dean of the school (who earlier in the year refused to introduce Tom Peters because he did not approve of Peters' writings), Lorenzo will give a speech interrupted numerous times by applause and receive a standing ovation at the end.

This is the same Frank Lorenzo who, in the decade of the 1980s, took Continental Airlines into bankruptcy twice and led Eastern Airlines to its final demise on January 18, 1991, when it closed its doors for the last time. It is not just any business executive who can take the same company into bankruptcy twice (losing $2.5 billion in 1990, at the time a record loss for a firm in the airline industry) and completely ruin what was once the third largest airline in the industry, Eastern.

Lorenzo was a hero not only to possibly naive business school students. Wall Street idolized him. When Texas Air bought Eastern Airlines in 1986, its "stock rose more than 50% in the days following the announcement."[1] His directors admired him: "Carl R. Pohlad, a Texas Air director, calls Lorenzo 'one of the most able business leaders I've met.'"[2] Even after his record in the airline industry was well established, other airline executives sought his counsel! Thus, for instance, in 1993, it was reported that "Bernard Attali, the chairman of Air France . . . had dinner with Mr. Lorenzo last fall in Montreal to seek advice on how to handle negotiations with labor unions and get rid of inefficient work rules," while other top airline executives wined and dined him, "eager to draw on his expertise."[3]

What had Frank Lorenzo done to earn such adulation from business school deans and students, Wall Street, and other senior executives? He fought unions and his work force with a vigor some describe as ruthless and had extracted a fortune of some $40 million, even as the company he controlled was going down.

Lorenzo is not the only business hero lionized for behavior that is far from consistent with achieving competitive advantage through people. When he was a rising executive at Ford Motor Company, Robert McNamara was known much more for his financial acumen than for his attention to or knowledge of operations and sensitivity to people issues.[4] Harold Geneen at International Telephone and Telegraph enjoyed a similar reputation. Through much of the past two or three decades, business heroes have been numbers people rather than people people, and those willing to slash employment levels and take on the work force have received much approbation even as they were occasionally obtaining less than spectacular business results.

Social approval is important to everyone, and high-level executives are no exception. To be praised for taking a hostile approach to dealing with the work force is likely to reinforce such behavior. We engage in a social learning process, in which we learn what behavior is appropriate by watching what others do and what happens to them. Seeing others lionized for fighting labor, for example, provides many managers with information as to what is valued and rewarded. Heroes are important, for they symbolize valued social ideals, patterns of behavior, and personal qualities.[5] The business press and business executives, who make heroes out of people who exemplify the opposite of the qualities and behavior necessary to achieve success through people, make it harder for a different way of management to emerge.

With business heroes like Frank Lorenzo, it is little wonder that change in how we manage people—change consistent with achieving competitive advantage through those people—is problematic. But there is, in fact, something firms can do to overcome this problem, at least in part. Obviously, no one can control what appears in the leading business magazines or the popular press, but organizations can influence who speaks to their employees and what literature and messages they distribute to both management and the entire organization. I have seen organizations, seeking to achieve success through people, spend some time screening potential speakers to ensure that the message being delivered is consistent with their intended strategy and culture. In a similar fashion, these same organizations distribute articles and books emphasizing the activities of business and other organizational leaders whose behavior is consistent with that necessary to manage people effectively. Firms can also be attentive to the people whom they put on their boards of directors and what messages their choices send to the organization. In short, heroes are important. For the most part, U.S. business has had inappropriate role models. Nevertheless, organizations can consciously send out more appropriate messages by their choice of speakers, literature, and people who play significant symbolic roles.

WRONG THEORIES

We may emulate the wrong heroes in part because we explicitly or implicitly subscribe to inaccurate, misleading, and potentially counterproductive theories of human behavior. Why should we care about theories of human behavior? Because, as Robert Frank noted: "Views about human nature have important practical consequences. . . . They dictate corporate strategies for preventing workers from shirking, for bargaining with unions, and for setting prices. . . . [O]ur beliefs about human nature help shape human nature itself. . . . Our ideas about the limits of human potential mold what we aspire to become."[6]
Frank makes the same point that Douglas McGregor did years ago in his book on Theory X and Theory Y management—that our beliefs and suppositions about human behavior act as self-fulfilling prophecies; people behave as the theories expect them to.

The discipline of economics, particularly its neoclassical versions, holds more dominance in the United States than almost anywhere else in the world. One might argue that this is because its views of human behavior are compatible with underlying social values and beliefs. Virtually all economic models of behavior view workers as effort-averse—or more simply put, they don't like to work, and without some form of external control or incentive, they will not perform useful labor. James Baron has perceptively noted:

> The image of the worker in these models is somewhat akin to Newton's first law of motion: employees remain in a state of rest unless compelled to change that state by a stronger force impressed upon them—namely, an optimal labor contract. Various incentive features of internal labor markets are claimed to provide forms of insurance that overcome workers' reluctance to work.[7]

Economic models and many lay theories of the employment relation emphasize so-called agency problems. "Agency theory holds that many social relationships can be usefully understood as involving two parties: a principal and an agent. The agent performs certain actions on behalf of the principal, who necessarily must delegate some authority to the agent."[8] Agency problems arise when "(a) the desires or goals of the principal and agent conflict and (b) it is difficult or expensive for the principal to verify what the agent is actually doing."[9] Since economic models presume that people don't want to work, but obviously those who employ them want them to, these models reflect differences in interests between owners or managers and other workers. Agency theory deals with the topic of contracts, or how to devise efficient systems for ensuring agent (worker) compliance, given differences in risk preferences between owners and employees, differences in access to information, and so forth.

Another dominant economic model of the employment relationship is transaction cost economics. This model seeks to explain why there are organizations at all, instead of recurrent contracting arrangements, as in spot labor markets. Transaction cost economics presumes that information and ability to foresee the future are limited, which makes writing complete contingent contracts either impossible or very expensive. Nor presumably can one rely on the parties in the exchange to simply work things out as events unfold; the perspective assumes that individuals exercise an extreme form of self-interested behavior— namely, opportunism: "By opportunism I mean self-interest seeking with guile. This includes, but is scarcely limited to, more blatant forms such as lying, stealing, and cheating. Opportunism more often involves subtle forms of deceit."[10]

One of the principal derivations of transaction cost reasoning is the presumed efficiency of hierarchy. Oliver Williamson, transaction cost theory's leading proponent (and someone frequently mentioned as a future Nobel Prize winner), defines hierarchy thus:

> Where the responsibility for effecting adaptations is concentrated on one or a few agents, hierarchy is relatively great. Where instead adaptations are taken by individual agents or are subject to collective approval, hierarchy is slight. . . . If one or a few agents are responsible for negotiating all contracts, the contractual hierarchy is great. If instead each agent negotiates each interface separately, the contractual hierarchy is weak.[11]

One of the principal claims of transaction cost reasoning is that the degree of contractual and decision-making hierarchy is positively related and that "the least hierarchical modes, in both contracting and decision-making respects ... have the worst efficiency properties."[12] Even as many organizations try to become less hierarchical and centralized to attain more productivity from their work force, one of the leading strands of economic theory, taught regularly in many of the major business schools and economics departments, argues for the efficiency of hierarchy. The inconsistency is transparent.

Moreover, the portrayal of individuals in these economic models is scarcely flattering: "Typically, such organizational economic actors seek personal wealth, status, leisure, or the like. . . . Accordingly, their behavior as potentially shirking or opportunistic agents can be curbed by vigilant monitoring, together with incentive schemes based around money, promotion, negative sanctions, and the like."[13]

The implicit and explicit recommendations of these models are scarcely consistent with the prescriptions to employ self-managing teams and delegate or decentralize authority, or in fact, with any system of governing the employment relation that relies on trust.

These perspectives on human behavior are incorporated in numerous policies and practices of the work place, in which an emphasis on control, discipline, limited individual incentives, and monitoring are evident. For instance, Macy's is a large department store chain that is in bankruptcy because it underwent a leveraged buyout that left it with an unmanageable debt burden. Performance is even more important for an organization in such straits, and today's competitive retailing environment presents a tough challenge.

What did Macy's do to encourage more productivity from its employees? One thing it did was to install strict attendance rules: "Under the policy started in March, Macy's equates a documented medical absence with a day at the beach, and arriving five minutes late with missing a whole day. . . . [T]he new policy has hurt morale around the El Camino distribution center."[14] This policy prompted Macy's employees to engage in informational picketing outside several stores and to file contract grievances through their union. Macy's also imposed higher sales production quotas on its salespeople, threatening to fire them if they did not perform up to the new standard. Yet the store did not seek their advice on how to actually improve sales performance. It seems unlikely that these procedures increased sales or reduced costs.

Surveillance and an emphasis on control and hierarchy have transformed much office work, but not always for the better or in ways consistent with what we know about how to obtain productivity. Many organizations have installed computer-based monitoring and control systems and, on occasion, listen in on telephone calls handled by reservation agents, bill collectors, customer service representatives, and telephone salespeople. "The Office of Technology Assessment estimates that more than 10 million workers in 1988 were subject to concealed telephone and computer observation. . . . [T]he congressional arm disclosed that the number of surveillance systems sold to businesses rose nearly three-fold to 70,000 from 1985 to 1988."[15] Whether such surveillance actually enhances performance is a matter of some dispute. However, studies indicate that it increases job-related stress and, consequently, workers' compensation claims:

> Video display terminal workers who labor under the constant scrutiny of secret monitoring devices suffer higher levels of stress-related medical problems such as ulcers, heart disease, fatigue, and depression. . . . [T]he study found that 43% of monitored workers are plagued by the loss of feeling in fingers and wrists and 51% suffer from stiff or sore wrists.[16]

This rate of medical problems was twice that for nonmonitored workers in similar jobs.

These views of human behavior, with their emphasis on optimal incentive contracts, encourage organizations to seek answers to many, if not most, performance problems by tinkering with the compensation system. By pressuring employees to produce in a narrowly measured way, threatening them with loss of their jobs if they do not, and offering large rewards if they do, organizations occasionally set individuals against each other and against their customers, with catastrophic results. For instance, a June 11, 1992 article on the front page of the *San Francisco Examiner* reported: "State consumer protection officials Thursday accused Sears, Roebuck and Co.'s 72 auto repair shops in California of systematically defrauding car repair customers and said they are seeking to suspend or revoke the company's license. . . . The investigation revealed a constant pattern of abuse."[17]

A breach of corporate ethics? A breakdown in managerial control? An unfortunate but random event? Possibly, but more likely the result of a system of incentive and control gone awry:

> The bureau said complaints about Sears had increased dramatically after the centers changed from hourly wages to a commission structure. . . . [T]he investigation showed that Sears instructed employees to sell a certain number of repairs or services during each eight-hour shift. . . . If they failed to meet these goals, their hours were often cut or they were transferred to other Sears departments.[18]

Once again, a performance problem—insufficient revenues and profitability—led to a hierarchical, control-oriented solution, and as in Macy's case, the results were not quite what the company wanted.

It is evident that the theories—agency theory and transaction cost economics—provided by contemporary economics for understanding the employment relation are fundamentally antithetical to the perspective one would have to hold in order to adopt the practices that are described in Chapter 2 or that characterize organizations such as NUMMI. It is also evident that the implicit prescriptions of these approaches guide much, although certainly not all, managerial action and public policy. Is it possible that these theories are essentially correct, calling into question the evidence and ideas presented above? The answer cannot be resolved on a once-and-for-all basis. Certainly in one important area—collective ownership—the evidence seems quite clear that both perspectives make predictions that are inconsistent with empirical observation.

Collective Ownership

As noted in Chapter 2, employee ownership is a characteristic of many high-performing organizations—for instance, each of the top five stock market performers from 1972 to 1992 is listed in the Employee Ownership 1000—for the simple reason that making employees owners diminishes the conflict between capital and labor and between owners and employees. Employees become, in some measure, owners, and labor also has capital in such a system. Regardless, both transaction cost economics and agency theory strenuously maintain that integrating ownership with management and work leads to *less* efficiency and productivity, not more: "Much of the relevant theory . . . argues against extending worker participation, suggesting that group rewards diminish individual incentives and undermine central control."[19]

There is the potential problem of free riding—if workers are owners and share proportionately in the earnings of the firm, there is little incentive for any single worker to be diligent. Shirking will not affect the total result very much, and because of his or her ownership, earnings will accrue to the person in any event. There is the potential problem of monitoring and control—because of the peer norms and equality in power that exist if the employees are also the owners, there will be little incentive to monitor and discipline individuals who don't perform adequately. There is the problem of insufficient bargaining over the terms and conditions of employment—the absence of an adversarial relation leads to less attention to the details: "A chronic problem with labor market organization is that workers and their families are irrepressible optimists. They are taken in by vague assurances of good faith. . . . Tough-minded bargaining in its entirety never occurs or, if it occurs, comes too late."[20] There is the problem of attracting managerial talent: "cooperatives are unable to retain superior managers, who are induced to leave by offers of better pay in capitalist firms."[21]

These problems of free riding, absence of hierarchical discipline and control, and scarcity of managerial talent are said to doom the cooperative organizational form. There is only one thing wrong with these arguments: there is quite a bit of empirical evidence to the contrary. In several European countries, founding rates of cooperatives have generally exceeded the birthrate for conventional firms in manufacturing:

> [I]n the United Kingdom there were fewer than 20 co-ops in 1975, but around 1,600 in 1986. Comparable data for France shows around 500 PCs in 1970 and around 1,500 in 1986. In Italy, the period from 1970 to 1982 saw the formation of some 7,000 new co-ops. . . . [D]uring the 1970s and 1980s . . . the rate of co-op formation . . . was 17.1% in France, 21.01% in Italy, 12.1% in Sweden, and 39.1% in Britain.[22]

Moreover, the existing empirical evidence belies the prediction of poor survival rates for cooperatives. One study of French producer cooperatives noted that between 1970 and 1977, only four such organizations failed; and in 1979, more than 30% of the French producer cooperatives were more than 30 years old.[23] The study concluded: "Our findings do not support the view that PCs are bound to fail. The prediction of rapid demise is refuted both by the low mortality rate of French PCs during the 1970s and by the ability of many . . . to survive for more than 30 years."[24]

In the United States, cooperatives are less frequently observed, largely because of legal conditions and restricted access to financing. Cooperatives do exist nonetheless. A study of 18 plywood plants in the Pacific Northwest that had cooperative ownership found that "the return to members per hour of work has been above the union average rate most of the time in most of the cooperatives, and at some time in all of them."[25] The study also found superior productivity in the plywood cooperatives compared to conventional ownership along a number of dimensions, including the "physical volume of output per man-hour of work, quality . . . of product, and economy of material and equipment use."[26] A study of the productivity effects of cooperative ownership and other participation schemes in France and Italy found generally positive results and "support[s] the proponents of participatory schemes rather than their critics."[27]

Exemplary case studies, both in the United States and in Europe, also speak to the potential effectiveness of a form of ownership that conventional economic theory says should not even exist, let alone thrive. The Mondragon cooperative system, one of the largest cooperative organizations in the world with more than 20,000 employees, is phenomenally successful.[28] Located in the Basque region in Spain, the cooperatives are active in the export market, exporting more than 40% of their production. During the 1974 recession, employment rose 7.5%, profits 26%, and exports 56%. Compared to the 500 largest Spanish capitalist firms, the evidence suggests that the Mondragon cooperatives have a much higher rate of value-added per unit of fixed capital, with a ratio more than three times that of the largest firms.[29] The Mondragon cooperatives are less capital-intensive—requiring less capital for each additional job—but more productive then the average large Spanish firm.

The John Lewis Partnership, a department store and retail chain in Great Britain, is the largest employee-owned firm in the world, with 37,000 employees and almost $3 billion in sales in 1989.[30] The firm is owned collectively as a trust for the benefit of past, present, and future employees. All its profits, after payment of preferred dividends and retained earnings, are distributed as a bonus to current employees in proportion to their pay.[31] Comparing John Lewis to its most successful British competitors—including Marks and Spencer, Sainsbury, and Tesco—is informative. Between 1970 and 1989, John Lewis's sales grew at a compound rate of 15.2% per year. "The partnership achieved the fastest sales growth from given additions to both labor and capital,"[32] performing better than its competitors in terms of rate of growth in factor productivity.

In the United States, 59% of the Reflexite Corporation's stock is owned by employees either as a group or as individuals.[33] Although an ESOP (employee stock ownership plan) rather than a cooperative, the firm, a manufacturer of reflecting materials and panels, gives its employee-owners a great deal of power and has achieved excellent financial results as a consequence. It has grown from net sales of $16.6 million in 1989 to $31.3 million in 1991, the year for which it was named Entrepreneur of the Year by *Inc.* magazine in its January 1992 issue. Employee ownership has permitted the company to develop and nurture a technology that Minnesota Mining and Manufacturing has still not been able to replicate, expand into new global markets, weather successfully a serious downturn in sales, and maintain profitability even in the face of both growth and economic challenges.[34]

This discussion of the effects of employee participation and ownership is important because if conventional economic theories can be so wrong about this issue, they can be—and probably are—equally wrong about other issues in managing the employment relation. By confronting the question of cooperative ownership, we see dramatically the effects of norms and resulting public policy on the structure of the economic landscape. With little public policy or other institutional support, the United States has lagged behind many other economies in developing ownership or governance forms that encourage participation and productivity. Considering the effects of employee ownership and cooperation provides even more evidence for the effectiveness of the principles outlined in earlier chapters.

SOME MORE USEFUL THEORIES

There are number of social psychological theories that are consistent with how effective organizations manage the employment relationship. They suggest that actions consistent with agency theory or transaction cost reasoning have a substantial likelihood of being counterproductive. These alternative theories invariably have excellent experimental support—although not all of them have been tested in field settings—and provide useful ways of thinking about potential policies and practices employed in managing the work force.

Attribution and the Self-Perception of Behavior

Several of these theories maintain that individuals act as lay or naive social scientists, attempting to infer causality for behavior, including their own, by examining the setting within which that behavior occurs. If some action is taken in a situation in which there is little or no visible external pressure to engage in the behavior (the so-called insufficient justification condition), people are likely to conclude that the behavior occurred because the individual liked it or wanted to—that it was chosen freely. By contrast, if behavior occurs in the presence of a great deal of external pressure—either positive in the form of monetary inducements or negative in the form of threats or sanctions—people are likely to conclude that the external forces both caused the behavior and were, in fact, necessary to produce it.

These self-perceptions affect the individuals' attitudes and subsequent behavior because people are likely to behave in ways consistent with their beliefs and self-perceptions absent other social forces compelling them to do otherwise.

Hence, if a person is asked to undertake a task under conditions of strong external pressure, the theory suggests that any initial intrinsic interest the person may have had in that activity is undermined by this pressure, and that when a person is subsequently presented with the same activity in the absence of strong external forces, he is less likely to choose to engage in the activity.[35]

The amount of reward or external pressure in a situation helps people develop perceptions of the causes of their behavior. When committed to a behavior despite the absence of strong external pressure, people behave as if they are committed—by having more favorable attitudes toward the job and performing better. In contrast, large extrinsic rewards can actually undermine intrinsic interest in and enjoyment of a task.[36] Compensation systems that pay people more equally or on a group basis, and thereby de-emphasize the importance and salience of working for money, are consistent with building stronger commitment to and interest in the organization and the job.

Surveillance is another form of external control that can undermine intrinsic interest in and enjoyment of work. A study of children reported that "adult surveillance during the time the child was engaged in the task was itself sufficient to produce a . . . decrement in subsequent intrinsic interest in the activity, as suggested by a self-perception analysis of their situation."[37]

Surveillance can affect not only self-perceptions but also the perceptions of others. In a classic study, subjects who were placed in a situation in which they monitored one subordinate more closely than another came to believe that the more frequently monitored subordinate in fact needed more surveillance and could be trusted less, even though there was objectively no difference in the performance or behavior of the two. Supervisors, then, have a fundamental dilemma:

> The supervisor, who presumably is concerned with the degree to which his subordinates will work without constant supervision, may become victimized by his own previous supervisory behavior. If his interactions with the subordinates have been largely confined to frequent monitoring of the subordinates' work efforts (and this may be an accidental by-product of the particular supervisory positions), then the supervisor has, in effect, denied himself the opportunity to obtain relevant information concerning their unsupervised work efforts. . . . [H]e will tend to perceive the

causal locus for the [subordinates'] work efforts . . . as being "outside" them. . . . Such an inference will obviously have consequences for his future interaction with them, and something like a self-perpetuating information loss may be the result.[38]

These findings make sense for a number of reasons.[39] First, if a manager, in fact, supervises closely, the best way to make sense of that behavior is to assume that the characteristics of those being managed necessitated the close supervision. Second, the situation makes it impossible to develop trust as there is no opportunity to observe whether those being supervised would work as well on their own. Thus, the almost inevitable inference is that those who are being closely watched cannot be trusted. The self-perpetuating nature of such an inference is clear. The way out of this dilemma is, almost as an act of faith, to exhibit trust, for that is the only way to learn whether trust is justified.

The situation gets even worse. Giving someone the job of surveillance provides that individual with a self-justification rationale not only for finding the need for surveillance but also, perhaps, for provoking or stimulating the proscribed activities. Thus,

> entrapment in certain situations may represent an attempt by a surveillant to justify the monitoring activity. When an individual commits himself to a position or activity, there seems to be a desire to increase the certainty that the chosen position or activity is appropriate and correct. . . . [S]urveillants who become involved in covert surveillance may feel a need to justify their actions by generating evidence that the surveillance effort is worthwhile.[40]

An experimental study of entrapment found that surveillance not only produces distrust and alienation but also can stimulate entrapment activities that actually increase the frequency of undesired behaviors and justify the close and intense supervision in the first place.[41]

A person who monitors another or administers rewards or punishments has power over that other individual. David Kipnis examined how such power affects the perceptions of the person with power both of himself and of the individual in the subordinate role. In an experimental study, he found that

- "[S]ubjects with power attempted to influence their workers more frequently than those without power. . . . [V]ery few subjects with power relied on personal persuasion. . . . These findings . . . support [the conclusion] that the availability of a punishing response encourages the use of such a response."[42]
- "[S]ubjects with power devalued the work of their workers. 72% of the subjects without power and 28% of the subjects with power were classified as giving above median appraisals of their workers. . . . [T]he more those with power attempted to influence their workers, the less they thought of their work."[43]
- "[S]ubjects without power expressed a significantly greater willingness to meet socially with their workers than those with power."[44]
- "[S]ubjects with power viewed their workers as being controlled by the subject's power, that is, the subject's control of pay raises."[45]

Monitoring or attention can signal not only distrust but also that the task is important and the organization cares about its performance.[46] This signal of importance can lead to enhanced satisfaction and performance. Obviously, however, the message that what people do is important is conveyed very differently from the message that people are not trusted.

The results from these studies suggest, first of all, that one should not expect those who have engaged in close supervision to suddenly say, in effect, "My past activities were a waste of time." As a consequence of those activities, they will come to justify their own behavior and to believe that their subordinates are not competent or trustworthy and that without their management efforts, performance would degrade. Changing this behavior requires some strong intervention as well as training, new information, and new work arrangements, for example, that permit individuals to change without having to admit they were wrong.

The Self-Fulfilling Prophecy

Expectations can have profound effects on behavior. Expectations of outstanding performance can actually increase people's job performance, while low expectations can diminish performance.[47] Expectations of interacting with someone who is thought to be attractive or intelligent can actually produce more sociable and intelligent behavior on the part of the other individual.[48] Through our own behaviors, we often produce the very behavior in others that we expect to observe.

Although the effect of expectations of shirking or opportunistic behavior on manifestations of those behaviors has not been empirically demonstrated, there is no reason to believe that these effects would not occur. Extraordinary levels of monitoring and surveillance can help communicate the belief that those subjected to such regimes are not expected to perform adequately. Second, electronic monitoring, close supervision, and tight control communicate a lack of trust. Those confronted with this absence of trust may come to view themselves as not trustworthy and then behave in ways congruent with this self-image.

A third effect is that through supervision and control, the organization communicates that it is responsible for controlling and determining performance rather than the individual who is monitored and controlled. This makes the individual feel less responsible for his or her performance. The feeling of diminished responsibility can produce diminished effort and certainly reduced levels of initiative taken on the organization's behalf. As a result, systems designed on the assumption that individuals are effort-averse, opportunistic shirkers are likely to help produce those very behaviors. It is in this sense that the values and theories that managers hold about the work force determine the behavior of that work force. These values and beliefs necessarily permeate the design of feedback, control, and incentive systems and therefore become self-fulfilling.

Reactance

Jack Brehm's theory of psychological reactance states that individuals strive to retain their freedom and their options of choice, particularly when confronted with circumstances that would limit them.[49] Reactance principles have been used to explain why as things become scarcer, they also become more valuable and valued by us. "As opportunities become less available, we lose freedoms; and we *hate* to lose the freedoms we already have.... [W]henever free choice is limited or threatened, the need to retain our freedoms makes us want them ... significantly more than previously."[50]

People react to constraints on freedoms in the work setting by desiring freedom and autonomy even more and by discerning ways to obtain them. The following reaction to computer monitoring provides a nice illustration of the principle of reactance in action:

> Now and then Harriette Ternipsede stands up, defying the stream of calls pouring into her telephone. When she does, her supervisors at the Trans World Airlines reservation office here call across the rows of sales agents and tell her to sit down. Although standing up slows productivity, it gives her relief from ... stretches of sitting at a computer terminal, and she says, "It's a way to show I'm a person."[51]

A truck driver for Safeway, the grocery store chain, used to enjoy his job because of the autonomy it provided. But "now a small computer on the dashboard of his truck ... keeps track of speed, shifting, excessive idling and when and how long he stops for lunch or a coffee break. As a result, the driver says he will retire early. He complains, 'They push you around, spy on you. There's no trust, no respect anymore.'"[52]

Strong external incentives, along with close supervision and machine-assisted monitoring, can provoke feelings of a loss of control or freedom and the need to restore some degree of personal control to the situation. Somewhat ironically, more attempts at direct hierarchical control can stimulate attempts to circumvent that control, leading, in turn, to additional efforts at surveillance in an expensive and largely wasteful cycle of behavior.

WRONG LANGUAGE

That language is a powerful, if not *the* most powerful, method of social influence is well recognized.[53] Confucius, when asked what he would do if appointed to rule a country, is reported to have said that the first thing he would do would be to fix the language. We see things according to how they are described. This is why Disney chooses language for use in its theme parks that reinforces its employees' understanding that they are in show business and terminology that helps them deliver high-quality service. There is no personnel department—employees are hired by "Central Casting." Everyone is a "cast member"; there are no bellhops, custodians, security guards, and so forth. People work "on stage," and most important, visitors are called "guests" rather than "tourists." It is more difficult to be rude to a guest—the very terminology evokes certain subconscious associations that tend to produce desired behavior.

Others have learned from Disney. At the Lakeway Resort and Conference Center outside Austin, Texas, a new management turned around what had been a declining facility. One of the things the center did was to "fix the language." When employees leave private areas (e.g., going from the kitchen into the dining room), there is a sign saying "On Stage" to remind them they will be in view. Maids are called "room attendants." The strategy was successful, and Lakeway enjoyed a remarkable turnaround.

In this context, consider carefully the language of much of economic theory and of traditional management. Ask yourself, does this language foster the right feeling, the right expectations, the right approach to managing the work force? The current language of management is filled with references to "restructuring," "rightsizing" (rather than "downsizing"), and similar terms for reducing employment levels. Negotiations with employees are almost always described in win-lose terms and with warlike language (indeed, one might wonder whether the extensive use of military metaphors in business in the United States has made partnering with suppliers more difficult, but that is a topic for another book). Under competitive pressure, firms seek to reduce costs and expenses, and almost invariably focus on labor costs and labor expenses, regardless of the proportion of total costs accounted for by direct labor. Reducing labor costs almost always seems to imply reducing labor rates—the rate of pay—which is not the same thing as reducing costs at all.

The dominant economic theories are also filled with language not apt to produce trust and cooperation, to put it mildly. Agency theory notes that "there is good reason to believe that the agent will not always act in the best interests of the principal"[54] and goes so far as to deny the reality of common interests and shared culture and experience that can constitute organizations: "[M]ost organizations are simply *legal fictions which serve as a nexus for a set of contracting relationships among individuals.*"[55] Transaction cost economics maintains that the problem of economic organization is a problem of contracting,[56] not a problem of motivation, commitment, the building of trust and cooperation, or solving problems of interdependence—each an alternative way of describing the problem of organization. Moreover, contracts involve costs, including "maladaptation costs incurred when transactions drift out of alignment . . . the haggling costs incurred . . . to correct . . . misalignments . . . the setup and running costs associated with the governance structures . . . to which disputes are referred, and . . . the bonding costs of effecting secure commitments."[57]

Disputes and conflicts loom large in the language and are therefore likely to loom large in the context of activity that is undertaken based on that language and the knowledge it represents. This is not to suggest that no disputes would arise absent a theoretical guide to behavior that assumes conflict and opportunism, but the self-fulfilling prophecy effects on behavior are real.

There is, in fact, empirical evidence that "Exposure to the self-interest model commonly used in economics alters the extent to which people behave in self-interested ways."[58] Economists defect more frequently in prisoner's dilemma games, give less to charity than other faculty, and are more likely to free ride in an experimental situation that permits free riding.[59] In short, "economists appear to behave less cooperatively than noneconomists along a variety of dimensions."[60] The evidence is that this difference in cooperation is produced, at least in part, by training in economics and is not simply a result of self-selection—those less prone to cooperate choosing to study more economics. It is scarcely surprising that training that stresses self-interested behavior, rampant opportunism, and conflicts of interest would produce less collaborative behavior on the part of those exposed to the training and the language used to express these ideas.

Recognizing the managerial importance of language, Karl Weick has argued:

> Managerial work can be viewed as managing myths, images, symbols, and labels. . . . The manager who controls labels that are meaningful to organizational members can segment and point to portions of their experience and label it in consequential ways so that employees take that segment more seriously. . . . Because managers traffic so often in images, the appropriate role for the manager may be evangelist rather than accountant.[61]

Managerial language is critical. This language both reflects and determines how people think about the managing process. Singapore Airlines is world famous for its service—"a standard of service that even other airlines talk about."[62] That service is attributable, in part, to how the senior management thinks and talks about its management style. Joseph Pillay, the chairman of Singapore Airlines in the late 1980s, noted that some of the key elements of that management orientation were: "First, we are above all a democratic organization. . . . [W]e are not authoritarian, autocratic, or paternalistic. . . . [T]here has to be delegation of authority down the line. . . . [W]e endeavor to create an environment in which responsibility . . . can be exercised effectively at all levels. . . . [T]raining and retraining is an unwavering object of the group."[63]

Now ask yourself, would you rather fly on an airline that uses that language about the management process or one that is obsessed with "contracting," "shirking," "free riding," and "principal-agent" problems? It is possible to hide one's values; it is possible that one's language or way of thinking won't necessarily reflect how one actually manages people; but neither of these prospects is likely.

IMPLICATIONS

A simple decision rule useful in thinking about the issues covered in this chapter (and for that matter, the topics to be covered later) is this: To what extent is a given policy, behavior, practice, and so forth consistent or inconsistent with what we know about achieving competitive advantage through people? If it is inconsistent, regardless of its other qualities, one should be cautious about embracing it. Conversely, to the extent that it seems to point one in a useful direction, one should embrace it. Simply put, if we are really serious about being able to overcome the obstacles to obtaining competitive advantage through people, we need to become much more pragmatic—as opposed to ideological or theoretical—about managing the employment relation.

It seems almost axiomatic that the work force is unlikely to be used efficiently and effectively in an atmosphere of distrust or adversarial relations. Thus, the above rule of thumb will often translate into: To what extent does whatever is being considered lead to a climate of greater mutual trust and cooperation or a climate of mistrust and conflict?

We have seen in this chapter that various perspectives on behavior at work are scarcely neutral on these issues. Many academic and lay theories of behavior presume conflict, mistrust, and deceit. Consequently, they are likely to lead to recommendations that either produce the very behavior they fear or, at a minimum, may cause the organization to incur extra monitoring, supervisory, and surveillance costs. In my work with companies, I have found the following exercise to be quite compelling. List the management practices or methods under discussion. Then, abstracting as much as possible from the specifics of the situation, ask people to consider what behavioral characteristics, what motivational assumptions, are consistent with those practices and methods—in other words, what model of behavior is implied if the practices or methods are presumed to be effective. This or some other mechanism is important for making people confront their implicit models of human behavior.

Once these models are explicit, one can proceed to the next question: To what extent is such a theory of human behavior either 1) consistent with what we know about individual behavior at work or 2) consistent with what would be required to achieve some competitive success through the work force? Although it still may be difficult to move to the next stage—recommending practices more consistent with the desired goals—this step will almost invariably generate an interesting discussion and at least begin the process of making the organization's behavior consistent with its strategy and with what it seeks to accomplish through the management of the employment relation.

Second, follow Confucius's advice, and fix the language. In particular, pay attention to language that separates people who otherwise need to work cooperatively. Be careful if you hear lots of third-person pronouns—"they," "them," or "those." Pay close attention to words that create status distinctions and barriers in ways that make people in critical roles feel as if they are less important or less responsible for the organization's well-being and performance. It is easy to scoff at Lakeway Resort's calling maids "room attendants" or Disney's use of "cast member." But language is not only an important tool of social influence, it is a vital first step to affecting behavior. An elevated title may help, although it certainly won't guarantee that we treat the individual with that title more seriously and with more respect.

Remember, ideology dies hard—particularly when it comes to evaluating issues of policy, both public and private. We react on the basis of belief rather than evidence all too frequently. This leads to poor policy recommendations and often terrible results. An example can make this point explicit.

"Everyone knows" that the labor market policies pursued by the United States and the United Kingdom during the 1980s were beneficial. After all, these policies relied heavily on free-market ideology and conventional economic reasoning. They sought to diminish the power of institutions, such as labor unions, that interfered with management's right to govern the enterprise as it saw fit, to weaken labor market regulations that introduce friction into the market, and in general, to rely on competitive market forces to produce good outcomes. Conventional logic is consistent with free-market ideology in pointing to the clear success of these public policies.

As you might have guessed, what "everyone knows" to be true in fact fades when confronted not with belief, faith, or ideology, but with evidence. A study notes that in the early 1990s, the British economy was mired in a deep crisis in spite of policies "introduced to free the markets, erode the position of organized labour, and sharpen the incentives for private enterprise."[64] By 1988, part-time or other nonstandard employment accounted for more than a third of the labor force.[65] By 1986, Britain had lost its position as a high-wage economy and had the lowest labor rates in Europe, comparable to Spain and Portugal and far below those of France, Italy, and Germany.[66] Moreover, the antiworker policies and low wages did nothing to improve productivity in terms of Britain's comparative standing. Between 1960 and 1986, the average annual percentage rate of change in the real value-added in manufacturing per person employed was 3.0% in the United Kingdom, the lowest of the major industrial countries except for the United States (at 2.7%) and substantially lower than in Japan (7.5%), France (5.0%), Italy (4.9%), and Belgium (5.5%).[67] There was no change in the underinvestment in training and the development of human capital. Thus, even though the Thatcher government had "sought to remove, weaken, or radically reform those institutions which in their view had . . . adversely affected labour costs, productivity, and jobs,"[68] the results were the opposite of what had been intended.

Similar findings are beginning to emerge in the private sector in the United States. We are slowly learning that the "intent" of policies or, for that matter, good hopes and best wishes are not sufficient. Corporate downsizing and other actions that make employment less secure do not inevitably produce higher levels of productivity or competitive success, nor do the weakening of employee voice and participation and the concomitant increase in the power of management. Margaret Thatcher may be another example of a "wrong hero," idolized for her adherence to a view of the employment relation that is embedded in a system of theoretical supposition and language that seem to lead to poor rather than beneficent outcomes.

At any level of analysis—government policy or firm-level policy—the question is the same: Do the policies make sense in terms of what we know about people and how to achieve competitive advantage with them, and do they contribute to building a less adversarial, more cooperative, and trusting work environment? In that sense, are they consistent with a strategy that seeks advantage through the work force? If the answer is no, then neither false heroes, ideology, nor inadequate theoretical conceptions of the employment relation will withstand confrontation with empirical reality.

Overcoming History

5

In the late 1980s, Boise Cascade, facing tremendous losses because of overcapacity and consequently weak prices in the paper industry, embarked on a total quality management effort that included training, employee involvement, and some decentralization—particularly with respect to operating decisions. The company's senior leadership seemed genuinely committed to the program, and for good reason. The paper industry is highly capital-intensive, with investments on the order of $500 million or more to upgrade and expand plants. With an investment of close to $1 million per worker, downtime or any inefficiency in the operation of machines is very expensive. Moreover, competition had increasingly moved to include quality and delivery as well as price. Yet in spite of the announced commitment, relevant meetings, dedicated leadership, and a clearly pressing business need, the program moved forward in fits and starts and was almost certainly not as successful as quickly as many had hoped. There was resistance on the part of middle managers in many of the plants and some cynicism on the part of both lower-level workers and managers that the company's commitment would wane. Why?

Obviously, there are many answers to that question, each with some merit, but one important piece of the puzzle is the company's history of relations with its largely unionized work force. In 1983, a strike at the company's De Ridder, Louisiana, paper mill was so violent and tense that the incoming human resource executive at the plant told me he and his family slept on the floor of their house for several months in case someone fired a gun through a window during the night. After its final and best offer, in August 1983, was rejected by the membership, which went on strike on September 4, Boise operated the plant first with management personnel and outside contractors and then, on October 19, announced it would hire replacement workers.[1] In July 1986, the company's paper mill in Sheldon Springs, Vermont, went on strike, and later that same month, its huge paper mill in Rumford, Maine, also struck—for 76 days. In both instances, the company quickly moved to hire permanent replacements for the strikers, and picket lines were patrolled by police to prevent trouble.[2] When the strikes ended soon thereafter, bitterness remained. In 1988, Boise Cascade took a strike at its Emmett, Cascade, and Council, Idaho, plants and also at a veneer plant in Independence, Oregon.[3] Again, the company attempted to keep the plants operating with managers and replacement workers. In 1989, the company faced violence at its International Falls, Minnesota, mill, which was being expanded using nonunion labor. In September, "hundreds of union protesters overpowered police forces, flipped cars and burned a temporary housing camp, causing an estimated $1.3 million [in] damages."[4]

The company's position during that time was that it was trying to undo earlier mistakes in which it had given in too quickly and too easily and therefore had experienced rapidly escalating labor costs. In a November 8, 1986, speech to the American Paper Institute's Presidents Forum, Boise's CEO noted that one of the greatest challenges facing the industry was "improving labor productivity while reducing our relative labor costs."[5] He observed that the company had made strides in the previous six years "to correct a labor situation" that had gotten out of hand, and because of a change in bargaining tactics, "we've begun to turn things around."[6] He went on to note the company's intentional policy of implementing final offers, operating mills during a strike by hiring replacement workers, and controlling both direct labor costs and indirect costs such as health benefits. He stated: "In my judgment, the discipline we've begun to exhibit over these last several years is in marked contrast to our weakness at the bargaining table for the 10 years prior."[7]

This is not a company with unenlightened management or one that was particularly unusual for the industry at that time. Indeed, many of the same sentiments and actions are expressed at General Motors and numerous other companies. However, it is clear that this history of conflict with the work force, a history of distrust, the habit of winning at the expense of the other side (on the part of both workers and management), makes implementing total quality or other variants of work place reform difficult.

Embarking on its quality program, one of the first things Boise Cascade did was to appoint a task force to review its strategy with respect to labor relations. The company recognized that this strategy was, in its application and results if not in intent, inconsistent with what it hoped to achieve with its work force. A legacy of conflict, however, is not readily overcome, and a declaration of new principles and intent must take into account a history all too vivid in the minds of the combatants on both sides.

The Boise Cascade case is a specific example of a more general issue that represents an obstacle to achieving competitive advantage through people—the need to overcome a history of management practices and relations with the work force that makes it hard to implement new, more cooperative practices. In many dimensions, this history is unique to the United States. It has produced a legacy of ideology and belief as well as of emotions, all of which will need to be recognized and changed if high-commitment work practices are to be implemented.

The history of the evolution of management practices in the United States contains several separate strands united by an underlying theme. The strands include attempts to deskill and routinize work to reduce dependence on labor; attempts to limit the power of employees and their organizations by law and intimidation; and attempts to assert and maintain management control in contests for power in the work place. The underlying theme was to reduce the firm's dependence on unreliable, untrustworthy employees and assert managerial prerogatives to govern virtually all aspects of the work place. That this history is inconsistent with current trends to decentralize authority and increase employee involvement is clear, as is the burden such a legacy leaves for those managing the modern organization. This chapter considers how the evolution of the management of work has created barriers to the development of new ways of managing. It also considers the implications of this history for management efforts to achieve competitive advantage through people.

THE CREATION OF THE EMPLOYMENT RELATION

In an economy in which more than 90% of us work for someone else, the idea of being an employee is quite unexceptional and the concept of the employment relation is assumed more frequently than it is examined. Such was not always the case: "We look back after wage labour has won a respected position by two centuries of struggle. We forget the time when complete dependence on wages had for centuries been rejected by all who regarded themselves as free men."[8] The earliest shops were located in people's homes. Individuals owned their own equipment and they worked for themselves, at times with the assistance of the family.[9] The idea of a regular workweek or a regulated workday was unknown. Production was via the craft system, which means that "most or all of the basic decisions about how to produce a product are made by persons who are themselves directly involved in physically producing it."[10]

By the late 1700s, a production method called the "putting out" system emerged. The system looks, in many respects, like the so-called network organization or virtual corporation now in vogue, perhaps illustrating the continuity of issues of management over the centuries.

"Under this system, workers continued to own their own looms or spinning wheels, continued to work . . . when and as they pleased, but no longer owned the raw material or sold the product in the market. Instead, the raw material was supplied to, and the product taken from, the worker by a merchant putter out."[11] In this system, the entrepreneur did not necessarily control or even understand the process of production but was essentially a trader standing between the various producers, the final product, and the market.

The outwork system failed because of problems such as poor-quality work, slack effort, waste, and theft.[12] It was replaced by a system of inside contracting, in which centralized work places—factories—were established so that monitoring of the production process, use of materials, and so forth would be easier in a concentrated location. However, those who worked within the facility were still independent of the factory owner.

> Inside contractors were in most respects similar to independent subcontractors. The inside contractor made an agreement with the . . . owners of a company to make a part of their product and receive a certain price for each completed unit. . . . Inside contractors had complete charge of production in their area, hiring their own employees and supervising the work process.[13]

Inside contractors typically did the production work as well as supervised those who worked for them.

In the late 1800s, inside contracting was the system employed almost universally by producers of small arms, the iron and steel industry, and many of the largest and most famous machine shops of the time (including Pratt and Whitney) and was used in such major companies as Singer Sewing Machine, Reed and Barton Silversmiths, and Baldwin Locomotive.[14] Within 50 years, however, inside contracting and its predecessor, the putting out system, had both virtually ceased to exist. Yet some 50 plus years later, in the 1970s and 1980s, contracting and other alternative work arrangements would enjoy a tremendous resurgence in popularity.[15] The question of why this happened is important because one of the most crucial decisions a firm makes is the boundary decision—what activities to include within the administrative hierarchy and what activities it will manage through contractual or market mechanisms. If we understand something about why these early forms of organization once disappeared, perhaps we can understand something about when they are most applicable today.

It is essential to first understand the difference between relying on these quasi-market mechanisms and the employment relation. The essence of the employment relation is that there is now someone else besides yourself who cares about your level of performance. For instance, in the inside-contracting system, in which the worker was paid by the number of pieces produced, the person could adjust his or her effort and hours to how much money was desired. If the person worked less, the merchant was not harmed because fewer pieces were produced and therefore less was paid. If the individual figured out a way to organize work more efficiently, he or she received the benefits of this insight. In an employment relation, on the other hand, "what the worker sells, and what the capitalist buys, is *not an agreed amount of labor, but the power to labor over an agreed period of time.* What he buys is infinite in *potential* but in its *realization* it is limited by the subjective state of the workers . . . by the general social conditions under which they work . . . and by the technical settings of their labor."[16]

In the employment relation, as long as workers have their jobs, they get paid. Thus, the owners of firms have the opportunity to increase profits by finding ways to organize work more efficiently, introduce new technology, and obtain more output from the labor process. The employment relation makes the task of management both necessary and important—there are no "managers" in markets, and work organized under the putting out or inside-contracting system was work organized in a marketlike fashion. In the employment relation, there is both a need and an incentive for labor to be managed or controlled, and "control is . . . the central concept for all management systems."[17]

There are a number of arguments as to why the employment relation supplanted inside contracting and the putting out system, but unfortunately, they are not fully satisfactory in explaining the change. One argument is that the employment relation is necessary to ensure technological progress and to take advantage of changes in technology. It is, however, not clear why independent contractors would not avail themselves of technological progress, and because of their intimate knowledge of and involvement in the production process, they might be better able to do so. In fact, a study of the Winchester Repeating Arms Company documented the extent to which contractors improved productivity and cut costs.[18] There is no reason to believe that contracting should be more prevalent in technologically less sophisticated industries.

A second argument is that the employment relation permitted owners to exploit labor more readily. This is also not plausible. Under a contracting system, firms could put contractors in competition with each other, negotiate fiercely to lower prices, and change the sourcing of other inputs. Once these contractors became employees, the organizations faced the task of supervising them and the threat that the workers, if treated too harshly, would organize into labor unions, quit, or sabotage quality or equipment. Although in times of high demand, outside contractors might be able to negotiate better prices, in times of slack demand, the reverse would hold.

A third argument relies on transaction cost logic, noting that the employment relation economized on the need, in a contracting system, to bargain repeatedly over the terms of the agreements. The problem with this argument is that there can develop long-term market relations that take on elements of the employment relation, in the sense of relying on trust and resetting or renegotiating terms only infrequently. Conversely, as anyone who follows professional sports will know, employees may also rebargain salaries with great frequency.

Access to capital must be a part of the story. Inside contractors and people working at home must, in many cases, have been fairly thinly capitalized. In the absence of the more efficient capital markets we now take for granted, investment in new equipment or even expansion would be more difficult. This logic suggests that we would observe more contracting out, then and now, under conditions of low capital investment—which accords with the observation that it is often knowledge work or other tasks with comparatively low technological intensity that are done by contingent employees.

Another part of the story is the illusion of control to be gained by internalizing workers. The control may or may not be illusory, depending on how people are managed, but there is always the perception that things within the firm's boundaries are more certain than those left outside. For whatever reason, the employment relation became the dominant mode of organizing work early in the twentieth century and continues to be. The question then, and now, becomes one of how to manage that relationship for the best outcomes.

THE SEPARATION OF PLANNING FROM DOING

In the employment relation, employees depend on firms for jobs and wages. Firms depend on employees for their labor power, at a minimum, and their ingenuity and skill, at best. In this situation, two approaches are possible: 1) a process of accommodation and partnership, in which a relationship of trust is built and mutual commitments develop that bind the parties to each other; or 2) a process in which each side tries to a) obtain a position of relative power (less dependence) with respect to the other and b) use that position to extract as much as it can from the relationship. It is, by the way, not necessarily the case that the first option is inevitably superior—it depends in part on one's time horizon and one's belief that a mutually advantageous way of working together can actually develop. Which form of managing interdependence emerges depends on many factors, including what others do, norms, and custom as well as one's belief that one can, in fact, succeed following the second, adversarial, strategy.

In the United States, for a number of reasons—including immigration (which made replacing workers easier), the absence of a labor party or a strong labor movement, a laissez-faire ideology, and a government that tended to take business's side in a fairly active fashion—employers soon determined to deal with their work force by gaining dominion over it: they managed dependence not by building a system of mutual interdependence but by acquiring power and dominance over the employment relationship.

This was accomplished in many ways. In firms in which the owner was also the manager, there was personal control, which was, for the most part, more benign than alternatives practiced in larger firms. This personal control was usually perceived as legitimate—after all, the owner had his or her money invested. Moreover, the personal bonds—the social relations—that inevitably developed when people worked together served to make the owner's control more palatable and, in most instances, less severe. For years, Henry Ford worked with his engineers designing cars and systems to build them—he had a real affinity for people, and it was reciprocated. In small firms, "the personal ties that owners . . . established with their workers in many cases tended to obscure the real . . . differences between them. Loyalty had a direct and personal meaning for workers, and many were reluctant to break the bonds it formed." [19]

In larger enterprises, foremen and other supervisors exercised control over the work force, and the methods they used were harsh, to say the least. The foremen had absolute discretion as to whom to hire, what jobs to assign to each employee, how to pay people, and whom to dismiss and for what reason. [20] Motivation, if it could be called that, was driven mostly by fear and the exercise of the foremen's virtually unchecked power: "The methods used by foremen to maintain or increase effort levels were known . . . as the 'drive system': close supervision, abuse, profanity, and threats. . . . Workers were constantly urged to move faster and work harder. . . . The drive system depended, ultimately, on fear of unemployment to ensure obedience to the foreman." [21]

The system encouraged a high rate of turnover and, indeed, depended on it—if someone wasn't doing the job, fire the person and bring in someone else. Workers were seen as interchangeable, necessary to do the work but certainly not a source of advantage. In 1913, the turnover at Ford Motor Company was 380% at the Highland Park plant, [22] and such turnover levels were typical.

The real problem with the drive system was that workers still retained too much power and control—as long as knowledge of the task and how to do it resided largely with the labor force, management could never be completely certain whether there was slacking or featherbedding.

"Management could control the labor process only if a 'transfer of skill'—from craft worker to manager—about production techniques occurred."[23] The best and perhaps only way to "transfer skill" was to analyze the work process and divide the work up into small component parts, each done by a separate worker. This permitted one to hire workers for each task with the requisite skills for that small task and to economize on labor rates. Second, once the work process was decomposed, it could be studied, analyzed, and most important, the precise way in which work was performed could be specified so that employees or machines could be instructed in how to do the work.

What was unique about the specialization that began to occur in the early twentieth century was that, for the first time, the planning of work was separated from its execution. The emphasis on planning work led to the golden age of engineering. Between 1880 and 1920, the number of engineers in the United States grew from 7,000 to 135,000.[24] Many of them "were responsible for developing new methods of organization and management," and "discussions of plant administration and cost accounting were found chiefly in engineering publications."[25]

This was also the time when Frederick Taylor developed his principles of scientific management, which were to have a profound effect not only on the practice of management but also on management language, ideology, and thought even to this day. The principles of scientific management are:

- "The managers assume . . . the burden of gathering together all the traditional knowledge which in the past has been possessed by the workmen and then . . . reducing this knowledge to rules, laws, and formulae."[26]
- "All possible brain work should be removed from the shop and centered in the planning . . . department."[27]
- "The work of every workman is fully planned out by the management . . . and each man receives . . . complete . . . instructions, describing in detail the task which he is to accomplish, as well as the means to be used in doing the work."[28]

Taylor believed that workers systematically shirked or "soldiered," to use his term. He believed that one answer to this problem was to pay people a piece rate and not cut the rate when they were more productive and earned more. However, the solution to the problem of shirking also involved obtaining "control over work through control over the *decisions that are made in the course of work.*"[29]

Current prescriptions to get rid of Taylorism are correct in intent but will be problematic in implementation unless we recognize where Taylorism and its associated practices, such as the separation of planning from doing and a finely grained division of labor, originated. These principles, and the discipline that foremen used to exercise and that the Boise Cascade executive mentioned in his 1986 speech, came from a need to influence the work process. In the early years of the twentieth century, as now, economic competition was ferocious and business failures were frequent. Achieving productivity was not a luxury but a necessity, and productivity depended then, as now, on people, equipment, and their interaction. Control in the work place was (and is) not a luxury but a necessity. The only choice—then and now—was how that control, how that performance, was to be obtained.

At that time, most firms and their managers chose a particular course of action—a Taylorist course whose residue still exists and that many firms are now struggling to overcome. The residue is real. One of the first things NUMMI did when it reopened the plant in Fremont, California, was to eliminate virtually all the industrial engineers. Similarly, when Volvo undertook its wide-ranging work redesign in the 1970s, one of the things it did was to specify that changes on the assembly line could not be instituted by engineers alone and needed the consent of the foreman as well. Both of these events reflect the fact that the separation of planning from doing became institutionalized in a profession, industrial engineering, in practices associated with work and plant design, as well as in an ideology that made it unthinkable—literally not thought about or considered—to actually ask those doing the work to participate in its design and control.

Moreover, the desire for control of the work place and the fear of becoming dependent on employees still dictate both management policies and behavior. Preaching work redesign without directly tackling the issue of alternative mechanisms of ensuring efficiency and control seems almost inevitably doomed to failure. Of course, team- or peer-based control, particularly when coupled with the sharing of productivity gains with those same people, can motivate more discipline than supervisors ever could. It is a different way of achieving the same thing, however, and it makes managers coming from the Taylorist tradition nervous. In this sense, recognizing where these practices originated, and how and why they are maintained, becomes an essential first step in successfully altering them.

RESISTANCE AND RESPONSE

The drive system, the arbitrary exercise of authority and favoritism by foremen, was not always for the benefit of the employers, as sometimes the foremen took bribes for hiring people or placing them in higher-paying positions regardless of their skill or suitability for the job. Moreover, the attempt to deskill work and exercise close control prompted resistance on the part of employees. Sometimes, they simply quit, which is one reason why turnover was extraordinarily high and why the employment relationship often more closely resembled a spot labor market than a continuing relationship. Sometimes, they destroyed machinery and the products being produced—something that still happens in some automobile factories and other plants. Sometimes, they developed elaborate schemes to cheat the employer (also something not unknown today) by theft, loafing, reorganizing work to permit some to take unauthorized time off, and so forth. Sometimes, the resistance took the form of collective action: forming unions, striking (with or without unions), walking off the job without warning, sitting down on the job, and more.

Confronted with these problems, employers had two choices. They could try to find another way of organizing work to prevent the problems in the first place, or they could counter the workers' resistance with their own moves in an escalating war of attrition. These same two choices face employers today. They can either try to understand and remedy the underlying causes of the problems, or they can treat the symptoms, often by tightening discipline and control over an already recalcitrant work force. Which method of dealing with work place problems is chosen depends on many factors, but certainly two of the most critical are the values and ideology of managers and the extent to which they believe they can actually prevail in a conflict with the work force.

In the United States, the ideology of control is quite strong. This perhaps helps account for why our country currently has the highest rate of prison incarceration in the world, and a black male has five times as much likelihood of being in prison here as in South Africa, the country ranking second on this measure. Crime is met with punishment rather than prevention, even though some 80% of those in prison never completed high school, and the correlation between dropping out and being in trouble is higher than the relationship between smoking and cancer. The emphasis on discipline and control remains to this day—witness the quotes from the Boise Cascade CEO at the beginning of this chapter.

The emphasis on exercising control, on struggling rather than finding a way to reach a more collaborative solution, is going to look particularly attractive to employers that have not only their own resources but the resources of the state at their disposal. Employer resistance to work place threats to their control was organized, coordinated, sophisticated, and for the most part notably successful. As one example, after labor trouble in the 1880s, Detroit employers formed a coalition designed to fight unionization and organization in plants. To get a job with a member firm, one had to apply through the association, which kept records on the employees of all member firms. "By 1911, the association's employment bureau had in its files names of more than 160,000 workers, a figure equalling nearly 90% of the Detroit labor force."[30] Detroit's employers were so successful in identifying and blacklisting troublemakers that the city developed an image as a good place to do business. Consequently, the Packard Motor Company moved from Ohio to Detroit in 1903, and in 1904, the Burroughs Adding Machine Company relocated there from St. Louis.[31]

On a national scale, the National Association of Manufacturers took the lead in two antiunion campaigns, the open shop drive of 1903 and the "American Plan," pursued in the 1920s. In the pre–New Deal era, organized labor faced up to 137 associations of employers either openly or covertly hostile to unionization and collective bargaining.[32] When faced with the threat of unionization, companies would organize company-sponsored unions as alternatives. By 1928, company unions had some 1.5 million members.[33] Firms also tried cooptation through a program of welfare capitalism by providing generous pensions, recreational services, health care, housing, and other services.[34] Finally, firms over time attempted to make control less visible and overt, substituting rules and procedures for the arbitrary authority of foremen and supervisors.[35]

But when blacklisting and political influence, company unions, welfare capitalism, and bureaucratic control were insufficient, and sometimes even when they were effective, employers frequently resorted to violence to intimidate workers, break strikes, and thwart unionization. Evidence from numerous sources indicates that the United States had the highest level of industrial violence in the Western world. Employers "hired company guards and railway police, armed men supplied by agencies like Pinkerton,"[36] and sometimes operated security systems that would have been the envy of many governments. Ford Motor Company employed "spotters" who worked on the assembly line but whose "real job was to keep a careful note of their fellow workers' badge number, and then to tittle-tattle on them in detailed reports."[37] One survey on labor violence in the United States noted that "in the bloody period between January 1, 1902, and September 30, 1904, 198 persons were killed and 1,966 injured in strikes and lockouts. Our own independent count, which grossly understates the casualties, records over 700 deaths and several thousands of serious injuries in labor disputes."[38]

One reason for the violence was the fact that the government, largely controlled by business interests at the time and comparatively weak at that, either sided actively with employers or did nothing to regulate their behavior with respect to fighting the work force. For instance, in Europe, police powers were reserved to the central authorities, whereas in the United States, governments tolerated the establishment and equipping of private police forces and security departments, whose function was often to discipline employees and fight the unions. Several states had laws that specifically permitted the deputization of privately employed police.[39] In Pennsylvania, "every railroad in 1865 and every colliery, iron furnace, or rolling mill in 1866 was granted by statute liberty to employ as many policemen as it saw fit . . . and they were clothed with all authority of Pennsylvania . . . and they were commissioned by the governor."[40]

In addition to permitting private firms to recruit and arm their own police forces, governments often came to the aid of organizations confronted by labor unrest:

> [S]tate militias, which were reactivated after the Civil War primarily to police labor disputes, were on active duty in at least 150 labor disputes between 1877 and 1900. . . . [F]ederal troops . . . participated in the suppression of several critical strikes, including the 1877 railroad strike . . . and two major pre-1933 attempts to form industrial unions—at Pullman in 1894 and in the steel strike of 1919.[41]

Nor is the heated level of dispute and the state's taking sides something that occurred only in the long-forgotten past. In the early 1980s, there was a strike against Phelps Dodge in Arizona. A Democratic governor, Bruce Babbitt, subsequently appointed secretary of the interior in the Clinton administration, called out the national guard and state police to help the company bring in replacement workers and keep the mines open. The state of Arizona arrested hundreds of miners and their spouses, but not one was ever convicted of a crime. Rather, the arrests were part of the state's attempt to assist the corporation.[42]

The contrast with the situation in other countries is dramatic. In 1932, 4 men were killed and 20 wounded when a march on Ford's River Rouge plant was met by the Dearborn police, whose chief formerly worked as head of the Ford plant police in Highland Park.[43] In Germany, by the 1920s, a codetermination law, granting workers government-mandated participation in the operation of firms, had been passed. In Britain, in 1894, a royal commission sanctioned collective bargaining, and in 1906, the Trade Disputes Act restrained the courts from intervening in labor disputes on the side of management.[44] In Sweden, the government passed a mediation law in 1905 and obtained agreement from private employers to recognize workers' right to organize. Finally, in France, between the 1870s and World War I, "the government took various steps favoring collective bargaining, including . . . government mediation of labor disputes . . . and a preference for conciliation rather than repression of labor disputes."[45]

There is a saying, "Be careful what you wish for, you may get it." Corporations actively sought, and still do, the intervention of the state in struggles against the work force. For the most part, this intervention helps ensure victory. Phelps Dodge won its strike in Arizona, as did the automobile companies in many violent disputes of the 1930s and Boise Cascade in the 1980s. However, the "victories" are illusory, for after the police go home and workers or their replacements return to work, after the newspaper headlines fade, and after the thrill of victory passes, the organizations still need to be productive, efficient, and competitive and to find a way to achieve competitive success in an increasingly difficult marketplace. The victories leave them disinclined to seek competitive advantage through the vanquished workers, who are often resentful and, at a minimum, fearful. Indeed, the residue of the industrial disputes affects productivity and performance negatively.

When the employer's victory cannot be achieved by force or with the help of the state, however, the situation becomes analogous to the arms race between the United States and the Soviet Union. Faced with the inability to win by fighting, the parties will eventually see the need to compromise and work together for the mutual benefit of all. It may not be a happy or comfortable détente, particularly in the beginning, but it will be détente nonetheless and a necessary precursor to developing more helpful practices for managing the employment relation. Thus, somewhat ironically, the very fact that government has so often and so vigorously helped employers has left those employers incapable of working out cooperative, accommodative arrangements with their employees—exactly those arrangements and practices that can now provide competitive advantage through the work force. It is not only an unfortunate irony but one that is still not fully appreciated by many managers who are still caught up in the idea of winning and forgetful of the price of victory.

LEARNING FROM THE PAST

Since the mid-1930s, U.S. companies have succeeded in reducing the proportion of the work force covered by collective bargaining, in passing legislation that restricts union power, in maintaining
their ability to hire replacement workers—in short, perpetuating their
dominance and control in the work place. They still enjoy government
assistance in the battle with the work force, and although the level of
violence is less than it was 100 years ago, the power of the state most
often favors employers in maintaining discipline and control in the work
place. Technological advances have raised the ability to exercise control
to ever higher levels, and the deskilling of work has continued apace in
numerous occupations. For instance, today medicine is subject to some
of the same processes of scientific management formerly applied to
other work—patterns of practice are monitored; there are attempts to
break the tasks down into smaller ones so that those for which a physician is not needed can be performed by nurses, physician's assistants,
or technicians; and in many of the larger health maintenance organizations, how physicians spend their time is monitored and controlled.

Despite our history of work place relations and what that history has
produced—Pyrrhic victories even as firms fail to achieve competitive
success through their work force—too little is learned. In part, that is
because there are occupations and professions—for example, labor lawyers who consult on union avoidance, discipline, and grievance procedures; experts who will re-engineer jobs; equipment manufacturers that
sell surveillance and control technologies—with an interest in pro-
claiming the past a success. In part, it is because the industrial landscape has come to resemble Vietnam—having experienced an escala-
tion in the level of conflict over the years, it is difficult for those who
initiated or at least favored the battle to admit that there might be a
better resolution to the war.

Certainly, much of the difficulty in overcoming our history and learning from it stems from a narrow, unsophisticated view of the issue of
control in the work place. At Boise Cascade, a senior manufacturing

executive and former manager of the De Ridder plant decided to let line workers have more responsibility for scheduling the machines. The plant produced different grades and types of paper, and one of its largest expenses was setting up a new product type. The machine operators, with their years of experience, understood better than the engineers how to schedule different grades of paper and how long production runs should be to limit downtime and quality problems. When they were given more control over their own schedules (and additional training in repairing machines), productivity improved. In one sense, this clearly represents a loss of control for management.

But if history teaches us anything it is that the control achieved through the application of Taylorist principles and management might was illusory. People could, and did, resist the imposition of control, for reasons we saw in the last chapter. The application of force to counter resistance merely elicits more resistance, expressed, perhaps, in more subtle ways, and the cycle continues. History shows, I believe quite clearly, that in the battles fought in and over the work place, there were truly no winners.

Overcoming this history requires being clear about those in the organization who want to perpetuate the past and what their economic interest is in doing so. It is not by accident that work redesign and restructuring often proceed more effectively when those with a stake in the conflict-filled past are not permitted a large role in the process. Most important, it requires really understanding how work systems evolved to solve control problems and how their failure to do so speaks more to their own limitations than to the need for control.

Consider again the case of New United Motor. There is an emphasis on production efficiency and on standardized work—indeed, NUMMI may be the ultimate example of Taylor's principles applied in a production setting. There are real advantages to standardized work, as described by a NUMMI manager:

> [R]educed variability and team assessment of the jobs result in a whole series of interconnected improvements. There are fewer injuries . . . since workers get an opportunity to examine all the possible sources of strain and danger. . . . We get improved quality because workers identify the

most effective procedure for the job. . . . We also get better inventory control because we have a much more finely-tuned and well-balanced process. . . . Standardized work . . . means that each worker in the team can refer to a good procedure for doing the job. . . . In the old days, absences killed quality because the replacement not only didn't know the job but didn't even have a procedure to refer to for doing it right. . . . [Y]ou can't improve a process you don't understand. And standardized work has the major benefit of giving control of the job to the person who knows it best—it empowers our workers.[46]

NUMMI workers work harder than they did at the old GM-Fremont plant and, in spite of that, like the job and the system better. Control hasn't been lost, but its locus has been shifted. It is no longer management or industrial engineers telling the people what to do—it is the people telling each other what to do, with as much professional help and support as they need and with clear quality and efficiency standards and objectives. NUMMI represents learning the lessons of the history of work in America—that control imposed from outside or above, regardless of the power behind that control, ultimately fails. For even if the enterprise achieves control and discipline, it may not achieve the learning, adaptation, and efficiency necessary to remain successful against the competition. The history of industrial conflict and the deskilling of work was recognized in NUMMI—which, after all, is populated by people used to working under the old system—and then a conscious decision was made to break with that history. George Nano, shop steward under both the old and new systems, noted: "The key to NUMMI's success is that management gave up some of its power, some of its traditional prerogatives. If managers want to motivate workers to contribute and to learn, they have to give up some of their power. If management wants workers to trust them, we need to be 50/50 in making the decision with them."[47]

NUMMI, Boise Cascade, and numerous other work places provide evidence that it is not necessary to take the past into the future. But these examples also remind us that in order to change the past, we must both acknowledge it and understand what it is that needs to be changed.

Labor Laws, Lawyers, and Litigation: Friends or Foes of Work Place Change?

6

There are fairly straightforward questions that need to be asked about labor laws and the legal system that regulates the employment relation as well as management's response to and participation in that system. Such questions, however, do not include: Are we keeping enough lawyers fully employed and wealthy? Does the system reflect some ideological beliefs in individual legal entrepreneurship? Or is the system congruent with economic theories of human behavior? (By the way, in the United States, the answer to these questions is, for the most part, yes.) Rather than ask those questions, it seems to me fundamentally important to ask the following: 1) Does the system of law governing the employment relation tend to promote and enhance changes that permit firms to obtain competitive advantage through people? 2) Does the system provide remedies proportional to the wrongs or injustices done? 3) Does the system, and organizations' use of that system, enhance efficiency? And perhaps most important, 4) are individual firms using the legal structure, imperfect as it may be, in ways consistent with achieving competitive advantage through their work force? All too often, the answer to these four very crucial questions is, unfortunately, no.

The system for regulating the employment relation in the United States is in many respects disastrous, providing neither efficiency nor equity, nor fostering change in employment practices in ways consistent with achieving competitive success through people. The system, however, is a given, at least in the short term. Although its pitfalls need to be considered, for it is an important barrier to changing work place policies, how many organizations choose to respond to and use it makes the situation even worse. Thus, the purpose of this chapter is to indicate how the legal framework in the United States acts to impede changes in work place policies that might provide substantial economic benefits and to indicate what organizations can and might do to operate more effectively.

WHAT THE LAW MIGHT DO

It is instructive to consider regulation of the employment relationship in the United States compared to many, if not most, other industrialized countries. Table 6-1 presents issues potentially within the domain of labor law and indicates where the United States fits in the context of other countries. By other countries, I mean Western Europe, Australia and New Zealand, and Japan. Obviously, these countries themselves vary somewhat, and not all, for instance, mandate codetermination. The table presents the central approaches of many countries in the industrialized world—the very countries with which the United States is or should be competing in product and labor markets.

What Table 6-1 accurately suggests is that many other countries have much more interventionist policies with respect to the employment relationship, and as a consequence, labor market decisions are often more centralized. The United States, consistent with both dominant theory (neoclassical economics) and ideology (laissez-faire), relies much more on the actions or lack thereof of individual organizations, operating in what they perceive to be their own best interests. Since readers in the

Table 6-1 Domains of Legal Regulation of the Employment Relation and a Comparison of U.S. Policy with That of Other Countries

Issue	U.S. Policy	Dominant Policy in Other Industrialized Countries
At-will employment	Accepted and fought for vigorously	Proscribed by law and limited by regulation
Training expenditures	At the discretion of individual firms	Encouraged by tax incentives
Training standards and practices	At the discretion of individual firms	Frequently established and enforced by government-sanctioned industry or occupation councils
Codetermination and employee participation	Not encouraged	Frequently mandated
Employee representation by an organization	Neutral to not encouraged	Encouraged by law and social policy
Use of contract and temporary workers	Not regulated	Limited in amount and duration of employment
Benefits (e.g., health, retirement)	Provided by employers at their sole discretion	Provided in many cases by government or by employers under mandate

United States have come to take this situation for granted, its potential problems need some exposition.

I assume that one intermediate goal of labor market interventions should be to encourage the development of trust and cooperation among the organizational members, including stockholders, owners, and managers. Even agency theory recognizes that "in most . . . relationships the principal and the agent will incur positive monitoring and bonding costs . . . and in addition there will be some divergence between the agent's decisions and those decisions which would maximize the welfare of the principal."[1] There are obvious efficiency gains from minimizing monitoring costs and decision divergence, and such a result is more likely with trust and cooperative behavior.

It is also reasonable to assume that, particularly now, firms face a very competitive market so that not being disadvantaged in regard to principal competitors is a virtual necessity. In many instances, there is a history of conflict between owners or managers and the vast bulk of employees, and even if there is not such a history in a specific case, the general history of the evolution of the employment relation in the United States, described in Chapter 5, has left a residue that must affect to some extent how employees view their employers. If nothing else, the recent rounds of massive layoffs would cause them to fear for their job security. Consequently, it is likely that employees and owners face a prisoner's dilemma situation—a situation in which the best joint outcome is mutual cooperation, but the best individual outcome (particularly if one cannot be sure that the other party will cooperate) is to try to exploit the situation and not cooperate.

Considering just a few examples from the table can illustrate how action that may be optimal for an individual organization can lead to collective difficulties. For instance, consider medical and retirement benefits. An organization for which direct labor constitutes a substantial fraction of its costs can, in the short run, obtain a competitive advantage by eliminating its health and retirement benefits. Of course, this advantage is likely to be short-lived, since its competitors cannot keep labor at a cost disadvantage and will be tempted to follow suit and also reduce benefits. If the firms are unionized, there will probably be bargaining and possibly even strikes over this decision, and employees are likely to feel disadvantaged to have lost a benefit they once enjoyed. Moreover, as firms cease to provide health or retirement benefits directly, the government will inevitably be called upon to do so. This means that those firms that continue to provide the benefits wind up paying twice—once directly and once indirectly through taxes to fund the benefits not provided by their competitors. At some point, it becomes uneconomic for anyone to privately provide benefits.

By contrast, in a setting in which basic benefits are either provided to all, through some form of government insurance scheme, or have to be provided by employers by law, these benefits are taken "out of competition"—there is no advantage to trying to cut them, so disputes about such issues are minimized. In fact, during much of the 1970s and 1980s in Sweden, Volvo and other large manufacturers benefited from being able to bargain only over local conditions and concentrate on job enrichment and productivity-enhancing efforts without having to confront vexing issues of benefits levels.[2]

The centralized provision of benefits or regulation of benefits levels, as the Swedish example suggests, does not mean that these levels will be set at an optimal overall amount. Nevertheless, it is interesting that in the United States, there is much discussion of medical insurance costs and who bears them and there are many concerns about efficiency and choice—but the question of what the present or alternative systems do to the relationship between workers and firms is for the most part, virtually ignored. What examples of some other countries illustrate is how the very conditions that are and are not open to question in the employment relation can affect the extent to which trust and cooperation more easily develop.

Consider at-will employment—the ability of employers to fire someone without cause. It might be desirable, for the reasons previously discussed, to offer security of employment at least to some degree as a way of producing more commitment and greater levels of effort on the part of the work force. However, if only one firm provides such an assurance, it may be subject to adverse selection—those most likely to be fired will seek employment at the firm because of the comparative benefit from doing so. If, however, by law all firms provide an approximately equal level of employment security, employment security will no longer be an inducement to work in one place rather than another, and consequently, no firm will be confronted with an applicant pool motivated in part by inappropriate reasons for working there.

Consider the case of training expenditures. One question is, if people are such an important asset, why would firms underinvest in training? In the absence of the ability to bind workers to the firm—and slavery has been abolished—there is always some nontrivial chance that the training provided and paid for by one firm will benefit a competitor that hires away the already trained personnel. In economic theory, consequently, general training is supposed to be paid for by the worker, who is the primary beneficiary, since that person can sell his or her enhanced skills for a higher wage, while firm-specific training, of use primarily only to a single employer, should be paid for by that employer. This is fine in theory, but what constitutes general versus specific training is uncertain in practice. The potential for firms to have their training expenditures wasted through labor turnover probably produces some underinvestment in training, to the detriment of the larger economy as well as of those firms participating in a labor market filled with underskilled workers. If every firm spends comparably on training, then training expenditures are also "taken out of competition" and are no longer a disproportionate cost burden. This is the explicit reasoning behind requirements (such as in Australia and New Zealand) that corporations spend a certain percentage of payroll on training or else pay tax at the rate of 100% on the specified amounts not spent.

Finally, consider laws and social policy that favor rather than hinder collective representation of employees. With such laws in place, employers are not tempted to decertify unions or fight unionization efforts. Such laws tend to equalize the power of the work place participants. With more equal power comes a greater likelihood of seeking cooperative, as contrasted with adversarial, outcomes. Cooperation and trust can only be built by reciprocal and reciprocated actions on both sides. In the United States, where laws and their application have tended to favor employers, and in a decentralized labor market in which organizations believe they may be able to reap some short-run benefit by weakening the economic position of their employees, it has historically been problematic to develop cooperative relations in the work place. For example:

> The American unions are angered by the activities . . . to promote a union-free environment. John T. Joyce, president of the bricklayers' union, said, "The leadership of American labor has yet to recover from the shock of discovery, during the labor law reform effort of 1978, that the acceptance by American labor of private enterprise is not reciprocated by management." He and others were incensed that management, including many who "preached cooperation," would promote a legal framework that frustrated union organization efforts.[3]

What this example illustrates is that the possibility of "winning" in the legal arena presents a temptation almost too great to overcome, and rather than cooperating with either workers or their representatives, management is likely to try to vanquish them at all costs. In this way, the legal framework tends to discourage the development of cooperation and trust.

WHAT THE LAW DOES: WRONGFUL DISCHARGE AND EMPLOYMENT AT WILL

In the United States each year, there are approximately 3 million terminations for noneconomic reasons. Under the doctrine of employment at will, "in cases of employment of uncertain duration, 'All [employers] may dismiss their employees at will, be they many or few, for good cause, for no cause or even for cause morally wrong, without being thereby guilty of legal wrong.'"[4]

The United States is the only major industrial nation in the world that adheres to the at-will doctrine to even a limited extent. "Canada, France, Germany, Great Britain, Italy, Japan, and Sweden have enacted legislation which requires that employers have 'good cause' before terminating an employment relationship."[5]

Even in the United States, the at-will doctrine has eroded. In the public sector, civil service reforms protected employees from arbitrary dismissal. In the private sector, the National Labor Relations Act of 1935 made it unlawful for an employer to discharge an employee for "participating in union activities, complaining about violations of the NLRA, or seeking to exercise any other right guaranteed by the NLRA."[6] The various civil rights acts, beginning in 1964, provide protection against dismissal on the basis of gender, race, religion, national origin, age, or disability. In 1988, Congress passed the Workers Adjustment and Retraining Notification Act, which provides for a 60-day discharge notice for layoffs. This act does not limit an employer's rights but does require prior notification.

In the absence of legislative limitations on at-will discharges except for certain protected classes (e.g., union members, minorities, older workers), the courts in numerous states, acting on their own, have broadened the exclusions to the at-will doctrine. "As of June, 1987, forty-two states recognize an exception to the common law doctrine . . . either based upon the employer's alleged violation of public policy or breach of an implied contract"[7] or based upon a covenant of good faith. Exceptions on the basis of public policy hold that people cannot be fired for acting lawfully—for example, refusing to lie before investigating bodies, refusing to fix prices, or in general acting in ways required by the law. Exceptions on the basis of express or implied contracts hold that people cannot be fired at will if either written or implicit contractual obligations are established in the employment relation. In one Michigan case, *Toussaint* v. *Blue Cross and Blue Shield,* the existence of an internal policy manual specifying that it was the company's policy to terminate only for just cause was held to create an implied contractual obligation on the part of the employer to follow that statement. Particularly in California, courts have been willing to infer contractual obligations from the general circumstances of an employment relationship, such as years of continued employment with positive performance evaluations.

The final judicially created exception, the implied covenant of good faith and fair dealing, if taken literally, virtually eliminates employment at will. In *Cleary* v. *American Airlines,* the California Court of Appeals in 1980 decided that

> an employee could be wrongfully discharged . . . because the discharge violated an implied covenant of good faith and fair dealing that is present in every employment contract, even at-will employment. The court held that this covenant requires employers to treat employees in good faith and not take any action to deprive them of the benefit of their employment without just cause.[8]

The courts have extended not only the conditions under which a contractual right to continue employment is presumed but also the remedies available to those wrongfully discharged, moving gradually to include tort damages for things like emotional distress and punitive damages, to deter future conduct. These judicial extensions and the expansion of monetary remedies have produced a proliferation in the growth of at-will employment cases. Unfortunately, as we will soon see, these cases have not really provided equitable financial benefits to those discharged, have been enormously costly in time and money, and have served to intensify the arm's-length, conflictual relationship between employers and their employees. Moreover, there is little evidence that the "problem" of wrongful discharge has even been solved.

As to the proliferation of legal actions, one article reported a growth in cases at the appellate level in the United States from 40 in 1980 to 450 by 1986, an increase of 1,000% in six years.[9] An examination of case filings just in Los Angeles County Superior Court for the months of March and April found an increase from 15 in 1980 to 39 in 1982, more than a doubling in two years, with a further increase to 78 by 1984 and 102 cases filed in these two months in 1986.[10] By 1989, one estimate was that there were 25,000 wrongful discharge cases pending in state and federal courts in the United States and that wrongful discharge cases doubled in the five years from 1982 to 1987.[11]

The RAND Corporation conducted what has probably been the most comprehensive study of wrongful discharge cases, examining 120 jury trials decided in Los Angeles County between 1980 and 1986, about 50% of the cases involving executive or middle management plaintiffs. Jury trials are obviously not a representative sample of wrongful discharge actions since many cases are settled prior to trial. Nevertheless, statistics from this sample are striking. On average, it took 38 months for the cases to come to trial,[12] with the trials lasting on average 10 days. From the time of the verdict to final disposition of the case, including appeals or final settlement, an average of 5 months elapsed for closed cases and 28 months for cases still open at the time of the study. Of the 120 cases, the plaintiffs won 81, and in 40 of the cases, punitive damages were awarded. The average total verdict was $436,626, and considering only those cases won by the plaintiff, the average award was $646,855. The largest award was $8 million, and the smallest was $7,000.

A statistical analysis trying to explain the size of the total award was notably unsuccessful, accounting for less than one-third of the variation.[13] The only three statistically significant predictors of the size of the award were the plaintiff's age and earnings, both with a positive impact on the size of the award, and the plaintiff's being female, which had a negative impact. Size of the employer had no effect. The inability of analysis to uncover systematic effects on award size reinforces the sense that there is a tremendous amount of chance involved, and while this may be fine for gambling casinos, it is probably a poor foundation for important public policy consequences in a domain affecting the employment relation.

Final payments were often reduced on appeal, particularly in the case of larger awards. Costs of litigation were substantial. The average fee to defend one of the cases was more than $80,000, with the largest defense fee being some $650,000.[14] In more than half the cases, the plaintiff's attorney worked on a contingent fee arrangement, taking 40% or more of the final recovery. The study found that plaintiff's and defense legal fees combined are, on average, larger than the amount actually received by the injured party.[15] Moreover, considering the time to trial and median award compared to the plaintiff's salary, the evidence is that "the typical plaintiff receives the equivalent of one-half year's severance pay. By inducing terminated employees to accept such a severance, employers could save $84,000 in defense fees."[16]

Note that these costs are direct costs, not the costs of managers' time spent preparing for the cases and testifying, nor the cost of disruption to the organization. This expensive system, filled with delays of unpredictable duration, produces, on average, puny awards to the injured parties. The RAND study is consistent with the results of a nationwide study of wrongful discharge conducted by the Bureau of National Affairs, using a nationwide database of personal injury verdicts between January 1986 and October 1988—a total of 260 cases. That study found that plaintiffs also prevailed in about two-thirds of the cases (64%), winning an average award of $602,302, with the verdicts ranging in size from $500 to $17.5 million.[17]

The financial costs, although considerable, are perhaps not the most significant because of the way the United States handles at-will employment. Recall that one theory under which wrongful termination actions are brought is that express or implied contracts are created by promises made to employees either in corporate policy manuals, literature, or handbooks or during the recruiting process. This has led to the advice to remove promises of permanent employment (and in fact, even the phrase "permanent employee") from all such literature. Moreover, prospective employees are frequently asked to sign, as part of the job offer, statements waiving their rights to sue for wrongful discharge or acknowledging explicitly that they can be terminated at will. A consulting firm, in a poll of 60 major firms, "found . . . that 75% proclaim their right to fire at will on job application forms or in employee handbooks." [18]

Based on its study of wrongful discharge law and cases, the Bureau of National Affairs developed a set of recommendations; consider the likely consequences—not legal but in terms of managing the work force—from implementing them:

> Do not make any statement concerning the length of employment. . . . Avoid statements that employment at the company should be viewed as a long term career. . . . Avoid references to job security, longevity, or career paths that employees will take. Avoid any discussion of the policies and practices for layoffs and terminations. Interviewers should *not* describe probationary periods of employment. [19]

A reasonable reading of these recommendations suggests that they are, as a whole, almost completely antithetical to what an organization would do to achieve competitive advantage through its work force. The fact that these recommendations seem natural because of the state of existing labor law leads to the conclusion that current labor law in the United States—on this issue, at least—hinders the development of high-commitment work practices.

Consider the cost to management and how it approaches employees. If managers spend a disproportionate amount of time worrying about being sued and having employees and job applicants sign statements waiving their rights; if management is more concerned about the legal technicalities of the language in employee handbooks and policy manuals than about their effects on motivation and commitment; if management, through this process, comes to see employees as potential legal adversaries, then that management will probably engage in behavior that creates a self-fulfilling prophecy of distrust, conflict, and litigation. Its policies will signal a lack of trust and mutual commitment, which will almost certainly be returned in kind. Such behavior almost patently contradicts the oft-stated claim that "people are our most important asset."

LAWS GOVERNING COLLECTIVE BARGAINING

When employees are represented by a union or other collective associations, the potential for conflict is increased. It is probably in the interests of the labor organization to prove to its members how important and necessary it is. One way of doing this is to provoke management into taking hostile positions that convince members that the collective organization is their best source of protection against an arbitrary and capricious management. With organized interests on both sides, it would therefore seem particularly important to have institutional and legal practices that would encourage cooperation and the development of trust—trust that is going to be even harder to come by in this situation. Unfortunately, existing U.S. law and practice in this domain mirror the experience in at-will employment—they almost guarantee the opposite result.

The National Labor Relations Act, sometimes called the Wagner Act after its sponsor, established the basic regulatory and legal framework for collective bargaining and also established the National Labor Relations Board "to supervise representation elections and to investigate and adjudicate charges of unfair labor practices."[20] Passed with the hope of ensuring labor peace and industrial harmony, the law and its implementation have had no such effect. Table 6-2 illustrates the increase in the volume of litigation activity between 1948 and 1980. Just between 1970 and 1980, the number of unfair labor practice charges filed doubled, the number of workers offered reinstatement to their jobs almost tripled, and the total amount of back pay awarded quadrupled, even as the

Table 6-2 Growth in Labor Relations Litigation

	1948	1970	1980
Number of unfair labor practice cases filed	3,598	21,038	44,063
Number of workers offered reinstatement	1,001	3,779	10,033
Number of workers receiving back pay	1,196	6,833	15,642
Total back pay awarded (in thousands of 1948 dollars)	$431	$2,324	$9,388
Back pay per worker (in constant 1948 dollars)	$360	$341	$603
Number of representation elections	3,319	8,074	8,240

Source: Robert J. Flanagan, *Labor Relations and the Litigation Explosion* (Washington, DC: The Brookings Institution, 1987), 29, 76.

number of representation elections remained virtually constant, the proportion of the work force covered by collective bargaining declined, and there was no difference in strike activity that could account for the huge upsurge in litigation.

Because of an approach to labor relations that emphasizes the legal process rather than desired public policy or organizational effectiveness outcomes, a structure has been created that is costly to operate. In 1983, the budget of the National Labor Relations Board was more than 50% larger than the budget of either the Securities and Exchange Commission or the Federal Communications Commission.[21] Moreover, the process itself works poorly:

> Under the NLRA, union organizing is to an important extent a legal process with an intricate set of rules . . . governing almost every aspect of conduct by unions and employers as they seek to influence how workers vote on the question of unionization. . . . The result has been a level of regulatory activity and litigiousness in labor relations that is *without parallel in the rest of the world.*[22]

The laws governing collective bargaining directly interfere with attempts to improve work practices. Because of a history of employer resistance to labor unions using, among other things, company-sponsored unions, the Wagner Act forbade employers to establish their own unionlike organizations. Two relevant provisions are:

1. "It shall be an unfair labor practice for an employer to . . . interfere with the formation of any labor organization or contribute financial support to it."

2. A "labor organization" is "any organization of any kind, or any employee representation committee which exists for the purpose of dealing with employers concerning grievances, wages, hours of employment, or conditions of work."[23]

Because of the conflict between unions and management over the very existence of unions, labor organizations have used any means available to fight back, and the Wagner Act provisions just cited provide one such mechanism. Taken at face value, they seem to forbid the kind of employee-management committees often used to tap employees' knowledge and enhance their involvement and commitment. In a case involving the Electromation Company, an NLRB judge ruled that the committees in the company—established "to deal with problems such as absenteeism and pay scales for skilled workers"—violated the law.[24] Although some experts believe that the facts of this particular case limit its generality, even if the ruling is subsequently upheld, it is nevertheless significant that we have laws and regulations that can get in the way of something that many firms and even broader public policy regard as desirable—the use of teams of workers.

It is, however, important to recognize that the provision was written to stop some management abuses, and although it really reflects and perpetuates a system of conflict, it is not its only cause. The Electromation case was brought by the Teamsters when it began an organizing drive at the company, a drive that was possibly encouraged by the firm's decision, following a year of losses, not to grant wage hikes to its employees. It was only after the employees objected that the committees were established. Thus, it seems clear that neither side is totally blameless in this particular instance. Nevertheless, the point remains that the regulatory environment and the law do not facilitate making important and necessary changes in work place systems and climate.

The contrast with the rest of the industrialized world is particularly instructive. Although other countries are more unionized than the United States and experienced the same growth in wages and economic competition as the United States, they did not experience the tremendous increase in litigation found here. Take the case of Japan, which ostensibly has a very similar legal framework—imposed on it by the United States at the end of World War II—but a very different way of operating. The right to organize labor unions and bargain collectively is constitutionally guaranteed in Japan, but there is no election mechanism comparable to that in the United States. Virtually all employers of any size have unions, albeit enterprise unions, and the idea of exclusive representation—which is why an election is needed, to choose some specific representation or none at all—does not exist. As a consequence, about 1,000 "new charges of unfair practices are filed each year, whereas 25,000–30,000 charges are filed against employers annually in the United States. Moreover, Japan has not experienced the sharp growth in charges observed in North America in recent decades."[25]

As in the case of wrongful discharge, all this legal and administrative overhead, in addition to being expensive and not producing a labor relations climate conducive to taking advantage of the skills and commitment of the work force, even fails to adequately punish violations of the intricate rules:

> The Supreme Court has ruled that Board Actions must be remedial rather than punitive, and that the objective should be to restore the status quo. . . . Thus, when employers are found at fault, the Board usually requires them to post cease-and-desist orders. . . . When workers have been illegally discharged, the Board typically orders their reinstatement with back pay. For an employer's refusal to bargain, it may issue an order to bargain.[26]

The absence of actual punishment means that companies can and do simply refuse to obey NLRB orders.

DOES THE PUNISHMENT FIT THE CRIME? DISCRIMINATION LAW

The United States has laws that forbid discrimination in hiring, promoting, or discharging based on a person's race, gender, national origin, religion, age, or physical or mental handicap. The law has two purposes: to protect less powerful members of society against harm in the labor market and to encourage organizations to use their human resources efficiently by taking advantage of all the possible talent available to them. The first purpose is by far the more important, but the second speaks to how these laws, by encouraging the full utilization of all human assets, can contribute to both organizational and economy-wide effectiveness.

The problem with these laws, in addition to occasional lax enforcement by the federal agency responsible (the Equal Employment Opportunity Commission), is the small economic gain to those who are harmed by discrimination. For instance, in 1977, the average dollars received per person benefited in cases settled by the EEOC was $1,170. This amount increased to $4,800 by 1982 and $5,848 by 1985. When one considers that these are the average benefits received in cases that were actually settled as opposed to cases in which charges were filed, and that the charges involved limitations in individuals' ability to find and hold jobs, the amount of redress is quite minuscule.

When one reads about the seemingly large judgments firms pay in discrimination cases, it is critical to compute the amount that each of the harmed individuals receives. For instance, on July 18, 1991, American Telephone and Telegraph settled a case charging bias against pregnant women for $66 million. "Under the terms of the agreement, AT&T will pay $60 million to about 13,000 current and former employees of Western Electric. About $6 million will go toward legal fees."[27] The award averaged $4,615 per person. Furthermore, the plaintiffs waited 13 *years* to get this modest amount, as the suit was originally filed in 1978! The present value of $4,615 discounted over a 13-year period is truly trivial. Or as another example, in 1978, the EEOC reached a conciliation agreement with General Electric providing for a payment of $29.44 million. However, almost $10 million of the settlement went for training, and there were more than 265,000 employees covered by the agreement. Even if all the money had gone toward paying back wages, the amount received would have been about $100 per employee.

There is little apparent relationship between the actual harm done to employees and the amounts received for wrongful discharge, for being subject to violations of collective-bargaining laws, and for being discriminated against. There is, consequently, little evidence that these laws (or others that I don't review here) fulfill some sense of equity, in terms of having the compensation to victims reflect in some proportional way the economic loss suffered.

WHAT ORGANIZATIONS CAN DO

We have seen that the system for regulating the employment relation in the United States is economically inefficient, incurring high costs that primarily benefit players in the legal system; we have seen that the system is scarcely efficient in its use of time; it is apparently capricious, with there being little predictability in terms of the amount received or how long it takes to receive it; the system does not seem equitable, in the sense of having punishment or compensation proportional to the damage inflicted or incurred; and most important, it continues to foster conflict between organizations and their workers, breeds distrust and suspicion, and therefore is inconsistent in important respects with what would be useful for building high-commitment and more productive work places. It is this last effect that is the most pernicious.

When General Motors was building its new Saturn plant in Tennessee, it decided to embark on an entirely new way of doing business with its employees. Implicitly following the NUMMI model, it severely reduced the number of job classifications, designed the work process to rely more on teamwork, and consulted with the United Auto Workers union on every major decision, from the choice of production technology to the development of advertising and marketing strategy. Much of this consultation—concerning the physical layout of the plant, technology, product design, and so forth—necessarily occurred in advance of the plant's actually being constructed and workers being hired. There's the rub. Without a work force in place to vote on representation, the UAW and GM behaved illegally under existing labor law. Without an election—impossible for a nonexistent work force—the union was not an authorized representative and hence could not legally bargain with the company. Fortunately, the union leader involved, Donald Ephlin, had excellent connections in the Labor Department and was able to keep the consultative process intact. The fact that this form of joint consultation is inconsistent with the existing legal environment, even when desired by both union and management and obviously beneficial to the interests of both owners and workers, simply makes the point once more about how the legal structure is an impediment to managing the work force productively.

Unfortunately, however, as much as they may complain about the present system, most organizations do little to change it—and in fact, frequently oppose reform. Moreover, by their own behavior, firms often act to compound the difficulties. There are alternatives. On the issue of reform, consider the case of employment at will and wrongful discharge. The American Civil Liberties Union has urged "states to enact legislation that would eliminate employers' right to fire at will, provide for arbitration, and limit damages"; the organization noted that "the average jury verdict in wrongful discharge cases is now over $500,000" while "the average decision under such a law would be $14,000."[28] Not only do the trial lawyers, as one might expect, oppose such a bill, so do organized business interests. It has only been Montana, of all the 50 states and the District of Columbia, that has enacted wrongful discharge reform, in spite of its having been discussed now for almost a decade. Somehow, firms would rather play legal roulette and maintain the present adversarial system.

It is also possible for the state to become more directly involved in mediating and resolving employment disputes, as it already is to some extent in the arena of discrimination. Although the creation of state agencies involves public expense, it may be more efficient than relying on the adversarial system of civil litigation. At least in a government-sponsored and -administered system, there is a chance of structuring interaction to preclude some of the animosity that necessarily evolves in legal proceedings. There is also the potential for a no-fault system as in the case of workers' compensation. Although that system is scarcely perfect, one might contemplate the alternative—a system for compensating occupational injuries that relies on the courts and tort law.

Public policy clearly has an important role to play in establishing a framework for cooperative relations in the work place and thereby making it more likely that high-commitment work practices will emerge. In this regard, the differences between the United States and most other industrialized countries are noteworthy. For instance, the following provisions are found in the constitution of Japan:

> Article 28 states that "the right of workers to organize and to bargain and act collectively is guaranteed.". . . Article 27 states: "All people shall have the right and the obligation to work. Standards for wages, hours, rest and other working conditions shall be fixed by law. Children shall not be exploited." Article 25 . . . states: "All people shall have the right to maintain the minimum standards of wholesome and cultured living in all spheres of life. The state shall use its endeavors for the promotion and extension of social welfare and security and of public health." [29]

These are not merely high-minded sentiments. These statements of intention, written not just into laws passed or repealed easily but into the constitution itself, provide a social context within which cooperative and trusting relations between organizations and their employees are encouraged by the state. The contrast with the situation in the United States could not be more dramatic.

Individual organizations need not wait for total system reform and rationalization to do things more consistent with achieving competitive success through their work force. The problem is not one of having too many lawyers and bad laws. To the best of my knowledge, lawyers don't work without clients. Organizations do not have to discharge employees at will without trying to pay compensation and without due process. There is no reason to pursue these cases all the way to trial and spend the several hundreds of thousands of dollars this often takes, and then to appeal decisions and drag the process out even more. These are decisions organizations make. Some have chosen a different course.

Following two narrow victories in union representation elections in 1946, the Northrop Corporation instituted an arbitration process that it follows to this day. According to the director of industrial relations, the process has a number of advantages: "I have come to believe that without final and binding arbitration, a system of internal grievance handling . . . runs the risk of losing credibility in the eyes of employees. . . . [T]he potential for grievances going to arbitration induces management personnel to think twice before taking an action which may generate an employee's grievance."[30]

One study of 78 nonunion businesses found that three-fifths had some kind of formal grievance procedure delineated in the employee handbook.[31] This proportion seems unusually large, and more typical estimates are that fewer than 10% of employers offer complaint or grievance procedures that provide employees with due process. Offering internal grievance and arbitration mechanisms not only can forestall unionization simply to obtain justice in the work place and provide an avenue for employee voice, but it can also head off problems before they become expensive. As the quote from the Northrop executive illustrates, such systems can even foster better management.

When the Portman Hotel opened in San Francisco in the late 1980s, its competitive niche was the luxury hotel market, a niche that was already fiercely competitive and becoming even more so. Portman sought to differentiate itself from the competition by instituting a system of personal valets, as can be found in many Asian hotels. The valets would provide an exceptional level of personal service. Portman, in other words, determined to achieve competitive differentiation through its work force. One thing Portman did was to sign an agreement with its workers:

> Every Portman employee was called an "associate" . . . and signed a contract. The . . . contract . . . covered both the associates' rights and responsibilities, making clear that the contract was binding, so that if any associate's rights had been violated, the associate could seek redress in court.
>
> The contract included a "bill of rights." . . . Other rights . . . had to do with terms setting the duration of employment . . . grievance procedure, the role of seniority, and policies pertaining to layoffs, terminations, discipline and general rules of conduct.[32]

This document is one example of what a progressive organization can do, if it wants to, in the way of unilaterally offering guarantees and procedures that seek to motivate and commit employees and to provide internal ways of dealing with issues in the employment relation rather than relying on the legal system or external regulators.

Why don't more organizations take this approach? Many have turned their employee relations over to attorneys who think in terms of cases won or lost, not in terms of resources expended and certainly not in terms of the effect of employee relations practices on the organization's competitive success. Once in a conflict, it is incredibly easy and seductive to think in terms of opposing positions and winning and losing. However, such a perspective is not inevitable. Recall that Lincoln Electric early in its history set up a council to hear employee suggestions and problems. Establishing internal mechanisms to build commitment while ensuring fair treatment is something that any organization can do, and many of the effective ones already have.

Employee Organizations: Their Effects and Role in Work Place Reform

7

No assessment of the factors that hinder and facilitate work place change would be complete without considering the role of organized labor. Seen as a villain by some and as a hero by others, the truth is actually somewhere in the middle. It does seem clear that, as with the legal environment, organizations can do things to make the role of organized labor more negative—or for that matter, more positive—than it would otherwise be. As with the evaluation of the laws and regulations governing the employment relationship, the evaluation of unions ought to be a pragmatic one—what are their effects and what is their behavior in the context of organizing the employment relation to achieve competitive success through the work force?

This chapter begins with an assessment of the effects of unions on important outcomes such as productivity, competitiveness, and profits, as well as wage levels and turnover. There is little evidence that unions have harmful effects on factors that would affect an organization's competitiveness, and indeed, there is some evidence that union effects may be positive. I next consider why, given these data, there is so much management resistance. This resistance brings its own response, and it can be seen that union behavior is in large measure a consequence of management behavior. This means that organizations have discretion to develop more collaborative relations or to expend resources fighting employee organizations, and this chapter considers examples of both responses. Finally, I examine alternatives to employee organization—including government regulation and intervention—and management's right to direct and manage without serious challenge by any other group. Although this latter situation is the one most often assiduously desired, there are both arguments and evidence that suggest it may not be as beneficial as at first thought.

The reader is cautioned that the subject of unions and collective bargaining is, in my experience, one that causes otherwise sensible people to lose their objectivity. I encourage a pragmatic approach to this issue as to all issues involving the organization of the employment relationship. We need to see what union effects really are, how employee organizations behave and why, and most important, why a German senior executive once said publicly in an executive program that he would rather have union members on his board of directors than bankers.

UNION EFFECTS

Estimating the effects of unions on organizations is not easy. This is because unionization is not some randomly assigned treatment that can be studied under controlled conditions, as one might study the effectiveness of a drug on some disease. Unions occur nonrandomly in the economy, and consequently, estimates of the effects of unions must account for the possibility that some of the conditions that produced unionization in the first place are also associated with the presumed effects of unionization. Fortunately, studies of union effects have become more methodologically sophisticated over time, and thus, estimates of actual effects are increasingly reliable and robust.

One other introductory proviso is in order. In thinking about union effects, one needs to keep in mind that unionization of the private-sector work force has declined drastically in the United States over the past several decades and that unionization in the United States is substantially lower than in virtually any other industrialized country, including those in Western Europe, Australia and New Zealand, and Japan. Given these facts, it is hard to blame contemporary economic problems on an institution that has diminished in importance in the economy. Moreover, in bemoaning our loss of competitive position to other countries, one can scarcely blame an institution that is almost invariably stronger in these other countries—although, as we shall see, union behavior may differ at least somewhat in some of them, largely because of a different social environment and response by management.

On Trade and Innovation

Is there any evidence for the commonsense supposition that unions have raised wages to noncompetitive levels and thereby compromised the position of U.S. firms in the world economy? Is there any evidence that unions, seeking to protect the jobs of their members, have retarded the introduction of technology that would enhance U.S. organizations' competitiveness? The answer to both these questions is, at least at the moment, no.

Thomas Karier studied 134 three-digit Standard Industrial Classification industries from the mid-1960s to the mid-1980s—when the economy of the United States became much more integrated with the world economy, accompanied by a rise in imports and exports—to see whether industries that were more unionized fared comparatively worse. He concluded that "heavily unionized industries are not found to have lost any more to imports nor gained any more in exports than comparable U.S. industries. . . . [I]ndustrial concentration appears to be a significant disadvantage."[1] In other words, industries coming into the period facing a less competitive environment fared worse in the intensified worldwide competition, but unionization had no effect.

Jeffrey Keefe examined the diffusion of seven advanced manufacturing process technologies, using a survey of the nonelectrical machinery industry. He concluded that union establishments were *more* rather than less likely to be using advanced technology. This effect occurred, however, because of the association of unionization with plant size and the use of shift work. With these factors controlled, Keefe observed no direct unionization effect on the diffusion of these advanced technologies.[2]

In specific industries, unions have sought to mitigate the effects of new technology on employment levels—for instance, in railroads, by maintaining the position of fireman even after diesel locomotives were introduced. By raising the costs or lowering the savings in employment obtained through new technology, unions may at times retard its introduction. However, systematic evidence on this point is sparse, and union effects are multifaceted. Keefe's study reviews the existing literature on the effects of unions on technology in a variety of samples, using a number of methodologies. A reading of the evidence indicates that the effects are mixed, and there is certainly no evidence that unions retard the introduction of technology in a consistent fashion. Obviously, the particular industry and competitive circumstances, as well as the particular union and management, matter a great deal.

Innovation relies, of course, not only on technology but also on changes in the management process. What is the effect of unions on work place reforms? Although the common assumption is that approaches like quality circles and employee involvement programs are more effectively deployed in nonunion environments, the limited available evidence suggests that this is not the case. Robert Drago studied establishments with quality circles in the metropolitan Milwaukee area, seeking to understand differences in the survival rates of quality circles (recall from the discussion in Chapter 3 that many work place reforms are difficult to diffuse and don't last long even when they are adopted).[3] His analysis revealed that unionization, however measured, was *positively* related to the survival of quality circles. In fact, the unionization variable was substantively more important in predicting the survival of quality circles than any other variable, including one assessing the extent of participative management.

On Wages

Unions do raise wages—this finding is scarcely surprising as raising wages is a stated objective of unions. The most comprehensive study of wage gains, reviewing some 114 studies covering the period from 1967 to 1979, concluded that 1) over the period, the mean union wage premium was 10.3%; and 2) the union-nonunion wage gap varied directly with the national unemployment rate, with union wage differences being greater in times of higher unemployment.[4]

Wage gains from union membership tend to be higher for low-wage workers such as young people, ethnic minorities, and lower-tenure employees. Although statistically significant, union wage differentials are comparatively small and are almost certainly not large enough to cause any significant macroeconomic dislocations. Richard Freeman and James Medoff noted that the small union wage premium, applied to the small fraction of the work force unionized, left a very small net effect on overall economic performance: "Our analysis, and that of others, shows that the loss of national output due to union monopoly wage effects is quite modest.... Our estimate ... suggests that union monopoly wage gains cost the economy 0.2 to 0.4 percent of gross national product, which in 1980 amounted to about ... $20.00 to $40.00 per person."[5]

On Productivity

What do unions do to firm-level productivity? The empirical evidence is less than definitive, but the general conclusion is that unions affect productivity negatively in situations in which union and management leaderships are not particularly competent and there is a great deal of conflict. However, unions affect productivity positively in settings in which management skills on the part of both the union and the firm are stronger. This is an important conclusion because it foreshadows a result we will encounter frequently in this chapter—the effects of unions depend very much on what *management* does.

Many studies of union effects on productivity use construction as an empirical setting. There are union and nonunion contractors, often operating in the same locale and building similar projects. Moreover, it is possible to assess the dimensions of a construction project—size, type, amenities—with greater precision, affording the opportunity to make more precise comparisons. One study found that union contractors were 30% more productive than nonunion contractors in the building of commercial office space but were not more productive in school construction.[6] A subsequent study found that the productivity of union contractors was 23% greater than that of nonunion contractors in the case of private hospital construction.[7] A study of the construction of 42 retail stores and shopping centers found that the square footage put in place per hour was 51% greater for union as compared with nonunion contractors.[8]

Research on productivity in 83 West Virginia coal mines in the 1920s indicated that unionism significantly reduced productivity at small coal mines but not at the larger ones.[9] The differential effect is consistent with other historical evidence that indicates that management and union leadership were both of higher quality at the larger mines. Another study of productivity in coal mining discovered that the productivity in union mines was 33% to 38% higher than in nonunion mines in 1965 but was 14% to 20% lower in 1975 and 1980.[10] One interpretation of these results is that the deterioration in union-management relations over this period, with the concomitant increase in industrial disputes and work place conflict, caused the change from a union productivity premium to a productivity disadvantage in a relatively brief period. These findings, and the findings on differences in productivity in construction, depending on whether there was private or government ownership of the project, reinforce the conclusion that management plays a key role in determining the impact of unionization on productivity.

Upon reflection, the fact that unionization often has a positive effect on productivity should not be that surprising. In the first place, the union effect of raising wages means that employers can be more selective and hire a better-quality, more experienced work force because they are paying better. Indeed, one study of hiring standards and union status concluded that "the data are compatible with the hypothesis that employers respond to union wage premiums by raising the educational component of hiring standards."[11] Just as Lincoln Electric and Nordstrom obtain better performance from a higher-paid and more skilled and motivated work force, so, too, do firms forced to pay higher wages by their union status.

Second, unions reduce turnover dramatically, which should leave the organization with a more experienced work force. This greater level of organization-specific experience and knowledge ought to translate into higher productivity. Unions reduce turnover because, with higher wages, it is more difficult to find an alternative better-paying job. Unions also reduce turnover because they tend to tilt the compensation package toward forms of deferred compensation and benefits such as pensions and medical insurance. Deferred compensation and seniority-based benefits and employment security encourage employees to stay on the job. In addition, unions positively affect working conditions and provide workers with a way of expressing and potentially addressing grievances short of simply quitting. Statistical estimates indicate that unionization reduces quits more than a 20% increase in wages would. Many studies report that unions have the effect of decreasing quit rates by 30% or more, whereas a 20% increase in wages decreases the probability of quitting by only about 10%.[12]

Unions can increase productivity because there is some evidence that, once working conditions are controlled, unions actually increase job satisfaction.[13] Unions reduce earnings dispersion in the work place.[14] Although some might argue that this decreases motivation, in fact, as we saw in Chapter 2, reduced earnings differences facilitate the development of team-based work organization and enhance cooperation in the work place. Moreover, the very fact of more employee control of the work process can enhance productivity. Participation in the design of work and the allocation of tasks may not only elicit more favorable attitudes but also enhance the effectiveness of the work process that results from a better division of labor and assignment of responsibilities. The higher union wage can act much as debt does in some theories—to discipline management and force it to become more effective. There are, then, a number of mechanisms that make finding a positive union effect on productivity not at all unexpected.

On Profit

Unions may increase productivity, but they also raise wages. The net effect on profitability is, consequently, unclear. The question is whether the productivity-enhancing effects overcome the wage premiums, or rather, do the wage gains overcome any increased productivity and result in a net decrease in profits?

Studying union effects on profitability is hard because "profitability is one of the most difficult economic variables to measure."[15] Accounting measures of profit often incorporate differences in how firms treat research and development, how they depreciate capital equipment, what inventory costing policies they use, and so forth, making benchmarking problematic. Some researchers have tried to use stock market price movements around events, such as unionization elections or the passage of labor laws, to measure union effects on shareholder wealth.[16] The problem with these studies is that the firms are scarcely a random sample of the population. Firms subject to union elections are already probably not managing their work force as well as they might—and it is therefore not clear whether the negative returns observed in such studies measure the effects of unionization or, alternatively, the provision to the public of information about the quality of management in a firm.

Some studies have investigated the effect of the percentage of unionized employees on the price-cost margin at the industry level of analysis, controlling for other factors that might affect profitability.[17] These studies indicate that unionization reduces profitability by between 14% and 37%. More detailed analyses indicate that unionization's effect on profitability occurs, not unexpectedly, primarily in highly concentrated, monopolistic industries. Unions appear to shift some of the economic rents obtained from a monopoly product market position from the shareholders to the employees. "Unionism has no impact on the profit-ability of competitive firms."[18]

MANAGEMENT RESISTANCE

Although union effects are often positive or at worst neutral, unionization efforts are steadfastly resisted by the management of virtu-ally all organizations. One extensive study of union certification and decertification elections reported that the typical consultant fee, paid to a firm to help management win the election, averaged $500 per employee.[19] Nor is this spending confined to the private sector. In a union decertification election in a public agency, where the expenditure of public funds made assessment of the costs possible, John Lawler reported that the agency spent some $10,000 on attorneys' fees and about $70,000 on two different management consultants. The campaign lasted more than a year and finally resulted in the removal of the union. As the bargaining unit consisted of 105 employees, the cost just for consultants and attorneys was about $760 per employee.[20] These direct out-of-pocket costs are not necessarily the largest expense—consider the turmoil in the agency's work force during the year that the campaign dragged on.

In 1990, the *New York Daily News*, at that time owned by the Tribune Company, determined that it wanted to take a strike to either eliminate the unions or else severely diminish their power at the newspaper. To prepare for the strike, and to ensure the ability to operate while it went on, the Tribune set up a dummy, or mock, newspaper operation in an-other location to enable replacement workers and management person-nel to be trained on the equipment and procedures so they could take over when the strike occurred. The eventual strike lasted months and cost the paper millions in lost advertising and circulation problems. Frank Lorenzo, preparing for a strike at Eastern Airlines shortly after he acquired the company, socked away $20 million in reserves in prepara-tion. The Phelps Dodge Corporation operated its copper mines in Ari-zona with replacement workers during a bitter strike. For months, the company had to pay for buses to bring workers in from nearby communities and for security guard escorts and helicopter rides.[21]

Why are organizations willing to spend real resources as well as substantial managerial time and effort to avoid employee collective representation? There may be several reasons. First, the mere presence of a union or union-organizing effort may send a negative signal about managerial competence. It is a common belief that good managers who know how to manage their people don't get unions. Given the prevalence of that belief, unions are not likely to be good for one's managerial career. This is precisely what Richard Freeman and Morris Kleiner found when, in 1986, they interviewed representatives of 243 firms that had held union elections in the Boston and Kansas City National Labor Relations Board districts during 1979 and the 1980s, as well as 33 comparable firms that did not experience an organizing drive during the period, included for control purposes. They wrote:

> The results show that an organizing drive and a union victory have definite impact on the careers of managers. Eight percent of managers in the sample of establishments with organizing drives were fired, and 10% in the subsample who lost the election to the union . . . compared to 2% in our control sample. At the other end of the spectrum, just 3% of managers . . . facing an organizing drive and none in the sample who ended up with a union contract were promoted, compared to 21% of managers in our control group. These findings . . . suggest that a union organizing drive signals stockholders and top management that the plant management is poor and should be replaced.[22]

If you are four times as likely to be fired and much less likely to be promoted, it is no wonder that a union or even a union election is not welcome and why managers are willing to expend substantial resources in fighting them.

Second, management, particularly senior management, in most U.S. corporations has almost no personal contact with unions except in an adversarial capacity, unlike the case in many other countries, particularly Japan. Indeed, many senior managers have had little contact with operations at all, having risen through the ranks of finance or marketing.

This minimal contact with the work force and with unions creates ample opportunity for negative stereotypes to develop.

Third, we saw in Chapter 5 that the history of labor relations demonstrates repeatedly that government is willing to back management, thereby legitimating resistance. Labor relations is a domain overrun with attorneys. One study reported that attorneys were the largest category of employer consultants on unionization and decertification elections, constituting some 45% of the total.[23] In spite of the rhetoric about alternative dispute resolution, attorneys most often see things in terms of "winning" and "losing," a posture that is consistent with the competitive culture of many organizations. If, as the late football coach Vince Lombardi said, "Winning isn't everything, it's the only thing," then pursuing conflicts almost without regard to the costs or economic rationale is natural.

Perhaps the statement I heard the most, as I talked to managers in both public- and private-sector organizations, is that a union or employee representation organization introduces a third party, an outsider, into the management-worker relationship. This intruder, coupled with a contract governing working conditions, constrains management's flexibility and interferes with its ability to manage effectively. I would have more sympathy for this view except for: 1) the absence of evidence that unions produce negative impacts on productivity or other indicators of organizational effectiveness, and 2) the fact that a potent and occasionally disruptive force is already present in most private organizations—namely, the shareholders and their representatives. There is an argument to be made that unions balance shareholder pressures for the betterment of the organization, and it is to this argument that I now turn.

ALTERNATIVE GOVERNANCE ARRANGEMENTS

The issues typically negotiated by unions—wages, hours, conditions of work including health and safety, grievance and discipline procedures, benefits, job definitions, and other aspects of the employment relation—have to be determined by some process. A useful way of considering the benefits and costs of unions is to compare employee associations to other ways of determining these dimensions of the employment relation.

One alternative to having these issues negotiated by employee representatives and the employer is to have them mandated or regulated by law and government intervention. Over time, it is clear that government regulation and enforcement have become more prominent. Today, there is a federal Occupational Safety and Health Administration, and many states have comparable agencies. Pension plans are regulated at the federal level to ensure their financial soundness, and since the 1930s, Social Security has provided some retirement income as well as disability benefits. Federal and state laws determine hours of work and what qualifies for overtime pay; federal and state legislation prescribe minimum wages; federal and state regulations determine licensing and qualification requirements for numerous occupations; and there are regulations governing work hours in occupations, such as trucking and flying, in which safety considerations are important. This is just a partial list.

Although there are some advantages to having government-mandated benefits and regulation of the employment relationship, there are two very important costs. The first is the absence of flexibility to adjust to changes over time, and the second is the difficulty in tailoring employment conditions to the specific circumstances of the firm and its work force. On the first point, laws and regulations, even laws such as those prescribing minimum wages, adjust only slowly and with great difficulty to changes in economic circumstances and in other business conditions. Laws require legislation, and getting legislation passed is at best a costly and cumbersome process.

On the second point, laws and regulations governing the employment relation and, for that matter, centrally provided or mandated benefits cannot be custom-tailored to an organization's specific circumstances. Nor are they readily adapted to the specific interests and needs of a given work force. Some employees may prefer benefits, others higher wages; some may want to trade wage adjustments for job security, others may not. Similarly, the particular technology and competitive conditions facing different firms and industries vary. The difficulty of making localized adjustments to specific circumstances is a big problem and, in fact, affects even collective-bargaining agreements that are industrywide. One of the advantages of the enterprise union model— prevalent, for instance, in Japan—is that the conditions of each firm and its work force can be accommodated in the specific terms of the employment relationship.

That government regulation provides at best a blunt instrument for determining the structure of the employment relation is a position that most managers endorse. Clearly, contracts negotiated at a local level that reflect the specific desires of the work force and the needs of the employer are preferable. But what about the other alternative, having conditions of the employment relationship determined unilaterally by management? In the absence of unions or government regulation and constraint, employers can potentially organize the employment relation for optimum efficiency, setting terms of employment in response to changing market conditions and adapting to the requirements of new technology and the competition.

There is something wrong with this story—namely, the evidence described in Chapter 3 about the slow diffusion of better ways of managing work and the often short half-life of work place reform. Why might firms not do the right thing, and how might employee organizations help solve this problem? There are at least two answers to these questions.

In the absence of some form of organized employee voice, management will inevitably act either in its own interests—for power and perquisites—or in the interests of shareholders. Using modern game theory and other tools of economic analysis, Masahiko Aoki has analyzed the structure of the Japanese firm (which he refers to as the J-firm) and compared it to the typical American firm (the A-firm). He proved the following:

> "[S]hort-run" share price maximization . . . does not necessarily lead to internal efficiency of the firm viewed as a coalition of the body of stockholders and the body of quasi-permanent employees. If all other resources of the firm, other than equity capital, can be realized from com-

petitive markets and priced there, share price maximization against market-determined costs will ensure internal efficiency. However, if human resources of the firm have come to be internalized . . . the well-being of the quasi-permanent employee will depend on various corporate policies such as investment, employment, and the like . . . In this situation, choosing strategic business policy to maximize share price, subject to the pay level . . . would not lead to internally efficient decision making.[24]

Unlike the typical U.S. firm, in which shareholders bear all the economic risk and claim all the residual returns after various inputs such as materials and labor are paid, in the Japanese firm, there is sharing of risk between shareholders and labor—labor rates fall (in the payment of the semiannual bonus) when profits are low. Most important, "Japanese management acts as an arbitrator between the body of stockholders and the body of employees, rather than as an agent of the former."[25] What is important is that Aoki demonstrated, both in the particular case of Japan and more generally, 1) how this arrangement has benefited the Japanese firm, 2) that this arrangement is, in fact, increasingly common in many industrialized countries, and most important, 3) that this arrangement produces better decisions in terms of the firm's overall efficiency over time. This latter result holds because "in order to generate the organizational quasi rent [extra profits], both bodies [stockholders and employees] need each other's commitment to the accumulation of financial and human assets."[26]

Capital is much more mobile than labor. This mobility means that, for the most part, providers of capital are quite fickle, which causes them and managers responding to their demands to take a very short-term view of things. And now we can account for the otherwise incomprehensible comment made by the German industrial manager at the beginning of the chapter as to how he prefers workers to bankers on his board. The bankers are interested only in getting repaid as quickly as possible, and similarly, shareholders, he claimed, were only interested in short-term dividends and profits. By contrast, workers understood that a large portion of their human capital was organization-specific. Committed to the firm over the long run, it was the worker representatives on the board who worried most about whether the level of capital investment was adequate to ensure long-run competitive success, whether enough earnings were being retained, and whether the firm was doing everything it could to prepare for the future.

I have spoken to few managers who, at one point or another, have not bemoaned the short-term financial pressures they are under, which often cause them to take actions inimical to the firm's long-term interests. Today, Levi Strauss is enormously profitable as an apparel manufacturer. Although some might attribute this enhanced profitability to the greater managerial incentives that came about because of its leveraged buyout, the Levi managers I have talked to attribute it, without hesitation, to the ability to make long-term decisions without having to worry about short-term stock market reaction. What managers who complain about short-term pressures emanating from the financial markets sometimes fail to realize is that employees, particularly when organized into a strong collectivity, can provide a countervailing force.

Donald Ephlin—a retired United Auto Workers union executive who, during the course of his career, headed first the Ford and then the General Motors department—was instrumental in the Saturn negotiations. He reported that one of the reasons why Ford's transformation during the 1980s was so successful is that many dimensions of its employee involvement efforts, and specifically training levels, were mandated by the contract it had signed with the UAW. The contractual obligation to maintain a certain level of training, as one example, meant that managers could not succumb to short-term temptations to meet budget or profit goals by cutting an expenditure that the organization had determined was going to be critical to its long-term strategic success. He argued that union negotiations and the resulting contracts enhanced the sustainability and the extent of institutionalization of work place changes. Absent the intervention of a third party—in this case, an employee organization—there was nothing to prevent management from succumbing to very real and potent short-term pressures and backsliding on work place change.

Employee organizations are likely, then, to take a long-term view of the enterprise and can counteract short-term financial market pressures.

Moreover, employee organizations may help create, through their very bargaining over specific contract provisions, the conditions that are likely to make work place reform both possible and effective.

In an extensive review of the existing empirical literature on the effects of employee participation, David Levine and Laura Tyson noted that participation customarily produced at least small, short-run improvements in performance and on occasion produced substantial, long-lasting improvements.[27] They identified four characteristics of the firm's employment relations system that are helpful for ensuring that participation positively affects productivity over time and, indeed, occurs in the first place: 1) some form of profit sharing or gain sharing, 2) job security and long-term employment, 3) measures to build group cohesiveness, and 4) guaranteed individual rights.[28] Each condition tends to be more prevalent in union settings because of what unions do. Unions typically negotiate for job security. By their very nature as collective organizations, unions seek to build group cohesiveness. Furthermore, their policies of wage compression help build social solidarity. Union grievance and arbitration procedures help ensure individual rights and due process in the work place. Although unions have typically not negotiated for profit or gain sharing, there has been more interest in such arrangements recently as employees recognize that they must share in the variability of organizational performance. Employee organizations can therefore enhance the conditions that foster participation and other useful changes in the management of the work force and create conditions that make changes in the employment relationship, however introduced, more effective.

UNION AND EMPLOYER BEHAVIOR

But what about the situations in which unions have fought work place change and contributed to inefficiency? At the Fremont plant of General Motors, there were thousands of grievances per year. Unions have frequently resisted moves to team-based organization of work and the reduction in the number of job classifications that is so necessary in order to have flexibility in the deployment of the work force. At Boise Cascade, the unions initially resisted changes in work organization and management practices at the De Ridder, Louisiana, plant that had been so wracked with conflict.

The answer is that, at least to some extent, union behavior is a function of the union's situation and how it has been treated by management. In this sense, the arguments of Chapter 4 about self-fulfilling prophecies also apply in this context—behavior not only is a function of the attitudes, values, and resources of a given social actor but also is importantly affected by how that actor is treated. Behavior is cyclical— action leads to reaction and interaction, an analysis that one can see in theories ranging from social psychology to game theory. In many instances, management seeks to exclude employee organizations from the process of control in the work place and attempts to decertify employee organizations or fight their very presence. In short, with such organizations under attack, there is often an understandable, even if unproductive, tendency for these organizations to hold onto whatever power and turf they control, to resist management at every turn, and to obstruct changes in the management of the employment relation. The question is not whether, under such adverse conditions, unions resist and delay changes in the management of the work force so necessary to achieve competitive advantage through people, but whether one observes this behavior under different conditions of less conflict and threat.

The case of United Parcel Service (UPS) provides compelling evidence on this point. UPS today has revenues in excess of $15 billion and since 1987 has been the largest transportation company and the largest air freight carrier in the world.[29] UPS competes on the basis of service and price—it underprices many of its competitors in the overnight package and letter delivery business and competes with the U.S. Postal Service in the package delivery business. Both factors depend importantly on its more than 160,000 employees. UPS is unionized:

> In 1919 Jim Casey [the founder], realizing that labor unions were unavoidable in the near future, invited the International Brotherhood of Teamsters to represent the UPS drivers and part-time hourly employees. He explained . . . "I think it's possible to be a good UPS member and

union member at the same time." Because of this early relationship, UPS was able to forge a flexible union-management partnership with such . . . features as variable start time . . . minimum work rules, working across job classifications, combinations of inside and outside labor, part-time employment . . . and mandatory overtime as needed.[30]

Although there have been labor disputes over the years, this initial commitment to not only making the union relationship work but, in fact, inviting the union into the company has served UPS well and has helped it achieve competitive success through its productive and motivated work force.

At UPS, positive relations with the work force and the union were established at the outset. At National Steel, a change in the relationship came late but still had positive results. In 1986, National, acquired by the Japanese NKK Corporation, instituted a set of new policies: 1) it promised never to lay off its workers; 2) it agreed to share sensitive financial information with its work force; 3) it instituted productivity gain-sharing bonuses; 4) it permitted the union leaders to write a two-page letter in the company's annual report immediately following the chairman's letter; 5) the company-owned executive club invited hourly workers to become members; and 6) it decentralized authority, so that in the plant, hourly workers act as foremen.[31] In return for these changes, National received more flexible work rules and a healthier labor relations climate, which has produced dramatic results: "Productivity . . . has improved to 2.95 man-hours per ton of steel—among the best in the industry—from 4.44 in 1986. Unexcused absenteeism has dropped by half, to 3.5%. Grievances have fallen 39%—and 80% of workers now attend company-sponsored financial meetings."[32]

Donald Ephlin has an interesting insight to offer. He notes that the union leadership in a plant reflects the management culture. Why? Because union officials must stand for election and are also employees of the firm. The climate and culture of the organization profoundly affect which union officials survive the election process and remain employees over time. Consider a union official who preaches cooperation with management and then confronts a firm that takes cooperation for weakness and exploits the union's position. Obviously, that official will not survive in office very long. Conversely, confrontational tactics will be repudiated by employees who face a management that seeks cooperation and a climate of trust and consistently expresses that desire through its behavior over time. It is not by accident that dissident union officials, seeking a more confrontational approach with management, lost the election at the Saturn plant and for a while lost at NUMMI, although recently, some of that slate were elected. In this way, management produces the union leadership and union tone that it then confronts.

For instance, in the past at General Motors:

> Management . . . jealously guarded against any encroachment upon the stipulations of authority guaranteed by the management-rights clause. This went so far that, in 1973, when the director of the General Motors department of the UAW asked GM local unions to post on their in-plant union bulletin boards a notice QUALITY PRODUCTS ARE OUR CONCERN TOO, a corporate executive called him to complain that quality is solely management's responsibility. He demanded that the bulletins be taken down.[33]

Although it is, in some sense, easy to blame unions for various obstructionist behavior and for excesses that caused productivity problems and job loss, both unions and management had agreed to a system that set up a labor-management environment in purely adversarial terms.[34] Once in place, the cycle of conflict and mutual obstruction was difficult to break.

In his study of work place reform in the shipping industry, which is heavily unionized, Richard Walton wrote about the role of unions in work place reform:

> The most prevalent view expressed by labor leaders is that it is up to management to create the conditions making it possible for labor to cooperate in innovative change. According to AFL-CIO Secretary-Treasurer Thomas R. Donahue:
>
>> For our part, we'd like to see the fullest degree of labor-management cooperation . . . but we'd like to see it based on mutual acceptance of the other side's right to exist . . . based on an acceptance of corporations' needs to be productive and to generate

capital for investment, production, payroll and profit, and based on an acceptance of worker needs to be . . . unintimidated in their rights to form unions or to be participants in forms of industry democracy. . . . But until those things are an accepted part of the labor-management scene, it seems to me silly to speak about labor-management cooperation.[35]

There is evidence that in the presence of cooperative behavior, unions can facilitate or at least be neutral with respect to work place reform. When confronted with a different management that pledged to solve work place problems and treat the employees fairly and with respect, and with a manager who liked to spend time in the plant talking to the workers about their ideas and concerns, the union at Boise Cascade's De Ridder plant no longer caused difficulties. Indeed, Boise has demonstrated that when management makes a commitment to work in a different fashion with a union and with the work force—a commitment that is, of course, going to be tested initially to see if it is sincere—it is possible to enlist the union to at least go along with changes required to achieve competitive advantage through people. That does not mean the union necessarily initiated such changes, but at least it did not obstruct them or cause problems.

At NUMMI, the very place in which there had been such intense conflict that some described it as a "war" between management and labor, under the new management there was a very different response on the part of the work force and the UAW, which still organized the plant. The new contract was some 80 pages long, compared to 250 pages for the old agreement.[36] There were many fewer grievances, and they were handled more easily at lower levels. Interviewed by Paul Adler in his extensive study of NUMMI, one worker noted:

"We're past the historically contentious issues we've fought over before, like wages and benefits. . . . [W]e've stopped beating up on each other and we've gotten down to the practical part of running a production facility. . . . If you go around the rest of GM's plants . . . the fact remains that workers are not involved in designing and managing the production process."[37]

The key that changed things was mutual trust and respect, the very same factors seen at Boise Cascade or at any other place where management-employee relations are going to be successful. George Nano, a union official under both the old and new system at the Fremont plant, put it this way:

> "We've learned that you don't have to have a thousand contract clauses if management makes a real commitment. Just look at the pages and pages in the old Fremont contract on safety and working conditions— things like when the toilets get cleaned and when the floor gets swept. And the plant was still filthy. Cooperation doesn't come from the contract—it has to come from the heart."[38]

This is not to say that changing the relationship with the work force will be easy or that in all cases the employee organization will behave responsibly. Even the most ardent advocates of a role for unions in governing the employment relation admit there are times when unions will behave as irresponsibly and uncooperatively as management sometimes does, even without provocation.[39] Nevertheless, analysis of the behavior of employees, organized or unorganized, inevitably needs to seek understanding of their behavior at least in part in management's own actions and intentions.

It is instructive to compare the case of NUMMI, just described, to that of the General Motors plant in Van Nuys, California. Although the plant, which produced Chevrolet Camaros and Pontiac Firebirds, is now closed, in the 1980s, both GM and the union sought to keep it open, in part by importing from NUMMI some of the same team-based work arrangements. However, the team system was never really successful in Van Nuys. The union opposed it, and union officials who favored cooperating with the company were voted out of office. The plant continued to suffer from high levels of absenteeism and warranty costs. One obvious difference between the two settings is that the NUMMI plant started with a clean slate—a new management team—albeit with the same work force and union leadership. Another difference was that "as a single-plant operation, labor and management could simultaneously bargain all aspects of the employment relationship, whereas in multiplant companies [the rest of GM] the wage and layoff provisions in the national agreement limit the opportunity to bargain over these issues simultaneously with productivity issues at the local level."[40]

The biggest difference was in the approach of the two managements. NUMMI took risks and gambled to win the trust of the union, maintaining its no-layoff commitment, for instance, even in the face of a 30% decline in production. By contrast, GM refused to make long-term commitments to either the workers or the plant, preferring to spend "millions of dollars to lay off workers whenever car inventories accumulate, without gaining the gratitude or loyalty of their workers."[41] A study comparing the two plants concluded:

> The crucial difference between Van Nuys and NUMMI is in the union and management strategies used to build trust.... The strategies adopted by the union and management are interdependent. Since the Corporation has greater long-run power than the union because of its ability to close plants, its strategy will tend to dominate the industrial relations path taken. The company's actions will set the boundary for how much trust can be developed.[42]

In some circumstances, employee organizations have promoted work place change and have even helped institute control in the work place. In some circumstances, employee organizations have served as a useful counterweight to the demands of bankers and shareholders for short-term actions that jeopardize the long-term economic viability of the company. In some circumstances, employee organizations help provide information that makes running the company more efficient and effective. These results are not guaranteed and are, at a minimum, a function of the behavior of management.

The MIT Commission on Industrial Productivity, seeking to understand problems of productivity and competitiveness in America through case studies of numerous industries as well as a systematic review of available empirical evidence of all types, concluded:

> While Germany, Japan, and most other highly industrialized nations competing with the United States have overcome conflicts over the rights of workers to unionize and to participate in enterprise decision-making, U.S. firms and unions continue to expend valuable resources and energies

battling over union organizing and the role of labor in society. This legacy of conflict has produced an adversarial pattern of industrial relations, one characterized by much conflict and little trust between workers and their employers. Research . . . has shown that this traditional pattern of industrial relations produces low levels of productivity and product quality in industries as diverse as autos, office products, and paper.[43]

As in the case of the legal environment, there are important environmental and societal forces that cannot be denied. There is also a potential for management to choose which course it will follow. In making this choice, it helps determine whether employees and their organizations will be obstacles or allies in work place change.

Resistance from Within

8

In 1988, the Southern Company, a large electric utility, implemented an innovative group-based profit-sharing plan in one of its divisions. In addition to splitting productivity improvements equally with employees on a basis proportional to the employees' salary, the plan entailed a "formal, two-level meeting structure designed to facilitate employee participation,"[1] the use of performance teams, and increased measurement of performance on numerous dimensions and sharing that information widely with employees. To evaluate the plan's effects, comparisons were made with a comparable division in which the new system was not implemented. The plan's specifics, however, are of less immediate interest than its results and what subsequently happened.

While the control division reduced costs by 2.67%, the division with the new incentive plan reduced costs by 8.61%, which, net of bonus payments, represented a cost reduction to the company of more than $2 million.[2] Comparing the two divisions on measures of productivity for operations, customer accounting, support services, marketing, and employee safety and health, "the experimental division outperformed the control division on all five percentage-of-goal-obtained measures . . . and in four of the five comparisons to the one-year baseline."[3] Furthermore, 72% of the employees in the division with the new plan expressed satisfaction with it. Yet in spite of its measurable success, the plan was discontinued not long after it was instituted.

Unfortunately, the mere fact of success is often not sufficient either to create changes in the management of the employment relationship or to sustain changes if they are implemented. Resistance to programs of work place change—even successful ones—is often intense. Part of the problem comes, as we have already seen, from outside the organization, from a legal and social environment not always conducive to the actions required to achieve competitive advantage through people. However, much of the resistance also comes from within. Understanding these sources of internal resistance and seeing how they might be at least partially overcome is the subject of this chapter.

An introductory word of caution is in order. Internal resistance to implementing the sorts of work place innovations described in this book is, in fact, part of a larger issue of organizational inertia and resistance to change. Problems in implementing "best practice" are scarcely confined to the subject covered here. For instance, Gary Johns explored what was known about a number of industrial psychology practices—recruiting, training, performance appraisal, and compensation—and the extent to which firms in fact did what industrial/organizational psychological research indicated ought to be done.[4] In the course of finding that much knowledge regarding industrial and organizational psychology was not applied, he noted that "there has been a strong tendency to view and portray innovations as rational, mechanical technologies for increasing the efficiency with which inputs are converted into outputs."[5] His work reminds us that the problem of administrative innovation is a general one, and few innovations, even technical breakthroughs, diffuse as easily or as quickly as one might expect. This chapter does not review the vast literature on innovation and its diffusion nor the almost as vast literature on organizational inertia and change. Rather, what is covered are issues that seem particularly relevant to the implementation of the types of changes in the employment relationship discussed earlier. The reader should be cautioned, however, that the more general treatments on diffusion of innovation and organizational change are also quite relevant to the issue at hand.

LOSS OF JOBS, STATUS, AND MONEY

One of the most pervasive themes in all descriptions of work place change designed to achieve better performance is the removal of layers in the hierarchy. Recall that at AMD's new submicron development center, there were four levels rather than the eight to ten found in a typical fab. At NUMMI, there are four levels in the hierarchy. Volvo's work reforms of the early 1970s removed, even at the initial stages, one layer of management. Lincoln Electric is characterized by wide spans of control and, consequently, fewer hierarchical levels. Ford Motor's experiments with employee involvement in the 1980s, changes that were significantly responsible for its financial success, involved taking several levels out of the organization's hierarchy. In fact, one of the biggest gains in overall productivity comes from eliminating layers of management. If one can achieve comparable performance without having managers watching managers watch others do the work, the gains are substantial. The jobs eliminated tend to be higher paid than the actual operating jobs that remain, and the output per person goes up substantially as there are now fewer people not doing work that actually adds value.

Needless to say, those who face the prospect of losing their jobs are not thrilled. Team-based management, one executive told me, is great for the team members—they have more interesting jobs and occasionally additional financial rewards. It is great for senior managers, who obtain the benefit of enhanced productivity and quality. The losers are the middle layers of supervision, who often face the elimination of their positions. Janice Klein examined attitudes toward employee involvement in nine companies. She reported that 72% of the supervisors believed the program was good for the company, and 60% believed it was good for the employees. However, only 31% believed it was good for the supervisors.[6]

Supervisors are not the only ones to face the elimination of their positions. In organizations that wage war on their work force, détente brings not only a "peace dividend" but also the elimination of the positions whose primary function was battle. At the General Motors plant in Fremont, California, in the late 1970s and early 1980s, between 5,000 and 7,000 grievances were generated during each three-year contract term. One beneficiary of this conflict was a local labor law firm that billed the company between $50,000 and $70,000 per month for its services. This was not the only entity with a stake in perpetuating conflict. Handling all the disputes required a significant employee relations staff in the company and a corresponding staff in the union. If you are in industrial relations and your job involves resolving disputes with employees, what do you do when the number of disputes is drastically reduced? It is unfortunate but true that a situation of conflict with the work force produces jobs that benefit from that conflict. This leaves the organization with individuals who have a significant stake in doing things the old way.

Not only jobs but power and status are at stake when organizations restructure the employment relation. Most companies that move to more participative work systems convey the decentralization in symbols of their culture such as the elimination of reserved parking, executive dining rooms, fancy offices, and other status distinctions. However, many organizations have, in the past, substituted titles and perks for interesting and meaningful work and real responsibility. Although the managers may, under the new system, actually be better off in terms of their job enjoyment, in the short term, all they see is the loss of status, a reward that may have been very important in the past.

It is not just status symbols but also real power that shifts under alternative ways of managing the employment relation. In plants in which workers analyze jobs and recommend changes, engineers and bosses who were used to giving orders become partners and helpers in attempts to simplify the work process. One of my colleagues, David Bradford, has written about the new manager as a coach.[7] It is an attractive and apt image, probably well suited to the new work arrangements. But for the many who have grown up with the image of "boss," "coach" is a foreign image, and they often do not like being more collaborative and sharing power. The loss of hierarchical, formal authority that often accompanies alternative work arrangements means that some lose power, and these individuals don't always like the loss.

In particular, they don't like the loss of power, status, and even hierarchical levels because it is often accompanied by a perceived loss in pay or the ability to obtain pay increases. Traditional compensation systems make the change to more team-oriented, participative, and less hierarchical work arrangements virtually impossible. Traditional pay systems reward people for how many others they supervise, either directly or indirectly. One of my friends has called it the "body count" system. Plans such as the Hay system assign points, and one of the better predictors of the number of points assigned to a job is its level in the hierarchy and the number of people controlled. In many organizations, the only way to get a raise is to acquire some managerial responsibility or move up the organization's hierarchy. This results, naturally enough, in a proliferation of hierarchical levels as a way of compensating valued employees more generously.

Perhaps one of the most bizarre and unfortunate illustrations of this principle occurred right at Stanford University in the business school. Secretaries occupy a key role in the school, as they understand the mechanics of putting together course syllabi, coordinating schedules, and assisting in organizing recruiting, as well as doing technical and other typing, answering phones, making appointments, and so forth. A lot of the knowledge—for example, the phone and computer systems and how things work—is quite institution-specific, so turnover is very disruptive. Yet turnover was high, particularly among the better secretaries, because there was a comparatively narrow salary range, and once someone had reached the top of that range, there was no way to earn more money, apart from the normal range adjustments each year.

Confronted with excessive turnover of precisely those people one didn't want to lose, the obvious answer would be to reorganize the job and increase the rate of pay. Stanford's answer was different. On the one hand mindful of the desire to be able to raise the pay of the better secretaries, and on the other hand bound by rules stipulating that the only way to raise pay was to reclassify the job, the school came up with a new position—"cluster coordinator." Secretaries were in clusters of offices, and the new position would coordinate the activities of the secretaries in each cluster. Since this new position had supervisory responsibility, it could be reclassified and paid at a higher rate.

Unfortunately, this elegant solution bred its own problems. Supervising and doing secretarial work are two different activities, and some of the better secretaries didn't want to supervise. Some who were passed over for promotion left immediately, so in the short run, turnover actually went up. Worst of all, now that supervisors had been created, the supervisors thought they should supervise, so the cluster coordinators held meetings with those in their cluster, with each other, with their boss, and so forth. Whatever efficiency gains accrued from retaining a few superior performers were almost certainly offset by the administrative overhead that was simultaneously created. Although this may be an extreme example, comparable situations are found in numerous organizations, in which positions are created or reclassified so that deserving employees can obtain raises.

On the one hand, the concern of those potentially experiencing new work arrangements that they will never be able to progress economically is valid and important, but one does not want to have more levels in a secretarial hierarchy than NUMMI has in its whole plant (the current situation at Stanford). Consequently, it is essential that pay systems change—and by that I mean the basis for pay must change, or else moves to eliminate layers of hierarchy, work in teams, and decentralize decision making are doomed to failure.

What Organizations Can Do

There are a number of things organizations can do to overcome the problem of loss of status, jobs, and income. The salary issue is potentially the most straightforward to solve, although it is often not tackled. One need not, and probably should not, pay a person by the number of employees supervised—what an incentive this is to pad the payroll! Moreover, one need not, and probably should not, make the number of levels reporting to a person the prime determinant of salary. There are other bases for pay, such as contribution or performance, and skill or knowledge.

For instance, Salomon Brothers has instituted a pay-for-skill plan in its back-office operations in Florida: "'Pay-for-skills values learning instead of control,' said Marc Sternfeld, a managing director. . . . Under the Salomon pay plan . . . pay will reflect an employee's specific job skills and a team's success in achieving performance goals that they have hammered out with their 'customers,' the traders in New York."[8] Other companies have broadened pay ranges so that outstanding performance can be rewarded without the need to create hierarchical levels. Even at Stanford, there is talk of instituting merit pay practices that will make it possible to enrich the jobs and increase the pay of outstanding secretaries without creating levels and changing the position in ways that no one thinks is desirable.

Pay is a sensitive issue, and the pay practices that reinforce hierarchy and stockpiling employees have their own supporters, including the compensation consulting firms that sell them. Nevertheless, it is absolutely clear that making pay less tied to hierarchy is an essential step if organizations are going to be serious about teams, decentralization, and enhancing productivity by having fewer people doing surveillance and more people doing the work.

The job loss issue is trickier but still can be managed. One solution is to bite the bullet and get rid of the redundant people all at once. When IBM spun off Lexmark—its printer, typewriter, and accessory subsidiary—into a freestanding company, the firm went from 5,000 to 3,000 employees mostly by laying off central office and manufacturing staff personnel, and then back to 4,000 people by hiring sales personnel to increase market penetration. If one is going to eliminate positions, it is certainly preferable to do this quickly rather than dragging out the process, prolonging employees' uncertainty and leaving potentially disaffected individuals in the organization.

An alternative is to try to find other positions for those no longer needed in their old jobs. Note, for instance, that Lexmark could have used at least 1,000 of the eliminated people to sell. When Jan Carlzon took over SAS Airlines in the early 1980s, he embarked on a project to change the organization's culture and operations in ways consistent with what has been described in this book. One of the things he did was to decentralize operations substantially and empower front-line employees to take whatever actions were needed to meet customer service goals and fulfill the company's vision of becoming the businessperson's preferred airline. These changes entailed eliminating departments and positions that had previously provided direction to those who would now have more responsibility themselves. In keeping with the Scandinavian culture, however, those whose positions were eliminated were offered other ways to contribute to the new mode of operating. For instance:

> SAS had a 40-person market survey department. . . . The department served a vital function as long as all the decisions were made by a few executives isolated from the customers. But once we passed responsibility out to the front line, we no longer needed so many market surveys. . . . So we gave those employees . . . the opportunity to work out on the front line or to take direct responsibility for certain flight routes.[9]

Even if the people moved to new positions aren't as productive initially as they might be, at least they are in jobs that are adding value more directly to the organization, and they are in positions that don't pose problems for others in front-line positions. In other words, even if the people are simply reassigned at their same salary to tasks that are more directly productive, the organization will be better off than when they were watching others watch others do work. Depending on how fast the organization is growing, its commitment to retraining, and its cultural values, people may be reassigned or let go, but in either case, the organization would be well advised to decide which course it will follow and communicate that directly and clearly to the work force.

Eliminating layers of management and changing the job of middle-level managers does not mean that none are needed or that they can no longer serve an important role. However, it does mean they need training, to develop new expectations about what their new tasks are and how they will be evaluated. Again, there are some lessons from the SAS experience:

The supervisor had not understood that his role had changed under our new organization. In the past he had issued orders and instructions to his staff. Now his job was to serve them by ensuring that they understood their department's objectives and that they had the information and re-sources required to meet those objectives. . . . We had let our middle managers down. We had given the front line the right to accept responsi-bility, yet we hadn't given middle managers viable alternatives to their old role as rule interpreters.[10]

Much of the loss of status can be countered to the extent that the organization has a clear vision and business priorities it is clearly com-municating. At SAS, a weak market position and financial losses left the firm facing an uncertain future. In such circumstances, a goal of provid-ing better customer service, linked to organizational changes that would make it possible to accomplish that goal, was comprehensible even to those who might not like all aspects of the change. The fierce worldwide competition in the automobile industry meant that at NUMMI, for in-stance, both supervisors and line workers understood that things needed to change for the plant to be viable. The clear communication of com-petitive information, including the organization's standing along rele-vant performance dimensions, and tying the changes in how people are managed to ways of improving those measures to ensure the organiza-tion's survival can go a long way toward overcoming resistance to the loss of power or status. It is better to lose some perquisites and power than to lose one's economic future because the firm cannot compete.

COSTS, BENEFITS, AND UNCERTAINTY

It is often the case that organizations institute efforts to change how they manage people when things are going poorly and, in fact, when many other changes have already been made and found to be insufficient. Thus, for instance, although there were early efforts at employee involvement, General Motors got serious about changing how it managed people, including embarking on the Saturn project, only after it had lost substantial market share and only when it was apparent that its massive investment in technology was not paying off as planned. Similarly, Boise Cascade launched its total quality effort after being confronted with massive losses and after investing more than $2 billion in new capital equipment, only to find persistent quality and productivity problems.

A Conference Board study of the problems plaguing many efforts at work place reform noted that "the units with poor records were those in which there were severe management problems and poor profitability prior to the new plan."[11] The fact that initiatives for changing how people are managed are often undertaken in adverse circumstances makes resistance to them and their subsequent failure more likely for several reasons.

As Machiavelli stated hundreds of years ago, "There is nothing more difficult to carry out . . . than to initiate a new order of things. For the reformer has enemies in all those who profit by the old order, and only lukewarm defenders in all those who would profit by the new."[12] Gains and losses are not viewed symmetrically—a loss of a given magnitude will be perceived more negatively than a gain of the same magnitude will be perceived positively. Or a loss of a given amount has more disutility than a gain of the same amount has positive utility.[13] This is why Machiavelli's statement holds true—those who face losses will fight those losses with vigor, but those who might profit from the new arrangements are less likely to fight as vigorously for their benefit. This condition is particularly likely to occur when the organization is facing difficulties already. Losses and potential losses—in jobs, in career and salary prospects, in status—will already be very salient to organizational members. In this context, change or reform will likely excite all the more those who already stand to lose. The very precarious nature of the organization's financial condition means that those who might benefit will not really see the benefit or believe in it with much conviction.

Moreover, the losses are likely to be concentrated while the gains are widely dispersed. In work place reform, supervisors may lose their jobs or at least their positions and power, and so will those who profited from the previous confrontational atmosphere such as company lawyers. However, the benefits will be distributed much more widely, over the newly empowered employees, the stockholders, and perhaps senior management. Except for this latter group, the others are not in a very good position to advocate change because of their lack of power.

Furthermore, the gains and losses are not equal in their certainty. The losses are immediate, visible, and certain. Eliminating the executive dining room and reserved parking, compressing the wage distribution, and decentralizing authority will occur first and will have certain impact. The potential gains in productivity and quality will come, if at all, in the future, and there is no certainty they will be realized. People abhor uncertainty and will obviously be reluctant to trade off uncertain future benefits for immediate losses. In fact, in discussing work reform, one manager admitted that although performance was not really adequate, it *was* known and predictable. This executive, at least, was willing to trade off the potential for a much better future level of performance, which entailed some risk, for the present level, unsatisfactory though it was—and I might add, that reaction is neither atypical nor incomprehensible.

These factors, as well as those discussed in the preceding section, explain why it is inevitably easier to set up effective management practices in so-called greenfield sites. At a new site, there are no entrenched interests who face losses. Moreover, perhaps as important, in a new site, everything is equally uncertain and in the future. The results from a finely specialized set of tasks administered in a centralized fashion are, absent the beginning of operations, no more certain or real than the results from a team-based production system with a great deal of autonomy.

Regardless, not every site can be developed *de novo*. One way of overcoming some of the perceived risk in moving to a new way of managing the work force is to begin on a pilot basis. In fact, that is what has often happened—at the General Foods pet food plant in Topeka, Kansas; NUMMI (which was to be a test site for the rest of General Motors); Saturn; specific factories of AT&T; Levi Strauss; and other firms. Although this prescription makes a lot of intuitive sense and certainly minimizes risk, it also minimizes the level of organizational commitment. In many instances, these successful one-site experiments fail to diffuse to the rest of the company. The results are characterized as being idiosyncratic or are not believed at all. Both the benefit from these experiments and the problem with them is that they are localized, which permits the rest of the organization to resist their diffusion.

The asymmetry of gains and losses means that organizations are often willing to try new ways of managing work only after things are already pretty desperate. But these circumstances create problems. Introducing work place change in a plant whose very existence is threatened means that the change is probably coming at a time of general fear and mistrust and that the situation is quite bad to begin with. Thus, the change will have many obstacles to overcome and may succumb at the first sign of trouble. This is what happened at Eastern Airlines in 1983 under Frank Borman. With the firm facing dire financial difficulties, Borman agreed to a radical change—the employees' unions were to receive four seats on the board of directors, and employees got 25% of the stock in the company in return for wage concessions and the right to participate in running the company. With more employee involvement, expensive supervision and monitoring were stopped, and in fact, at Boston's Logan airport, all managers were taken off the day shift, which was then run by the leads. The new way of operating saved over $100 million annually through productivity improvements, suggestions, and reduced supervision costs.

Unfortunately, when financial troubles returned in 1985—the company was too leveraged and still faced too much low-cost competition—Borman and his colleagues quickly reverted to form, taking an adversarial stance with respect to the unions and the work force. A reform born under economic adversity and a great deal of pressure could not survive additional stress because not enough time had passed and not enough change in beliefs and culture had occurred to maintain it.

Adopting work place change under adverse financial circumstances sends a mixed message to the work force, which is supposed to be at once the beneficiary of the new management practices, as well as the group that must do things better if the organization is to succeed or, perhaps, even survive. On the one hand, there is evidence of the need for change. On the other hand, the economic pressures are often so severe that the employees have legitimate fears for their jobs. The tone with which such reforms are introduced often has an undercurrent of threat—get more productive and produce higher-quality goods or services or you'll be out of a job. Employees may believe that the problems they are expected to fix completely through their own efforts are the result of management mistakes—this was certainly the perception, and quite probably the reality, at Eastern Airlines. They may react poorly to the increased pressure. Thus, ironically, it is the organizations that are doing well that have the slack and the environment of trust and goodwill in which to change how they manage the work force and therefore have the greatest chance of being successful.

There is one other important source of uncertainty that creates resistance to achieving competitive advantage through people. That is the fact that in order to obtain the benefits, many practices and policies must often be changed—what a colleague, John Roberts, has referred to as the issue of complementarity. When I presented the various practices of effective companies in Chapter 2, I noted that the existence of some practices required the existence of others, and that they reinforced or built on each other. One cannot have empowered employees without also having trained employees if one wants the change to be effective. Nordstrom, Lincoln Electric, NUMMI, and other examples are characterized by complex, interdependent systems for managing the work force for competitive advantage. This means that it is difficult to achieve great results by changing only one thing. Yet the necessity of changing so many things—structure, compensation, employment practices, salary levels, training, and so forth—makes the possibility of successfully implementing a fundamental change in the management of the employment relation much more uncertain and risky. This raises the stakes and provokes resistance. I have often heard people say, "We can't change everything, so let's not change anything." Complementarity clearly raises the risks and the uncertainty. However, it also means that if a company is successful, others will find it hard to imitate that success and may not even attempt to do so.

Uncertainty and the different views of costs and benefits are real effects. Changing senior leadership can convince people that the organization is serious about doing things differently, and it can also introduce additional uncertainty into the system that counteracts the fear of new work place management methods. Perhaps in the end there is no substitute for simple courage. Jan Carlzon, who was responsible for the remarkable turnaround at SAS, put it best: "Those who always choose the safest path will never get across the chasm. They will be left standing on the wrong side. . . . [C]orporations must dare to take the leap. . . . Having a clearly stated strategy makes the execution much easier. It is a matter of courage . . . with a large portion of intuition."[14]

FAILURES OF PERCEPTION: MEASUREMENT AND CAREERS

The resistance from within also derives from perceptual blind spots. Although inaccurate registering of the situation has many causes, two of the more important are organizational measurement systems and career practices. What we see, and how we see it, is very much a function of what is measured and how that measurement occurs, as well as our own particular background and education, which have taught us to look at some things a certain way and ignore other things. Given background and measurement, positions that amount to resistance to alternative ways of managing the employment relation are perfectly understandable and even predictable. This suggests that measurement and career processes, which so profoundly affect perceptions, are important targets for change by those seeking to alter the management of the work force.

Measurement

Several years ago, a study of cost-accounting procedures in manufacturing indicated that traditional managerial accounting practices were producing information that was almost worse than no information at all. The information was causing managers to make important decisions about pricing, product mix, and process technology based on distorted, misleading data, producing decisions that were worse than if the managers had used their intuition without the "benefit" of the cost-accounting data.[15] There is almost no question that the situation is the same, if not worse, with respect to managing the employment relation.

Part of the problem is that costs associated with the work force are just that, costs, and there is no way of realizing offsetting benefits in the customary accounting system. For instance, money expended on training is treated as an expense. Since profits are revenues minus expenses, the quickest way to increase profits is to cut expenses, and one of the easiest expenses to cut is training. If a firm buys a piece of equipment, however, the piece of equipment is probably going to be treated as a capital asset, added to the balance sheet, and depreciated over time. If its useful life is five years, then only one-fifth of its cost will be expensed in the first year (holding aside considerations such as accelerated depreciation and other tax gimmicks). Consequently, money spent on depreciable equipment will affect reported profitability less than the same amount spent on training—or for that matter, on other personnel costs such as recruiting and selection, paying higher wages to attract a higher-quality work force, and so forth. There is, then, a systematic bias toward investing in machines or buildings rather than people. Perhaps more significant, there is the sense that money saved on training, recruiting and selection, or wages is money that really does flow directly to the bottom line. Effects on productivity, customer service, or quality will appear later and may never appear in a way that permits them to be paired with the earlier decisions that caused the results.

Bad information will almost certainly produce bad competitive strategy, and this is surely the case with respect to strategy that seeks to obtain competitive advantage through the work force. The problem is compounded by the fact that many organizations place great emphasis in performance evaluations and financial rewards on managers' achieving budgeted financial performance. This performance pressure leads to deferring capital investment, skimping on maintenance, and cutting back research and development expenditures. However, adverse effects on these dimensions of preparing for the future are somewhat mitigated in many organizations. Capital investment and even research and development may be covered by separate budgets, and making the numbers in the short term by deferring maintenance or other investments for the longer term is a well-known response that can be and often is discovered. Because of both ideology and language that see labor as a "cost" rather than an investment, and because of the rarity with which firms think systematically about achieving competitive advantage through people, uncovering the same degree of short termism with respect to managing the employment relation is less likely.

Many of the important gains from changing the management of the work force are gains in responsiveness and flexibility, quality, and customer satisfaction as well as in productivity. "Yet all but a few companies—most of them owner-managed—still base capital decisions on classical return-on-investment calculations that seek to recover funds only from savings, not from gains in business."[16] Unfortunately,

> [r]eplacing people with machines and chipping away at waste and inefficiency no longer go very far. . . . [S]uch cost-saving measures contribute no more than 20% of a manufacturer's competitive advantage. Twice as important are long-term changes in the structure of a company, such as . . . better worker management.[17]

Because of the potential for measurement to mislead managers with respect to making decisions on the employment relationship, I once expected to find that differences in the measurement system in different firms would distinguish those that were effective in achieving competitive advantage through people from those that were not. Thus far, however, I have had no confirmation of this idea, mostly because I know of no organization that has a measurement or accounting system that produces data useful for making work force decisions effectively. Rather, what distinguishes some firms from others is whether the firm has managers with enough wisdom, insight, and courage to ignore the occasionally misleading messages produced by short-term budget and expense reports and to persevere in building a more effective work system anyway.

There is another measurement problem that leads companies to do the wrong thing with respect to managing the work force, and that is a consequence of the perils of spreadsheet analysis. As an example, suppose I put the reader in Frank Lorenzo's place after he purchased Eastern Airlines. Lorenzo and Eastern's president, Philip Bakes, believed they could cut 30% out of Eastern's $1.7 billion labor bill, with some $265 million coming from the machinists.[18] If, in fact, one could cut $265 million in annual costs, the value to the company would be immense. Given a corporate tax rate of about 34%, Eastern's after-tax profits would increase $175 million. At even eight times earnings—a conservative, but realistic valuation for the cyclical airline industry— cutting the machinists' wages the targeted amount could increase the capitalized value of the company by some $1.4 billion. Could an increase in value of that magnitude have been ignored? Faced with that analysis, it is little wonder that Lorenzo, or almost anyone else, would be tempted to take on the machinists and the rest of the work force.

The problem, of course, is that the estimates of what can be cut, and the nice spreadsheet simulations of the economic consequences, don't take into account the process by which these cuts will occur and the consequences of that process. In the case of Eastern, a war with the work force in a service industry produced customer defections and employee morale and productivity problems that precluded the realization of any financial advantages. Doing what-if scenarios on financial models of the firm creates a sense of reality. However, such models, and their assumptions, are not reality, and achieving results requires confronting the realities of the labor force and the marketplace.

Careers

The less actual experience one has in the nuts and bolts of a business, the easier it is to be misled by numbers or hypothetical financial scenarios. One of the things that actual operating experience in any environment provides is the ability to tell which measures and numbers are useful and which are not; to know which assumptions are feasible and which are just wishful thinking; and to understand the process by which the particular product or service is actually produced. Thus, career systems that emphasize promotion from within not only provide advantages in terms of managing the employment relation but also make it more likely that strategies for achieving competitive advantage through people will be understood and pursued. It is no accident that a number of the organizations that have been most successful in achieving competitive advantage through people—such as Lincoln Electric, Nordstrom, Wal-Mart, and NUMMI—have promotion-from-within policies and managers who are experienced in the industry operations.

Promotion from within lessens the social distance between leaders and those being led. It diminishes the likelihood that those setting the organization's direction will behave contemptuously toward the work force or that those in charge will regard the contributions of the work force as unimportant. One of the reasons why Japanese companies have, for the most part, been successful in achieving competitive advantage through the management of the work force is because these organizations not only promote from within but have a truly remarkable link between the work floor and the management hierarchy. William Gould, in a book on Japanese labor law and industrial relations, noted:

> The overlap or slight blurring of hierarchy and of blue collar and white collar is reflected even among company directors. One out of six Japanese company directors was once a union leader. Clark writes: "Of 313 major Japanese companies . . . 74.1 percent had at least one executive director who once served as a labor union leader." [19] . . . Not only have managerial personnel held positions of leadership in company unions; in some instances they have climbed the ladder to a position from the national federation itself. For instance, the international affairs secretary for the Japan Auto Workers . . . whom I first met in 1975, was in charge of sales for Nissan when I returned to Japan in 1978. [20]

The mobility between management and labor means that "almost anyone who has worked for a Japanese company has been a member of a union at some point." [21] This means not only that there will be less adversarial relations but also that senior management, having worked on the floor, will have more respect for the ideas of first-line workers and more appreciation for the potential of such workers to contribute to the organization's strategic success.

There are obviously exceptions to this rule—Herb Kelleher of Southwest Airlines is a lawyer and did not work his way up in the airline business by flying planes, doing airline marketing, or serving as a flight attendant; nevertheless, he has a real appreciation for the importance of the people in the organization and has developed a culture that has produced outstanding financial and customer service success. Such a pattern is more likely to be the exception than the rule, however. Companies that seek competitive advantage through their work force are well advised to put in place people who have some understanding of that work force and the jobs they do. Otherwise, resistance to achieving competitive advantage through people may be generated because those in a position to advocate or implement such a policy will have no contact with or knowledge of, and therefore may have developed contempt for, the lower-level employees who are so critical to such efforts.

Internal inertia interacts with history and with the external environment to make changing the organization of work difficult. In the absence of strong external pressures and encouragement, in the presence of a history of adversarial relations and control, there is often even more internal opposition. The study of change of any kind offers one clear insight into overcoming internal resistance. I have seen few introductions of any change—a new product, a new technology, or a new way of managing the work force—that do not have a "product" or "project" champion behind them. There must inevitably be someone who sees what needs to be done and has the skill and power to get it accomplished. It is for this reason that I often observe organizations that seek to change how they manage the work force begin by locating someone, outside or inside the company, with the values, skills, and perspective to implement this change and then putting this individual or others in key positions to make the change. A champion is not necessarily going to be enough, and we have all seen people ground down by an organization and its resistance and inertia. Yet getting the right people to advocate the change would seem to be virtually a prerequisite if the substantial inertial forces that almost inevitably exist in organizations are to be overcome.

PROSPECTS FOR CHANGE

III

The Promise of the Quality Movement   9

We have seen that people are an increasingly important source of competitive advantage. This is a source of success that is difficult to duplicate and consequently is sustainable over time. We have seen that there are practices for managing the employment relation that tend to characterize effective firms, and in spite of the evidence for their effectiveness, diffusion remains slow and inconsistent. It is evident that there are numerous barriers—ranging from the wrong heroes, theories, and language to history, a legal system, and sources of internal resistance—that make it hard to become more effective in managing the employment relation. A reasonable reading of the evidence would appear to suggest that the fundamental problems in achieving competitive success through people are more social and political than they are technical—we often know what to do but, for a variety of reasons, have difficulty doing it. Issues of implementation loom large, particularly in comparison to problems in figuring out what to implement.

To the extent that the problems of managing the work force are social and political, it seems sensible to evaluate various efforts at work place reform in terms of their ability to solve these implementation problems while promulgating practices consistent with what is required to achieve success through the work force. By that criterion, it appears that the quality movement offers a great deal of promise and, indeed, accomplishment. In evaluating quality programs or, for that matter, any other effort at work place change such as the application of sociotechnical systems approaches[1] or employee involvement programs one should be careful to compare those programs not to some ideal but to the situation that would exist in their absence. In other words, just because a program does not solve every problem or move the organization all the way, particularly initially, to where it wants and needs to be does not mean that it is a failure. A program fails when it produces either no sustained change or else change that is dysfunctional and ineffective. Some remediation of problems in managing the employment relation is certainly better than nothing at all.

Many observers and critics of the quality movement miss its essential point. It is not about a set of specific processes—such as statistical process control, benchmarking, Pareto diagrams, and so forth—although these techniques for implementing quality are clearly significant. Nor is it about managerial practices that are completely novel or unique to the practice of total quality. In fact, many observers rightly note that what is prescribed in most quality programs are simply fundamentally sound ways of managing, including managing the employment relation, that have been around for a long time. Cecil Parker, the former head of human resources for Compaq Computer and a consultant to SEMATECH in its quality efforts, once observed that "total quality" is nothing more than a label for practices that organizations ought to be following anyway and that many already did. What "quality," "total quality management," and any other terms one uses to describe some aspect of the quality movement have done is to provide political and social impetus in the context of a systematic program of policies and practices. These two features—systematic practices and social and political impetus— are precisely what are often required to solve implementation issues.

Robert Eccles and Nitin Nohria have aptly noted that "many progressive management concepts have been around in some fashion or another for quite some time,"[2] and that "when it comes to the basics of management, there is little new under the sun."[3] What is important about management concepts such as total quality is not so much their novelty or even their conceptual completeness but the framework they set forth and the language they use, and whether they generate useful action.[4] "Action is always the final test."[5] The quality movement is fundamentally a way of using language and ideas to mobilize actions that are often talked about but not as frequently implemented. In this regard, "the primary task of managerial language has always been to persuade individuals to put forth their best efforts in a collective enterprise with other men and women."[6] The argument developed in this chapter is that the quality movement is one way, albeit not the only way, of overcoming some of the barriers to implementing more effective management of the employment relation. It provides people with a model, social support, and powerful language—and the evidence is that it works.

This is not to say all is perfect. In a country in which fad diets come and go, we seek instant results. Because of issues of interdependence among changes in work practices, and because of long-standing values and theories that often point us in the wrong direction, results are not always immediate. Faced with the absence of quick results in a context that basically still holds to old ways of thinking, quality programs are as likely to be abandoned as any other work place reform effort. Quality programs and the quality movement have not effortlessly and permanently solved implementation problems. However, as this chapter suggests, the quality movement has probably done more than almost anything else to stimulate serious efforts at work place change in ways consistent with achieving competitive success through people. How and why it has done so are what we next examine.

RIGHT THEORY

The quality movement and the Malcolm Baldrige National Quality Award, given each year by the U.S. Department of Commerce, emphasize the importance of human resources, promulgate appropriate behaviors with respect to managing the work force, and explicitly critique approaches to management that tend to be inconsistent with achieving competitive success through people. In this sense, they set the right conceptual tone for managing the employment relation.

Numerous connections can be made between quality and how organizations manage the employment relation. The Baldrige Award itself makes the connection explicit. In summarizing the findings and purposes of Public Law 100-107, the act that established the award, the National Institute of Standards and Technology noted:

> [I]mproved management understanding of the factory floor, worker involvement in quality, and greater emphasis on statistical process control can lead to dramatic improvements in the cost and quality of manufactured products. . . .
>
> [Q]uality improvement programs must be management-led . . . and this may require fundamental changes in the way companies . . . do business.[7]

Of a total of 1,000 points in the 1991 Baldrige Award competition, 150 points were assigned to the general category of Human Resource Utilization, with another 100 points for Leadership, which includes quality values, senior executive leadership, and management for quality.[8] The only two areas that had more points than Human Resource Utilization were Customer Satisfaction (300 points) and Quality Results (180 points). It is quite likely that the net effect of an emphasis on customer satisfaction requires attention to the well-being of the work force, since it is difficult if not impossible for unhappy, unmotivated, uncommitted, and uninvolved employees to produce satisfied customers.

The emphasis on effective human resource utilization comes from its connection with achieving outstanding quality results:

> Meeting the company's quality objectives requires a fully committed, well-trained work force that is encouraged to participate in the company's continuous improvement activities. Reward and recognition systems need to reinforce participation and emphasize achievement of quality objectives. Factors bearing upon the safety, health, well-being and morale of employees need to be part of the continuous improvement

objectives and activities of the company. Employees need to receive training in basic quality skills related to performing their work and to understanding and solving quality-related problems.[9]

The Baldrige Award not only emphasizes the importance of the work force in the quality process, but it promotes practices that are consistent with achieving competitive advantage through people—such as an emphasis on training and skill upgrading, employee participation and involvement, and rewards contingent on achieving important performance objectives. Within the Human Resource Utilization section, the two most significant areas are employee education and training and employee involvement. In the section on employee involvement, emphasis is placed on:

a. management practices . . . such as teams or suggestion systems . . . the company uses to promote employee contributions . . . individually and in groups.
b. company actions to increase employee authority to act (empowerment), responsibility, and innovation. . . .
c. key indicators . . . to evaluate the extent and effectiveness of involvement by all categories and types of employees. . . .
d. trends and current levels of involvement by all categories of employees.[10]

The implicit and explicit theories of human behavior that undergird the quality movement do not emphasize the Newtonian conception of human behavior and the need to apply optimal monitoring, rewards, and sanctions in order to get people to act appropriately. Rather, they emphasize intrinsic motivation as contrasted with external control. For instance, W. Edwards Deming is one of the most respected and best-known writers and consultants on quality. Indeed, in Japan, a quality prize is named after him. Deming emphasized the process of management and the relationship between management and the work force, and took a very different view of human behavior than one would see in typical agency theory or transaction cost treatments:

Deming fervently believes in the "intrinsic motivation" of mankind, and that it is management's policies that often serve to demotivate employees. Instead of helping workers develop their potential, he asserts, management often prevents them from making a meaningful contribution to the improvement of their jobs, robs them of the self-esteem they need to foster motivation, and blames them for systemic problems beyond their control.[11]

Several of Deming's 14 points concerning how to build quality recognize the importance of the work force and recommend actions quite consistent with what successful companies that seek advantage through their work force have done:

6. Institute modern methods of training on the job. . . .
7. Institute modern methods of supervising. . . . Barriers that prevent hourly workers from doing their jobs with pride must be removed.
8. Drive out fear. . . . [P]eople must not be afraid to ask questions, to report problems, or to express ideas. . . .
10. Eliminate numerical goals for the work force. . . .
12. Remove barriers that hinder the hourly workers . . . including not knowing what good work is, supervisors motivated by quotas . . . and no response to reports of out-of-order machines.
13. Institute a vigorous program of education and training. . . . [P]eople must be continually trained and retrained.[12]

Philip Crosby, at one time vice president of quality at International Telephone and Telegraph (ITT), also recognized the importance of the work force in quality efforts and recommended approaches consistent with the practices reviewed in Chapter 2. For instance, his 14 points include the use of teams, recognition, supervisory training, and pushing things up the hierarchy only if and when necessary.[13]

The quality movement recognizes the importance of the work force, promulgates a more constructive view of human behavior and motivation, and explicitly critiques a financial/economic orientation that hinders the achievement of competitive advantage through people because of its assumptions and practices. The writings on quality address directly some of the measurement illusions described in Chapter 8 that get in the way of implementing work place changes and form a source of internal resistance. It is very difficult to introduce and maintain effective human resource management practices in an environment in which cuts in training, staffing levels, recruiting effort, and wages all appear to provide immediate positive financial returns.

Deming has been particularly critical of financial measures and in some instances has succeeded in getting these measures replaced:

> In Deming's view, the traditional financial mentality is the greatest impediment to quality management in the United States, because it deflects attention from the long-term interests of a company's operations and because traditional financial and accounting measures offer managers few of the insights they need to plan for the future. . . . The Deming-style manager learns to probe behind the numbers, knowing that numbers don't give you answers, only the questions that need to be asked, and understanding that in the short term figures can be dressed up to suit almost any occasion.[14]

Deming is merciless with managers who use financial system measures exclusively, and there is evidence that his influence has affected a number of companies.

One firm that Deming helped transform was the Ford Motor Company. In 1988, Ford Motor sold nearly as many vehicles as it did in 1978 but used about half as many production workers to manufacture them.[15] "By far the most important and impressive factor in Ford's increased productivity involves increased cooperation by its work force."[16] As the 1980s began, however, this result was far from assured. Ford was dominated by finance,[17] a legacy of Robert McNamara, Arjay Miller, Tex Thornton, and the other so-called whiz kids who came to Ford from the Pentagon following World War II. Financial calculations, regardless of their commonsense implications for the company's reputation and long-term sales success, dominated decision making.

Thus, for example, rust was a problem that plagued U.S. automobile manufacturers. At Ford,

> [t]he company knew of the rust problem and knew how to fix the problem. In 1958 Ford had developed a rust-resistant paint process. . . . But the manufacturing men in Ford's domestic operations couldn't convince the finance department that the process, which cost $4 million per plant, was worth standardizing at all the company's plants. . . . Ford's bean counters hadn't figured out a way to calculate the cost of a happy cus-

tomer. . . . [R]ust problems often occurred outside the period covered by the company's warranties, so the company figured it wouldn't have to pay for the problem! As of 1973, only a fraction of Ford car plants were equipped with the . . . system.[18]

Fifteen years after a process for addressing the rust problem was developed, Ford had not adopted it because the company could not demonstrate a return on the investment.

In a case that was to generate enormous amounts of bad publicity for Ford, the Pinto car model was found to explode with some regularity when involved in rear-end collisions because of the design and placement of the gasoline tank. Evidence introduced at a liability trial documented that Ford had performed a cost-benefit analysis comparing probable liability awards from death and injury verdicts versus the cost of correcting the problem.[19]

Ford's quality efforts during the 1980s changed the company's culture dramatically. Quality became "job 1," and considerations of customer satisfaction rose in prominence. At the same time, Ford transformed its employee relations culture, ridding itself of the traditional adversarial relations with its unions and embarking on major and sustained employee involvement and team efforts. This emphasis on the work force, in the context of the quality efforts, bore striking results:

> In the mid-1980s, while GM spent $3 billion equipping its metal stamping plants with highly automated machinery designed to replace workers, Ford concentrated on increasing the productivity of its . . . work force. "GM was determined to minimize the role of the hourly people," says Peter Pestillo, the Ford executive vice president who heads labor relations. "Our goal was to maximize the contribution of the hourly people." The outcome: GM's highly automated stamping plants now produce half as many stamped parts per worker as Ford's.[20]

The quality movement offers both a philosophy and activities as part of a program. The philosophy is consistent with an emphasis on achieving success through the work force and with the specific policies and practices that we have seen are necessary or at least useful. Moreover, the quality movement, in both its philosophy and practices, directs attention away from models of behavior and monitoring practices that are inappropriate if the employment relation is really to serve as a source of advantage.

RIGHT HEROES

The quality movement offers business heroes that are more consistent with progressive ways of organizing work. As such, it provides models that are consistent with achieving success through people and that embody many if not most aspects of the application of high-commitment work practices. A few selected examples make the point.

Milliken & Company is a privately owned major textile manufacturer with 14,000 employees that won the Baldrige Award in 1989. The company emphasizes achieving excellence through its people using effective practices in managing the employment relation. The profile of the company accompanying the award notes:

> Milliken has achieved a flat management structure in which associates working primarily in self-managed teams exercise considerable authority and autonomy. Production work teams . . . can undertake training, schedule work, and establish individual performance objectives. . . . [A]ny of Milliken's associates can halt a production process if that person detects a quality or safety problem.[21]

This way of organizing work has permitted the company to reduce the number of management positions by 700 between 1981 and 1989.

In a booklet describing the company used in recruiting, Milliken again emphasizes the importance of its people and its philosophy toward its work force:

> [I]n the process of arriving at new levels of quality, nothing supersedes the inner working of the human being. . . . There is an emphasis on finding the best people for every career and on continuing education. . . . At Milliken, people are called Associates—not employees—implying the importance of each one as a contributor to our common objective. . . . All of this assumes a participatory management approach. This is an approach which starts at the very top of the organization and works its way down. This participative management approach allows all Associates . . . to make immediate contributions.[22]

The Wallace Company—an industrial distributor of pipes, valves, fittings, and other products for the chemical and petrochemical industries—won the Baldrige Award in 1990. Effective human resource management was an important part of its quality strategy. Employees in this firm, too, were referred to as "associates," and the company emphasized decentralization and employee empowerment:

> "Empowerment" is a key theme in the Wallace approach to business. All associates are allowed to make customer-related decisions of up to $1,000 without seeking higher approval. Customer-related decisions on values greater than that can be made without approval in time sensitive situations. . . . Associates working in the warehouse can reject shipments if the material is either defective or the shipment is incorrect. . . . Wallace spent more than $2 million on formal training and education from 1987 to 1990.[23]

This $2 million expenditure on training is a large amount considering the company had a total of only 280 employees at the time.

Motorola is famous for spending more than $100 million per year on training and maintaining its commitment to upgrading the skills of its work force at all levels through good times and bad. Solectron, a contract manufacturer in electronics, operates in a very low-margin, competitive environment. Nevertheless, its employees receive 90 hours or more of training each year. In short, the Baldrige Award winners are organizations that train, practice decentralization and employee involvement, and pioneer less adversarial relations with a work force that is often organized on the basis of teams. They offer different models than the Taylorist approach traditionally followed and, as such, provide better heroes for the business community to emulate.

RIGHT LANGUAGE

Language frames how we look at things, what concepts we employ to describe and analyze them, and how we react emotionally. One of the problems with much of traditional management and, for that matter, modern economics is that it is filled with Taylorist language—words and terms that denigrate the capacities and motives of employees and presuppose a conflictual relationship. In this regard, the quality movement offers much-improved language. It is a powerful call to action and change and incorporates a terminology more consistent with building competitive advantage through the employment relationship.

In terms of language that provides a call and a strong motivation to action, the Baldrige Award is again a good exemplar. On the cover of the 1991 application guidelines is a quote from President George Bush: "The improvement of quality in products and the improvement of quality in service—these are national priorities as never before."[24] Inside the pamphlet, the findings and purposes of the public law establishing the award present a stirring call to action on the part of U.S. businesses:

1. The leadership of the United States in product and process quality has been challenged strongly . . . by foreign competition, and our Nation's productivity growth has improved less than our competitors' over the last two decades.
2. American business and industry are beginning to understand that poor quality costs companies as much as 20 percent of sales revenues. . . .
3. Strategic planning for quality [is] becoming more and more essential to the well-being of our Nation's economy.[25]

Inside the front cover of the pamphlet, Robert Mossbacher, secretary of commerce, stated, "Quality is the key to increasing our exports around the world and to a strong economy that assures job growth."[26]

The very word "quality" itself has nice properties. Who can be against quality? Who wants their company to become a low-quality organization? Furthermore, the quality movement has legitimized management practices that have been around for a long time but have not generated a lot of support, perhaps because of the language. "Worker empowerment," "employee participation" or "participative management," "employee voice," "equity and fairness," "due process," "high-commitment work practices," and similar terms often used in describing the employment relation somehow seem to smack of coddling the work force, socialism, or communism and fail to tap into most managers' ideology and values. The language of quality and the political support behind the quality movement overcome some of these problems, at least to some degree.

What is the "language" of quality? "Customer" is one term often seen in quality programs. Peter Drucker noted that "the purpose of a business is to create a customer and to satisfy a customer."[27] The first of Deming's 14 points is that "quality is defined by the customer."[28] The orientation of providing service to customers, both internal (such as other departments that use one's product or service) and external, shifts measurement and attention in important ways. "In a finance-minded company, the shareholders replace the customer as the principal focus of management."[29] Refocusing on customers helps break the often short-term and narrow financial focus of many organizations.

Another important word is "process." This term orients management away from results to the steps, the process, that produce those results. It is a term that focuses on helping employees improve the process, through training, redesign, or other changes. "Every job in an organization is part of a process. And only by understanding the role each job plays in the company's customer-driven strategy can the process be improved."[30]

Another quality word is "teamwork," which is often a part of quality improvement programs. Obviously, teamwork orients managers to think about implementing self-managing work teams, group and other aggregate measurements and incentives, and away from a focus on individual performance in isolation. The problem with an individualistic focus is that for most jobs in interdependent systems, performance is very much a function not only of the individual's own ability and motivation but also of the behavior of coworkers and the system in which he or she works. Deming noted: "Industry desperately needs to foster teamwork. The only training or education on teamwork our people receive in school is on the athletic field. Teamwork in the classroom is called cheating."[31]

Quality programs and the quality movement emphasize constancy of purpose or persistence, a valuable trait in a setting in which results may not occur rapidly and patience is often in short supply. "Constancy of purpose . . . entails an unequivocal long-term commitment to invest in, and adapt to, the challenging requirements of the marketplace. It is the antithesis of managing for short-term financial gain."[32]

There are many other words and phrases associated with the quality movement such as "continuous improvement," "reducing variation," and so forth. Perhaps one of the most important, useful for reorienting how we think about managing the employment relation, is the idea of "building in" as contrasted with "inspecting out" quality. Traditional management—and even current programs to rein in health-care expenses—are heavily focused on control and inspection. It is a posture that presumes and produces distrust of employees, emphasizing rewards and sanctions, and is control- rather than commitment-oriented. Many companies fail to recognize that inspection and control are expensive—it is not only in health care where resources are wasted in having people watch others do the work. "Deming . . . points out that inspection is an expense that can be reduced, and in some cases even eliminated, if a process is kept under control with a minimal level of variation."[33] This change in orientation was an important part of Ford Motor's successful turnaround in the 1980s:

> "Ford had always been heavily involved with statistical methods, but we used it to measure output. There was too much measuring results, rather than process conditions," said Mel Rowe, a veteran Ford man who was a quality control expert at the company for twenty-three years. . . . "Deming said that's not where you should use statistics, you should use it upstream. Deming influenced the whole corporation in this."[34]

By changing the language of management, the quality movement tends to direct attention toward process, constancy, customers, teamwork, and problem prevention. This change moves us away from the scapegoating, finger pointing, and control orientation that is otherwise too typical and tends to destroy employee motivation and initiative.

RIGHT ENVIRONMENT

Changing the management of the employment relationship has been hindered by a lack of institutional and social support. The quality movement has, to some extent, overcome these problems. One problem has been the message sent by the government. Except for a brief period during the New Deal, the government—including the court system, police, and prosecutors—has generally been hostile to employee organizations and, except for wrongful discharge cases, has not been supportive of worker rights. With the Baldrige Award, the federal government articulated support for the quality movement and, implicitly, for more employee involvement and training. There is now discussion of a national training policy and even tax incentives to encourage training. Contrasted with many other countries, the U.S. government has tended to take a very hands-off attitude toward work place change and reform. The Baldrige Award marks the first, small, tentative step toward involvement in encouraging the adoption of more effective practices for managing the employment relation.

Perhaps the biggest effect of the Baldrige Award has been to encourage firms to learn and borrow from others in a more systematic and coordinated fashion. The award and the general discussion about quality management create publicity and information for stimulating and directing change efforts. One of the requirements for those winning is that they provide seminars and information to all who ask about their own quality improvement efforts (although they can and do charge for this activity to cover their costs). This encourages learning from others and begins to build a network of companies doing interesting and innovative things in managing their work forces. This process seems to be having some effect:

> Xerox talks to over 100,000 people a year, many of them customers and suppliers. All come seeking information and advice. . . . The award has created a common vocabulary and philosophy bridging companies and industries. Managers now view learning across the boundary lines of business as both possible and desirable. The abhorrence for anything "not invented here," once a source of corporate uniqueness and pride, is being replaced by an unabashed zeal for borrowing ideas and practices from others.[35]

This sharing of information and the legitimization of building networks of collaborative learning and action help overcome one of the biggest barriers to the diffusion of work place innovations, the absence of an organized institutional support system. In an insightful book about one form of work force management innovation, Robert Cole posed the following question: "[I]n the main period under investigation, 1960–1985, American firms moved much more slowly and less effectively in adopting small group activities than Swedish and, especially, Japanese ones. Why was this the case?"[36]

The answer is complex and multifaceted, but certainly one piece of the puzzle concerns the infrastructure created—or not created—in the three countries to diffuse this particular work place innovation. In the United States, "President Nixon established the National Commission on Productivity by Executive Order on 17 June 1970."[37] Nixon based the commission on the Swedish tripartite model of involvement on the part of people from industry, labor, and government to work collectively to solve problems of inflation and productivity. However, "the commission was given token funding, never exceeding $3 million a year, and did not receive a legislative mandate until . . . 1975."[38] In that year, Public Law 94-136 established a National Center for Productivity and Quality of Working Life. The center was to encourage demonstration projects and participative work arrangements, and the use of groups and teams was an important element. However: "The commission's goals were not to be achieved. Congressional funding was erratic, and in 1978 President Carter disbanded the commission on grounds that 'it hadn't been sufficiently productive.'"[39]

Labor and business in the United States both tended to oppose governmental intervention with respect to the structuring of the employment relation. In Sweden, the government played a much more active role, both in providing funding for research and demonstration projects and through legislation encouraging, and at times mandating, the development of more cooperative working relationships. In Japan, the infrastructure was built not so much by government—although government provided tacit encouragement and a climate of moral support—but by the collective action of business firms that developed strong federations to share knowledge of more effective ways of managing work and the employment relation. Cole noted:

The Japanese and Swedish corporations . . . were more oriented to collective solutions to the start up, operations, and research and development costs associated with small-group activities. They seem to have had a greater appreciation of the economizing benefits associated with collaborative activities than did their American colleagues.[40]

Richard Walton's study of innovative change in the shipping industry documented the tremendous achievements of Japan, which started in a very uncompetitive position and emerged with one of the strongest industries. He argued that "institutional arrangements were uniquely favorable for Japan and played a major role in explaining Japan's innovative performance."[41] As one example:

The mechanism devised . . . to chart the future seafarer system, the modernization committee, was itself an impressive innovation. . . . [I]t included labor, shipowners, government, and a representative of the public. It enabled members . . . to learn from other countries, negotiate the issues, and discuss proposals with their constituencies.[42]

It is clear that the Baldrige Award and the quality movement provide some help in forging a stronger institutional structure to encourage learning from others. It is also clear that the quality movement does not really completely solve the problem of developing collaborative relationships among the various constituencies that are often necessary to solve both quality issues and work place reform problems. Nevertheless, by encouraging and indeed requiring some degree of sharing information and learning from others, and by providing governmental support and hence social legitimacy to this process and to the values of the quality movement, the total quality process and the Baldrige Award in particular have helped change the environment in a direction that makes the adoption of work place change more likely.

WILL THE PROMISE BE FULFILLED?

The quality movement has several things going for it. With the Baldrige Award, it taps into the competitive spirit of businesses and their managers. This is, after all, a competition with judges, rules, and prizes. It provides a philosophy, standards, and processes—a clear road map for change. By emphasizing measurement and indicators, the quality movement helps quantify what otherwise might appear to be amorphous and incomprehensible. The quality movement alters the language of management in some useful ways and offers a different theoretical conception of work and organizations that helps move businesses away from Taylorist paradigms. It encourages the development of social networks that facilitate learning and change. As one member of the board of overseers of the Baldrige Award wrote:

> In just four years, the . . . Baldrige . . . Award has become *the* most important catalyst for transforming American business. More than any other initiative, public or private, it has reshaped managers' thinking and behavior. The Baldrige Award . . . provides companies with a comprehensive framework for assessing their progress toward the new paradigm of management.[43]

Yet the quality movement faces some obstacles. In its emphasis on customers and employees it provides a challenge to the traditional preeminence of shareholders, a position reinforced by law, economic theory, and custom. Some, for instance, have noted that the Baldrige Award does not consider profitability or indicators thereof and have criticized the award for that reason. The quality movement, like all attempts to change organizations, requires time, and its proponents take a long-term, strategic view. This approach may be useful, but it certainly flies in the face of short-term pressures to make budgets, meet profit objectives, and advance one's career. Although the quality movement is consistent with the idea of changing the employment relation in ways designed to achieve competitive success through people and has a lot of political and social support behind it, these changes face entrenched ideology, values, and history. A survey by Ernst & Young suggests that "the 'total quality' movement . . . is floundering. . . . Despite plenty of talk and much action, many American companies are stumbling in their implementation of quality improvement efforts."[44]

Thus, this chapter is entitled "The *Promise* of the Quality Movement." The quality movement, although clearly helpful, remains a promise that is as yet only partly fulfilled and one that faces substantial obstacles.

Making the Change   10

The constraints of the environment, the legacy of history, old ways of thinking, and internal resistance are all real and potent factors. Some firms overcome these forces and find a more effective way of operating, and others do not. For those organizations that would prefer to be like Southwest Airlines rather than Eastern Airlines, like Ford rather than General Motors, or like Nordstrom rather than Macy's, research and experience provide some lessons. However, recall that if making changes to achieve competitive advantage through people were easy, everyone would do it and the advantage would be neither as large nor as sustainable as it presently seems to be. There are no magic formulas or quick answers. However, there are some ways of thinking about the challenge that are helpful, some experiences that are instructive, and some pitfalls to avoid. That is what this concluding chapter is about.

IT'S MANAGEMENT

At one company-sponsored management training program, toward the end of my time with the executives covering material on managing the work force, I was treated to a litany of reasons why nothing along these lines could be done at this organization. No one questioned the evidence of effectiveness or the logic of what was discussed. Rather, the executives emphasized the constraints imposed by unions, the investment community, government regulations and laws, and other factors beyond their control. In as nice a fashion as I could, I noted that managers are well paid to solve problems, not to complain about them. I can hire people for $10 an hour (or less) to stand around and complain about foreign competition, government intervention, a poor work ethic, difficult unions, and similar issues. It is the responsibility of management not only to recognize the very real constraints and problems that emanate from the environment but also to do something constructive. The first step in making the change, then, is owning up to the source of many of the problems with productivity and work force management, and to where the responsibility lies for fixing these problems—management.

The tendency is to blame others. If medical costs are too high, it's because doctors are greedy, improperly monitored, or both. If manufacturing productivity is low, it's because workers are lazy and have lost the old work ethic. If service is poor, it's because one can't find good help these days. At General Motors, for example, "In 1981, even as Pontiac was beginning to work with Deming and to seek a new cooperative approach to management, Smith [the GM CEO] made this assessment of the company's problems: 'Without question, noncompetitive labor costs represent the single biggest disadvantage we must overcome.'"[1]

These diagnoses invariably miss the point: "'There is nothing wrong with American labor, but there is something seriously wrong with American management,' said Sheridan M. Tatsuno, president of Neoconcepts

Inc. of Fremont and the author of a recent book on Japanese corporate strategy. 'We should seriously consider the way we run our plants and manage people.'"[2]

Even managers are coming to recognize that problems—and solutions—begin with the management: "About 80 percent of the top managers at 221 companies surveyed by *Productivity* magazine in 1980 cited 'poor management' as the key reason for lackluster productivity. . . . This is not so much an indictment of managers per se as of the management techniques used today to combine labor's input with that of technology and capital."[3]

For change to occur, it is imperative that organizations and those that manage them recognize that they indeed have a choice in how they manage their work force. In the industrial relations literature, there is an increasing emphasis on "strategic choice"—the idea that firms are major initiators of industrial relations practices and that they have a choice as to how to compete.[4] It seems clear that during the 1980s, many of the larger U.S. corporations decided to pursue cost-minimization strategies. In a difficult economic time, they used that economic stress to wage war against unions, if they had any, and against their work force more generally, with layoffs, wage concessions, and an aggressive posture of union avoidance and minimization of interference by the government in the work place. Ironically, in spite of (or perhaps because of) the downsizing and restructuring of management and a shrinkage in real income during the 1980s, "white collar productivity decreased."[5]

Firms, and nations, can choose competitive strategies and ways of managing the employment relation that promote cooperation or, alternatively, conflict:

> Competitive strategies that stress low costs and low wages produce high levels of labor-management conflict, reinforce low trust, and inhibit innovation and improvement of quality. The corollary to this lesson is: Competitive strategies that stress value added (e.g., enhanced quality) and/or product innovation require high levels of motivation, commitment, and trust in employment relations.[6]

Recognizing both the choices available and the important role of management is a necessary precondition to changing how organizations manage the employment relation and whether they obtain competitive advantage through people. This is not as easy to do as it might at first appear. Recognizing the possibility of doing things differently, and accepting management's responsibility for the present condition, can be threatening to those who were, after all, present when the old choices were made and who are implicated in the present levels of performance. It may not be easy, but it is essential.

A DIAGNOSTIC FRAMEWORK: INTERNAL AND EXTERNAL CONSISTENCY

I have found the following questions to be a useful diagnostic device for helping managers think about the policies and practices used in their organization:

1. What is the organization's strategy? What is it doing to distinguish itself from its competitors? What are its intended distinctive competencies and differentiating features?
2. What skills, abilities, attitudes, and behaviors will be required from the work force at all levels in order for the organization to effectively execute its strategic intent? What does it need to do in order to be effective, given its particular strategy?
3. What are the organization's current or proposed policies and practices with respect to: a) recruitment (where and how it attracts employees); b) selection; c) compensation, including the use of long-term incentives, group versus individual incentives, variation in pay by hierarchical level and by department, pay for skill or knowledge, pay for performance practices, and so forth; d) career development, including movement through jobs and progression through the organization; e) training, including who gets trained how often and on what subjects; f) employment security, layoffs, and the firm's obligations to employees; g) the use of contract,

part-time and temporary-help-service employees; h) ownership, including the use of employee stock ownership plans; i) performance appraisal and review, or feedback more generally; j) the degree of task specialization and division of labor; and k) the organization of work, including the use of hierarchy, teams, and other ways of achieving coordination and control?

4. To what extent are these policies and practices internally consistent—compatible with each other?
5. To what extent are the policies and practices likely to produce the skills, competencies, attitudes, and behaviors necessary to execute the organization's intended strategy?
6. To what extent are the policies and practices consistent with what we know about achieving competitive advantage through the work force?

What these questions ask managers to do is to assess two fundamental elements: 1) To what extent are the organization's policies and practices for managing the work force internally consistent with each other? and 2) To what extent are these policies and practices externally consistent, in that they are likely to produce the kinds of skills and behaviors necessary to compete given the organization's intended strategy and the competitive environment it faces? Some examples of internal and external inconsistency can illustrate how to use this simple and straightforward diagnosis to help avoid or solve problems.

The Portman Hotel, built in the late 1980s in San Francisco, proposed to succeed in the highly competitive luxury hotel segment, charging prices that were high even for this segment, by providing an outstanding level of personal service through a new position, that of personal valet,[7] modeled after Asian hotels and the Regent chain in particular. These individuals would be assigned to floors to execute the organization's policy of "no rules" for guests—to do whatever was required to attend to the guests' needs and solve their problems. Portman advertised extensively and made working in the new hotel sound like an exciting way to enter the hospitality industry. It obtained over 9,000 applications, from which it recruited some 300 staff, including about 70 personal valets, of whom 20% had some college education and 15% had completed some trade school.

The hotel had succeeded in attracting an educated, motivated work force to execute its strategy. There were only a few small problems: 1) it paid the personal valets $7.50 per hour, the same wage paid to the average hotel maid in San Francisco; 2) to save money on staffing when the hotel was not full, personal valets were moved around to different floors so they never worked as a team; and 3) to economize on staffing, the hotel did not hire any excess staff, so that 80% of the personal valet's time was actually spent on maid's duties rather than on providing extra service. Portman's wage and work organization policies were clearly inconsistent with its strategy, and indeed, the wages and work organization were incompatible with the recruiting and the quality of people it had attracted. Turnover—devastating in a high-service, strong-culture setting—ran at a rate in excess of 80% in the first year, and service suffered as a consequence. The hotel was subsequently sold.

Another example of external inconsistency—a mismatch between the organization's strategy and its work force management practices—helps explain the failure of People Express in the mid-1980s.[8] Started in the period following deregulation in 1978, People Express in the early 1980s was a widely studied business case, featured in numerous articles in the popular press and on the ABC television program "20/20." It was established with the goal of achieving competitive advantage through its work force, who were very carefully selected and trained. Frequently, 100 people would be interviewed to find 1 new employee, and prospective employees had to go through five weeks of unpaid training and then score more than 90% on a test to be hired into this elite organization. The organization promised cross-training and cross-utilization of people, and the basic structure emphasized self-managed teams.

Self-managed teams require mutual trust and time to communicate and work together in order to be effective. However, People, almost from its very inception, grew at a rate that was not sustainable, given its culture and how it proposed to manage its work force. When rapid growth brought many signs of strain—such as employee illness, family problems, and other symptoms of burnout—the response of founder Don Burr was to grow even faster. This strategy of rapid growth was incompatible with the systems for managing the work force designed to achieve competitive advantage through people—for instance, rapid growth is incompatible with a 1/100 employee selection ratio and with extensive cross-training—and led ultimately to the organization's demise. It was acquired by Texas Air as it slid into bankruptcy.

The diagnostic process described above can also often reveal internal inconsistencies or incompatibilities in various practices. Two of the more common inconsistencies encountered concern wage levels and issues associated with the use of teams. ESL is a 30-year-old organization with about 2,300 employees and annual revenues of approximately $300 million. For the past 15 years, it has been a division in the TRW Avionics and Surveillance Group. ESL is in the business of doing advanced signal recognition and analysis, systems integration, and hardware and software engineering for the Department of Defense, although it is now trying to transfer its technology to civilian product and service applications. The organization hires highly trained and skilled people, many with advanced technical degrees. Moreover, the nature of its business is fundamentally dependent on people—there are no factories, products, or brands to provide it with some market power, although obviously, it does enjoy a very fine technical reputation.

Recognizing that it is a skills- and people-dependent business, ESL takes recruiting and selection very seriously. Indeed, at any time, many of the projects are understaffed, which hinders the timely completion of their work. People are a large component of the firm's costs, and as competition became more intense, the organization changed its salary goal to be at the fiftieth percentile in salary in Silicon Valley. When ESL went through the diagnostic process just described, it quickly confronted the fact that paying at the fiftieth percentile was not consistent either with its aspirations for the quality of the people it hoped to attract or with the fact that being understaffed imposed large costs on its projects and customers. As a consequence of this analysis, the firm is rethinking its compensation strategy and its effects on other elements of its management system.

Many organizations have moved to install teams. ESL, for instance, has a number of quality action teams (QATs). Organizations often have difficulty, however, in implementing team concepts in either appraisal or compensation systems. Thus, they wind up sending mixed and confusing messages—on the one hand, teams are important and we expect you to be an effective team member; and on the other hand, you will be appraised as an individual and compensation will be based on individual merit. Taking teams seriously would seem to imply the use of peer appraisal and would certainly imply that at least some portion of an employee's compensation should depend on the team's results as well as on individual performance. Yet organizations sometimes have problems making their performance management and compensation systems congruent with how they have decided to structure and organize work.

These examples illustrate the types of issues that can be uncovered by using this straightforward diagnostic process. It is a process that calls attention to the importance of policies and practices often overlooked or taken for granted. It demands that management systems be evaluated comprehensively to assess whether the elements are all pointing in the same direction and to see whether the organization is doing things that will enhance its strategic capabilities.

CREATING THE PERCEIVED NEED FOR CHANGE

It is imperative that people perceive a need to do things differently, or else nothing will happen. If implementing practices to achieve competitive success through people were going to occur effortlessly, they would be in place already. There are at least three ways to promote a perception that change is necessary: 1) showing data indicating that current practices either are not effective now or are not likely to be in the future; 2) providing an analysis of the evolving overall competitive strategy of the organization and the implications of that strategy for how the firm manages its work force; and 3) furnishing some type of external stimulation, in the form of either plant visits to other companies, reading, seminars, or information from industry or professional associations—in short, some external models and data indicating that better ways of managing the employment relation are available.

Data

Information is an important impetus to change—although, by itself, it is not always sufficient. One source of information comes from the Baldrige evaluation process. A substantial number of companies, including Boise Cascade and ESL, perform an annual or biannual self-evaluation in which they score themselves as objectively as possible against the various Baldrige Award categories. This provides specific information about comparative strengths and weaknesses and can be used to discern trends as well as to indicate how far the organizations are from being world-class in terms of overall quality and various management process dimensions. Companies that use the Baldrige criteria in this fashion have almost invariably reported that it is a very useful exercise.

Another useful technique is the "obituary exercise," which involves having people write an obituary, including the when, how, and why of the organization's eventual demise. This is a good way of getting people to project themselves into the future and identify the problems or threats that could lead to the organization's death. It therefore serves as an effective means of thinking about what needs to be changed.

Many organizations have begun computing "customer satisfaction indexes," for both internal and external customers. This is a consequence of following the exhortations to become more customer-focused and is consistent with the quality movement. For instance, the Solectron Corporation is an incredibly successful contract manufacturer headquartered in Milpitas, California, with current sales in excess of $800 million per year and a historical growth rate of more than 50% per year. The firm, which won the Baldrige Award in 1991, assembles circuit boards, subassemblies, prototypes, and even complete products for electronics manufacturers. Once a week, it gets each of its customers to grade it on various dimensions of performance. Based on these grades, it computes an overall customer satisfaction index (CSI). At the time it won the Baldrige Award, its average CSI was in the low 90s (out of

100). Solectron then set itself the goal of improving to the high 90s, but the CSI plateaued and even declined slightly. When incremental efforts on the part of the very dedicated work force proved insufficient to improve its scores, the company looked to more fundamental changes in its structure and its ways of managing people. The change was clearly motivated by the data on customer satisfaction and its trend over time.

At ESL, it was not so much hard data on performance or customer satisfaction but what was happening to the defense business that prompted a recognition of the need for change. The phrase "Everyone knows about the Berlin Wall" is commonly heard in the firm. The fall of the Berlin Wall came to symbolize the changes in the world that would mean a decrease in defense spending and, for ESL, a need to take its technology and knowledge and apply them to commercial endeavors.

Linking the Need for Change to Competitive Strategy

A second way of demonstrating the need for change is by tying the change to an analysis of the firm's competitive environment and its evolving strategy for succeeding in that environment. For instance, Solectron began as a contract manufacturer at a time when the principal advantages offered by outside manufacturing sources were lower overhead, lower wage rates (and consequently labor costs), and the ability to absorb fluctuations in demand not readily accommodated by the customer's more permanent manufacturing setup. With this focus, the company was organized into separate divisions, each servicing a small group of customers for a particular part of the assembly, prototype design, testing, or other aspect of the manufacturing process.

However, as in many other businesses, the complexity and systems nature of the business expanded over time. As customers increasingly outsourced more and more of their manufacturing requirements, they came to look to their outside vendors for worldwide manufacturing capability and wanted each vendor to offer a single point of contact with a seamless set of internal boundaries. Not only the nature of the business evolved, but so, too, did Solectron. With its significant growth, there was always the possibility of some job shop arising to outcompete it on price. Furthermore, the business became increasingly dependent on materials rather than direct labor. Thus, the competitive strategy evolved over time to emphasize quality and customer service, not simply low-cost production—although that obviously remained important. This evolution in strategy brought new requirements for upgraded skills and organizational capabilities, and the recognition of this prompted the company to embark on an important change effort.

At ESL, the "Berlin Wall" phenomenon meant that in order to survive and prosper, the firm would need to alter its competitive strategy to emphasize commercial business. However, servicing commercial customers and competing in a commercial world, as opposed to DOD, obviously would require new skills—for instance, marketing and sales—as well as a new mind-set. One part of the mind-set would have to encourage more entrepreneurial behavior, which would affect how the firm recruited, trained, and compensated its work force. Therefore, again, a change in strategy provided the impetus for rethinking how the firm managed the employment relation and how it could make its practices more consistent with the strategy it was pursuing.

Advanced Micro Devices built its submicron development center to become a more important player in semiconductor technology. This represented an important strategic shift for a company that had been content to be sales-oriented and a good second source for chips that were designed by others (for example, Intel). This shift in strategy caused a re-examination of AMD's management processes and resulted in the development of a new work organization, as described earlier in this book. In each instance, a strategic change, clearly evident, was used as leverage for re-evaluating other aspects of the organization, including how it managed people, and for stimulating a recognition of the need for change.

External Stimulation and Information

Often, the preceding two processes are helped by some form of external model or stimulation to assist the organization in appreciating alternative possibilities. At Advanced Micro Devices, one of the champions of the new form of work organization went on a study visit to Japan and came back convinced that elements of the management process that he had seen would be useful in the new facility AMD was building. At Solectron, some key managers had read Senge's book on the learning organization.[9] They saw the applicability of these ideas and, more important, developed language for articulating the need for change and the direction the change should take.

At ESL, a number of the line managers attended an off-site training program in which they were forced, really for the first time, to think about the organization's human resource management practices. They saw the questions outlined earlier in this chapter regarding the strategy, the behavioral and skill requirements to execute the strategy, and how what the organization is doing is internally consistent or inconsistent with the strategy. As soon as they did this diagnosis on their own company, they got excited because they immediately saw numerous problems. At the next regular presentation of human resource material, they spoke up loudly and subsequently made a presentation to their colleagues who had not attended the off-site training. This provoked a lot of discussion within the organization, and this discussion and focus on the issues, as much as anything else, have stimulated re-examination and change.

Be it a company visit, a book, exposure to training, or something else, obtaining information and models from outside the organization is invariably an important component of the stimulus for change. Coupled with data and strategic necessity, such external information provides evidence that change is needed and gives tools for understanding the direction and specifics of change that will achieve competitive advantage through people.

FIRST THINGS FIRST

There are probably not sufficient data to generalize with certainty, but my own field research and reading suggest that successful changes in work force management usually involve actions taken early on in the process, and it is to those actions that we now turn our attention.

Establishing a Philosophy, Goal, or Vision

Change efforts invariably confront entrenched ways of thinking and policies and practices. Uncertainty and risk are inevitably associated with change, and results may not always occur immediately. To succeed, then, it is important that the organization or the person championing the change have a clear view of the goals and philosophy that form the foundation of the work place reform effort. When Volvo embarked on its major innovations in work redesign in the late 1960s and early 1970s, Pehr Gyllenhammar, its president, was clear about the fundamental philosophy that would guide the change efforts:

> In Volvo today we need to recruit about one-third of the whole workforce to keep going every year. We need to have about one seventh of our workforce in reserve because of absenteeism. . . . [A] lot of people leave us because they are not satisfied with their jobs. . . . [N]o group in society has until now considered job content and work environment. . . . Factory work must be adapted to people, not people to machines.[10]

At Advanced Micro Devices, the first step in establishing the submicron development center was to create a vision of how the place was to operate. Jim Doran, the head of the facility, said the firm concluded that to fully realize a return on its tremendous capital investment, the SDC had to operate differently. The goal was to enlist people's heads (their intelligence and thinking ability) and their hearts (their commitment and involvement), not just expect their hands to be extensions of engineering technology. They collectively created a vision that embodied the following principles: 1) continuous rapid improvement; 2) empowerment; 3) seamless organizational boundaries, or in other words, no functional silos that separate units or activities from each other; 4) customer centrality; 5) high-performance expectations; and 6) technical excellence.[11]

At Solectron, the change process also began with a presentation of a new vision for the Milpitas, California, facility—the largest unit and soul of the company's worldwide operations. That vision included a commitment to a set of values: measurement and evaluation were to be predicated on value-added, not hours worked or the number of people controlled; security of employment was to be achieved through growth in the business and by developing additional flexibility in both the people and the organization; and there was to be one scorecard for the site. The vision also encompassed organizational aspirations: reducing the number of layers in the hierarchy and relying extensively on self-managed teams rather than hierarchy for control and coordination. Moreover, there was a commitment to an open and supportive style.

The simple fact is that it is hard to get anywhere if you don't know where you are going. Successful change, consequently, almost invariably begins with a process of figuring out key objectives and an underlying philosophy that can guide the tactical decisions and provide a framework for the organization as it proceeds.

Making Change with Immediate Impact

One way of ensuring that changes in how people are managed will persist is: 1) to begin in areas where there will be immediate, visible results and 2) to make the changes in ways that generate support and commitment widespread enough to make going back to the old ways almost impossible. At Solectron, for instance, the implementation of teams in the packaging division resulted in a productivity gain of about 17% virtually overnight. This is less surprising than it might at first appear. Many, if not most, organizations have processes and standard operating procedures that have accreted over time, have possibly been designed by those who are not doing the work, and have not been rethought or re-examined even as new equipment, new tasks, and new performance pressures were introduced into the system. In such a setting, giving employees with proximate knowledge of the work process an opportunity to share ideas and influence the redesign of the process can often produce immediate, significant gains. These first gains will obviously be the easiest to achieve. Nevertheless, by beginning in areas where improvement is most readily achievable, the demonstration of significant results helps reinforce the commitment to making the change.

Once the work force experiences working under high-commitment work practices, it becomes almost impossible to go back to the old way. At Solectron, the new way of organizing work was preceded by a series of seminars, ostensibly on the learning organization but really about barriers to achieving further gains in productivity and effectiveness. This raised the possibility of the firm's moving to different high-commitment and flexible work arrangements. These seminars, conducted with both managers and hourly workers throughout the facility, generated a sense of excitement, enthusiasm, and hope for the future that had the effect both of providing reinforcement to those leading the change and of making it almost impossible to backslide. For instance, the person conducting the seminars and internally helping lead the change effort at Solectron received the following electronic-mail message from an hourly employee: "On behalf of [division] employees, I would like to thank you and [another manager] for quality training and better future for employees' careers. I am so delighted and optimistic. . . . I should say, 'God finally heard our prayers.'"[12]

The preceding statement reflects enthusiasm and the desire to participate more fully. It indicates how and why these changes work. Individuals want to be part of something great, to feel that they are contributing, and to be given responsibility. Other messages of basically the same tone demonstrated that it would be literally impossible, at least with the same work force, for the company not to move forward with its commitment to implement its vision of a different way of organizing and managing the employment relation.

Starting Activities

Some managers are great at articulating a goal or direction but then never do anything. For changes in the employment relation to evolve, something has to happen. It is particularly useful if the activities are consistent, in terms of the process, with the values being implemented. Action of some sort is essential early on in the process in order to achieve and maintain momentum because taking action, including simply holding meetings and forming work groups, represents a form of behavioral commitment. This commitment tends to ensure persistence.

One of the first things Advanced Micro Devices did was to create teams and charge them with the responsibility of solving the problems that inevitably emerged as the new work organization evolved. The fact that it was teams, not a (or even a few) manager(s) solving the problems was obviously consistent with the new values. Moreover, all the teams' activities built involvement and commitment broadly throughout the unit, creating an almost self-sustaining momentum.

In an analogous fashion, as soon as everyone had heard about the new vision for Solectron's Milpitas facility, activities began that were consistent with getting things accomplished. One task force tackled the job of defining the new organizational structure—how to actually implement the team concept and redo decision processes on the production floor. A second group quickly worked on developing a job-posting system. In order to offer more employment security, it is critical that one part of the organization isn't laying people off even as another is hiring similar types of employees. Because of the culture of strong subunit autonomy, job posting had not previously been done—and the group working on this implemented a system that would afford both opportunities for enhanced career development and greater employment security throughout the total organization. Yet another group began working on the compensation system, first assessing what was in place, determining what people understood about what was in place, and then working toward making the compensation system consistent with the work culture that was desired. Another group investigated the use of temporary and contract workers by, again, beginning with an assessment of the extensiveness of the practice and moving toward asking whether the practice was or was not consistent with the organization's strategic objectives and vision.

Activities like these surface information and share that information widely. They involve people from various parts of the organization and, as such, begin to increase the amount of cross-unit communication. By involving people in the process, commitment builds, and of course, these groups tackle and solve real problems. The lesson of Solectron, Advanced Micro Devices, and other organizations changing the employment relation is that it is vitally important to stop just talking about things and at some point actually begin doing them.

Experimenting

Each organization and its circumstances are unique in terms of the organization's history and culture, the characteristics of its work force and management, and the particular strategy, technology, and customers it confronts. Organizations will change and learn at different rates, and different ways of implementing some general principles will be needed in the various settings. It is therefore unlikely that everything can be planned completely at the outset, and successful organizations seem to be those that are open to change, innovation, and learning as the process progresses.

Work reform at Volvo eventually took the form of 1) improving the role of the foreman and relations with his work group; 2) developing meetings, almost like quality circles, in the plant; and 3) reorganizing the work into small, self-managing groups with responsibility for allocating tasks among themselves. However, these changes, although they fit together well and produced good results, were not all planned or known at the start. Describing the work redesign efforts at Volvo, Bo Adolfsoon, the general manager of the Lundby truck production plant, noted:

> We didn't know this was where we were going when we started. We just sat down and began to talk, developed some ideas and tried them out. When we saw what was successful we would extend it. It took much patience and a willingness to move one step at a time and see where it led. This kind of process is demanding on management and workers alike. Many times we asked ourselves, "Shall we go on?" [13]

At ESL, a number of managers told me that the real point of analyzing the various management practices and their relationship to each other and to the organization's strategy was, at first, not to "fix" compensation or training but to ask questions, to learn. One senior executive noted that it was critical to design an activity that creates a relatedness so that everyone can understand the common purpose, see where the firm is, and develop a shared understanding of the problems and what needs to be done to fix them.

Many attempts to change the employment relation begin with major pronouncements and a sense that there is some "program." Indeed, many companies have embarked on various changes, ranging from total quality management to work redesign, in a programmatic, almost cookbook, fashion. This is a recipe for disaster. First of all, some managers now feel their career is tied up with the success of the program as introduced. This commitment diminishes flexibility. And the idea that there is a formula, some pat processes or practices, diminishes the exploration, the experimenting, and the potential for learning and custom tailoring the ideas to the specific context that are so essential for real success.

It is critical to recognize that the organization will and should retain its competence in the process of diagnosis and change long after the initial changes in the structure, the compensation system, the training programs have been changed yet again in response to new competitive pressures, new strategic initiatives, and work force demands. The learning in the teams and task forces, the insights achieved, and the working relationships forged across disciplines and subunits are the permanent gains from the activity of altering how the work force is managed.

PROBLEMS AND PITFALLS

There are numerous potential problems and pitfalls along the road to work place reform, and I have already discussed a number of them earlier in the book—for instance, in Chapter 8, on internal resistance. There are a few additional issues that warrant particular mention at this point.

Strategic Persistence and Faddishness

Although the basic principles and ideas that help us understand how to manage the work force for competitive advantage are quite seasoned, that is, in fact, a problem. I often hear managers respond to some specific idea by saying, "Why, that isn't anything new. That idea's been around for a long time." Gravity is also an idea that has been around for a long time, but I don't hear people saying, "Well, we can ignore gravity. After all, there's nothing new there." Rather than asking about the novelty or trendiness of some practice, managers would be better advised to ask two simple questions: 1) Are we doing it? and 2) Does it make sense? If the answer to the first question is no and to the second yes, then it is probably something reasonable to consider regardless of its newness.

The search for "new and improved" may be useful in marketing and perhaps even purchasing soap powder, but there is not much evidence that it serves us well in thinking about managing people for competitive advantage. Rather, the search for novelty leads to flitting from one program to another, creating what one executive called "the fad of the month." Worse than this lack of consistency in direction and purpose, the lust for novelty for its own sake can lead to discarding approaches that are effective and useful simply because they are tried and true.

One of my pet peeves in this regard involves the area of training. Lacking any better way to evaluate education, and without the necessary skills and interest in developing effective metrics, training people often evaluate programs by the newness of the material. Have we changed the program, the instructors, the concepts? If not, we should. Change, when it is needed for some purpose, is obviously great, but change for the sake of change itself can be counterproductive. Consider the following example.

With the increasing success of Japanese companies in the world economy, a search began to understand the secrets of their success. In the course of this search, we learned that the Japanese adopted the teachings of W. E. Deming when his work in the United States was ignored for many years. Now comes research that argues:

> W. Edwards Deming, Joseph Juran, and other American experts have rightfully earned their place in the history books for their significant contributions to the industrial development of Japan. However, the United States Training Within Industries (TWI) programs, installed in Japan by

the Occupation authorities after World War II, may well have been even more influential.[14]

TWI consisted of three standardized training programs developed by the United States during World War II to boost industrial production quickly:

> The first, Job Instruction Training (JIT), taught supervisors the importance of proper training of their workforce and how to provide this training. The second, Job Methods Training (JMT), focused on how to generate and implement ideas for methods improvement. The third, Job Relations Training (JRT), was a course in supervisor-worker relations and in leadership.[15]

The particular value of these programs derived, first, from the fact that they were apparently successful in getting good management practices actually used and, second, from the fact that, because of their standardization, they could be readily exported to new settings and implemented rapidly. The evidence from their use in the United States is that they were spectacularly effective. For instance, one Texas shipbuilder reported that over a four-year period, it could attribute a 45% increase in production, a 78% reduction in training time, a 69% reduction in scrap, and a 70% reduction in accidents to TWI.[16]

What happened to these programs in the United States and Japan? In the United States, 1945 saw the end of the federal government agency responsible for the program because the war effort was over. With little foreign competition—the industrial base of future competitors was destroyed—and with little respect for anything not new, the TWI programs virtually disappeared in the United States. Not so in Japan, however, where they are still widely used and virtually unchanged. In 1990, some 66,700 people graduated from TWI courses in Japan, and in 1991, the number was 64,000:

> In 1992, even though the programs have changed little since their arrival in Japan, they are well-respected in Japanese management circles and are viewed as important enough to the national interest to be overseen by the Ministry of Labor, which licenses instructors and upholds training standards. . . . Indeed, the Japanese government is now developing plans to export the TWI courses *back to the United States.*[17]

The material in these programs is timeless: "the principles of instruc-
tion, continuous improvement, and human relations."[18] Yet how many
organizations in the United States would keep the same program, essentially unchanged, for almost 50 years, regardless of whether it was working? We seek novelty for its own sake. This is a serious problem in the
domain of making work place changes that will provide sustained competitive success over time. New isn't necessarily bad, but it isn't necessarily good, either.

Framing: Asking the Right Questions

Strategic persistence is one example of a broader phenomenon—asking
the right questions about work place change initiatives. In particular,
since the general cultural bias is against seeing the work force or the
employment relation as a competitive weapon, there are often attempts
to discredit work place change. These attempts seldom survive close
scrutiny when the right questions are asked. Below are three of my fa-
vorites.

When I happened to mention to a colleague that Solectron had
achieved a 17% increase in productivity in one of its divisions, his immediate response was, "Sure, but that's just an example of the Hawthorne
effect. How long do you think it will last?" The appropriate response
is, of course—I hope it lasts a long time, but even if it doesn't, some
improvement for some period of time is better than no improvement
at all. After all, if I told you I would increase your salary for some period
of time by about 20% over what it currently is, after which it would fall
back to its current trajectory and no lower, and that I couldn't tell you
how long you would enjoy the extra money, I doubt many of you would
say, "That's all right. Since you can't guarantee me an increase of this
magnitude forever, I'll pass this one up." Of course, how we manage
the employment relation will need to evolve and change over time as
circumstances change. However, a significant improvement that then
forms the foundation for subsequent learning and improvement is not
something to be dismissed out of hand. If your competitors do it and
you don't, you may not be around long enough to ask if it's still working.

A second problem is comparing the new system to an idealized condition and then rejecting it if it falls short, which it inevitably will. The relevant comparison is, of course, not to some ideal state of the world but to the organization's own recent past. If things are better, even if they are not yet perfect, under a different way of managing the employment relation, then this improvement should be vigorously embraced and used as a foundation for further improvement, not discarded. This is, after all, what continuous improvement is all about.

Finally, it is important to frame things in terms of gains or losses. Obviously, bigger gains are better than smaller ones, but an improvement of even 5% is better than nothing, as long as it is substantial enough to cover whatever costs might have been incurred in the implementation process. The tendency to go for the so-called home run in product development is well known and has caused numerous companies problems that are now well documented. The same difficulty exists with respect to changing how we manage people at work. Obviously, organizations should set high expectations, and there are, in most instances, substantial gains to be realized. However, any improvement is better than none.

System Fragility

Because of the complementarity among the elements required to manage people effectively for competitive advantage, some observers have noted that such systems are inherently fragile. For instance, talking about the diffusion of the system of lean production and its associated human resource elements, John Paul MacDuffie and John Krafcik noted:

> Lean production is . . . fragile with respect to its dependence on human resources. As lean production diffuses . . . it is highly vulnerable to the mass production assumptions and mindsets that have dominated managerial and engineering practice. . . . Unless managers keep the skill levels of the workforce high, unless they create a culture of reciprocal commitment in which workers will be willing to contribute to process improvement . . . lean production will quickly deteriorate. . . . [I]n practice lean production is not weaker or more prone to breakdown. . . . [M]aintaining

a constant awareness of lean production's "fragility" is . . . critical to preserving this resilience and flexibility.[19]

This stands in contrast to most management systems, which are quite robust. Think about your own organization. If it is typical, it probably has large numbers of people who aren't really doing their best, whose wisdom and insight are not being used, but nevertheless, the organization continues to function. On the one hand, getting rid of the surplus people and management that permit organizations to function with people working at some fraction of their potential produces great gains in productivity, but on the other hand, it eliminates the slack in the system. With managers watching managers watching other managers watching people do the work, one need not worry too much about commitment, training, or anything else—there is so much redundancy in the controls and the staffing that mistakes will probably be uncovered, and there are plenty of people to fix the problems. Such is not the case in high-commitment, team-based work systems with less redundancy of either control or personnel. It is in this sense that such systems are fragile, and the problem of complementarity among the various elements looms large.

The solution, however, is to recognize the interdependence among the various practices involved in managing the employment relation, not to be content with a redundant, unproductive, but robust system. I have found few intelligent managers who, once they begin to think about people as a source of competitive advantage and go through the diagnostic process described earlier in this chapter, aren't able to quite reasonably figure out what to do to manage the various interconnections and interdependencies. The problem of fragility and complementarity is compounded by the failure of many managers and many organizations to give proper attention to these issues.

The Role of Management

A final possible problem is the role of the manager under these high-commitment work arrangements. Why would anyone want to be a manager when line workers at Lincoln Electric can earn more than $100,000 and when the role of the manager appears to be diminished and constrained?

The answer was provided by an executive at Solectron presenting the ideas for new work arrangements, which involved eliminating layers of the hierarchy and a new role for self-managed teams. He noted that one does not add much value merely overseeing $7-an-hour direct labor. Under the new work structures, managers have both more time and more responsibility for planning, preventing problems, learning about and implementing new technology, coaching and training employees in more effective practices, and most important, the strategic thinking that managers complain they never have time for. The key insight in this comment is the idea of value-added. Managers, indeed, add much more value when they use their skills and experience in planning and problem solving rather than in direct supervision.

THE ROLE OF HUMAN RESOURCES

Although one might think that human resources, of all functions, would be taking the lead in changing work arrangements so that organizations can achieve better competitive results, this is not invariably the case. Moreover, even under the best of circumstances, human resources can play an important supporting role but can seldom be the only champion for these ideas if they are to succeed. That is because of its traditional role in organizations.

Hewlett-Packard is an enormously successful electronics manufacturer with 1992 annual sales of over $14 billion. In the early 1980s, the company was prominently featured in several books because of its particular management system and culture that, over the years, have produced excellent results.[20] The foundation of the company's success is the "HP way": "Bill Hewlett once put it this way: 'I feel that in general terms it is policies and actions that flow from the belief that men and women want to do a good job, a creative job, and that if they are provided the proper environment they will do so.'"[21]

Although Hewlett-Packard has depended on its work force and how it is managed for its success, it has not placed excessive reliance solely on the personnel function to maintain this competitive advantage. The company was founded in 1939, incorporated in 1947, and went public in 1957. Yet in 1956, almost 20 years after its founding, HP still did not have a personnel department. That year, at a management meeting, the founders, Bill Hewlett and David Packard, once again rejected the idea of having a personnel director. There were two fears. One was that the personnel function would take responsibility for worrying about how people were managed away from line managers—this was, after all, a company making sophisticated electronic equipment and dominated by engineers who had more technical skills and interests. The second fear was that the line managers would be willing to give this responsibility up.[22] After some further discussion, the personnel function was created in the company, but making line managers responsible for how people are managed remains an important part of the culture—for instance, today HP managers are held accountable for the results of employee surveys in their areas. It is also part of the culture of Procter & Gamble, an organization in which there are few personnel specialists; rather, people rotate into and out of that function from line management positions.

At its best, the human resource or personnel function can 1) call attention to the importance of the management process and the various policies, practices, and systems that support that process; 2) provide information and expertise on best practices in other companies and furnish analytic support for diagnosing and recommending solutions to problems arising in the employment relation; 3) participate in business decisions and facilitate change that is consistent with the underlying values of the company; and 4) do much of the necessary administrative work involved in employment. At worst, human resources can interfere with line management and not champion effective ways of managing work. General managers need to be sensitive to both possibilities and recognize the capabilities and potential of those with whom they are working.

One problem with expecting the human resource function to take the lead in championing change in the employment relationship is that,

to use the apt phrase of one general manager, often "they have a ser-
vant's mentality." By that he meant that, as a low-power unit, sometimes staffed with people who had failed in other functions, sometimes
seen as overhead, and simply put, in a vulnerable position, human resource personnel were used to fulfilling the requirements given to them
by others. They seldom had enough strength and self-confidence to
really assume a major, leadership role in initiating change in the organization. Obviously, there are many important exceptions to this, but if
one thinks about the history of the personnel function in many organizations, it can quickly be seen that, in a way analogous to the case of
unions, companies pretty much got what they seemed to want—a weak
department that served a primarily clerical function and didn't cause
too much trouble. The fact that, in some instances recounted below,
human resources has been more than this is a tribute to the quality of
those individuals working in those particular companies. However, one
should not expect change to be led solely by the human resource or
personnel function.

The senior vice president for human resources at Advanced Micro
Devices helped champion the change in the way work was structured
when the firm opened its new submicron development center. At Boise
Cascade, the human resource manager from the De Ridder, Louisiana,
plant moved with the plant manager when he became vice president of
manufacturing for the entire division, and the human resource manager
continued to work with the manufacturing manager to champion
change throughout the paper division. At Hewlett-Packard, the personnel function has helped to maintain the HP way in the face of short-
term competitive and financial pressures that threatened this culture.
Moreover, it has taken the responsibility for improving the process of
management and teamwork and for facilitating and measuring the accomplishment of this goal.

The human resource function at ESL has done a number of things
to help the organization align its policies and practices for managing
the work force so they will be consistent with each other and with the
firm's evolving strategy. First, the director of that function determined
that the unit should serve as a model for the rest of the organization, or

in other words, it should live by the values. Thus, he removed one layer in the organizational structure of human resources. The function worked toward having no barriers or boundaries within itself or between itself and the rest of the organization that inhibited coordination. The director supported his staff members' development of different and multiple skills, even if such skills were not strictly necessary in their present positions. Most important, he worked to make sure that everything the department did was focused on serving the organization's strategy. This is a change from the past when, for instance, training would be planned by using needs assessments—what people thought they needed—without necessarily establishing any direct connection to the organization's strategic objectives. One useful framework for accomplishing this strategic alignment was to list the strategic objectives on one axis of a matrix and then, on the other axis, list the training (or in another analysis, compensation) activities that supported each one. This provided a quick way of seeing 1) what activities weren't needed and 2) where there were gaps in the sense of strategic objectives that were not being served.

Contrast these positive activities on the part of human resources to support change in the organization and management of the work force with two other, less than positive, examples. In a conference room in North Carolina, the following people gathered to field test a presentation for a new management training program in a major pharmaceutical company: 1) two people from an external consulting firm who were hired to help design the program; 2) another outside consultant from out of state who works with the company in various capacities; 3) the director of corporate training; 4) two of his key staff people; and 5) two managers of the type who were actually to be the audience for the program. These latter two individuals, heavily outnumbered by the personnel specialists and consultants, seldom spoke. Among the rest, particularly the internal human resource staff, the discussion about the training did not focus on whether it served some strategic need in the company, how the message fit with the organization's culture, or other similar strategic questions. Rather, the discussion centered on whether the program should use cases from outside the pharmaceutical industry, how old the cases can be and still be acceptable, and so forth. It should not surprise the reader to learn that development of the management training program was behind schedule. The initiative for the program came from a senior line manager who wanted to develop the organization's managerial capabilities. The staff in the room were all fairly new to the company, since their predecessors had been terminated for not getting the task done.

This is an example of a fumble—a senior executive had both a good insight and a good idea. The insight is that in a high-technology business like the drug industry, people are important assets. He also recognized that in a technology-based company, people had not necessarily been either hired or promoted on the basis of their managerial skills but, rather, on the basis of their technical abilities. Consequently, the organization faced a critical deficiency—management skill—in a domain that might have great consequences. The manager, then, logically concluded that what was needed was management development training and an emphasis on building the firm's organizational capability. Therefore, he turned over the execution and accomplishment of this objective to his internal human resource people. Fearful, indecisive, and most of all, not thinking about tying their effort to the firm's basic business processes, these individuals wasted money and probably did little to further their careers in the company.

Lost opportunity and wasted money are not as harmful, however, as the other role human resources sometimes plays—keeper of the rules and the internal representative of outside lawyers. It is a nice strategy for a powerless group to use—seeking to acquire more power by relying on external legal or regulatory threats or attempting to maintain the integrity of various systems and procedures. Thus, in some firms, the fights are over salary—can line managers actually offer the salary necessary to attract people with the ability to do important jobs, even if such salaries violate the established position structure and salary ranges? In other organizations, the fight may be over recruiting sources and processes—will managers be able to recruit from competitors, noncitizens, or from other nontraditional sources? In some instances, the fight is over dismissal procedures.

For instance, in one case, a person obviously and clearly unqualified was hired for a secretarial position in a large organization. How the mistake in hiring occurred is not as interesting as what subsequently happened. When the organizational subunit discovered its hiring mistake in the first week the new person was on the job, it was told by the firm's central personnel function that there had to be a long, arduous process of counseling, documentation of performance deficiencies, and meetings—even though the secretary was obviously still on probationary status. It took seven weeks, and countless hours on the part of numerous people, to finally terminate the employee. When queried about the incident, the relevant human resource representative blamed the hiring department for not doing an adequate job in its initial screening, cited the organization's general policies, and criticized those who complained about the incident. The head of the human resource function remarked, "Seven weeks isn't too long to get rid of a poor performer."

The simple question to ask about the human resource function is this: Is it adding value, is it solving problems, is it serving the organization's strategic business needs? If the answer is no, then perhaps management would be well advised to turn its denizens loose on the competition to do their damage elsewhere. If the answer is yes, then the function can serve as an important partner in making changes designed to help the organization achieve greater productivity and performance. In any case, the smart general manager will make sure he or she knows what the situation is and whether human resources will be an ally or an obstacle to change.

THE CHOICE: CHANGE OR CONTINUING PROBLEMS

Old habits and old ways of thinking die hard, particularly when they are consistent with important social values and ideology as well as with implicit theories of behavior. Business discourse and business education, particularly in the United States but elsewhere as well, rely, even if only implicitly, on a neoclassical paradigm that is "utilitarian, rationalist, and individualist."[23] It is utilitarian in that the maximization of one's own utility presumably guides behavior; it is rationalist in that goals, rather than means, are emphasized in decision processes; and it is individualist in that the presumption is that the individual is the decision-making unit and collectivities are either not recognized at all or seen merely as collections of individuals.[24]

However, this is only one possible conception of the firm. Ronald Dore wrote:

> Contrary to the individualistic utilitarian assumptions of most . . . writing, "the company" can be seen, not simply as an arena, not simply as an institutional device that allows a variety of stakeholders to pursue their separate interests, but also as a reified entity. As such it can be the object of loyal sentiments and can be seen as itself having interests that transcend the interests of all possible . . . stakeholders.[25]

Because our theories guide our actions, and our actions, in turn, produce reactions on the part of others, we create the behaviors we expect to observe, occasionally trapping ourselves and our organizations in a self-fulfilling prophecy of adversarial relations with a work force that is increasingly critical to competitive success. The two central themes of this book have been: 1) managers and their organizations have the opportunity to choose a different course, and 2) they are likely to choose a better way only to the extent that they focus on pragmatic questions of performance rather than abstract ideologies and theories that delimit the field of vision and the range of options seriously considered.

Although we may not like to admit it, the legacy of Frederick Taylor lives on in our academic theories, our social values, and the daily actions many managers take in managing the employment relationship. Yet this need not be the case and certainly should not be for those organizations that hope to survive in a world of increasing competitive pressure. Konosuke Matsushita, the founder of the Matsushita Electric Industrial Company—a firm with a 250-year plan, organized in 50-year segments, and one of the most successful industrial corporations in the world—was asked to give a speech addressing the competition between firms in the United States and Japan. Quite old at the time, he spoke much more candidly than is sometimes the case:

"We will win and you will lose," he says. "You cannot do anything about it because your failure is an internal disease. Your companies are based on Taylor's principles. Worse, your heads are Taylorized, too. You firmly believe that sound management means executives on one side and workers on the other, on one side men who think and on the other side men who can only work. For you, management is the art of smoothly transferring the executives' ideas to the workers' hands.

"We have passed the Taylor stage. We are aware that business has become terribly complex. Survival is very uncertain. . . . Therefore, a company must have the constant commitment of the minds of all of its employees to survive. For us, management is the entire workforce's intellectual commitment at the service of the company. . . .

"We know that the intelligence of a few technocrats—even very bright ones—has become totally inadequate to face these challenges. Only the intellects of all employees can permit a company to live with the ups and downs and the requirements of its new environment. Yes, we will win and you will lose. For you are not able to rid your minds of the obsolete Taylorisms that we never had."[26]

The lesson applies to more than competition across national borders. Those firms that are locked into Taylorist ideology and practices are not likely to succeed in competition with such firms as Southwest Airlines, Hewlett-Packard, Lincoln Electric, Nordstrom, and the many others we have seen in this book that succeed through their people. Although shaking oneself free of old habits and ways of thinking is certainly not easy, the potential rewards are great. In any event, the competition may permit no other alternative.

Notes

Chapter 1

1. Michael E. Porter, *Competitive Advantage* (New York: Free Press, 1985), 1.
2. Ibid., 4.
3. "Investment Winners and Losers," *Money*, October 1992, 133.
4. George Stalk, Jr., and Thomas M. Hout, *Competing against Time* (New York: Free Press, 1990), 141.
5. Billie Jo Zirger and Modesto A. Maidique, "A Model of New Product Development: An Empirical Test," *Management Science* 36 (1990), 867.
6. Stalk and Hout, *Competing against Time*.
7. Presentation by Peter Thigpen at Stanford Graduate School of Business, February 26, 1991.
8. Edwin Mansfield, Mark Schwartz, and Samuel Wagner, "Imitation Costs and Patents: An Empirical Study," *The Economic Journal* 91 (1981), 907–918.
9. Ibid., 909.
10. Ibid., 913.
11. Maryann Keller, *Rude Awakening: The Rise, Fall, and Struggle for Recovery of General Motors* (New York: William Morrow, 1989), 213.
12. Richard Pascale, *Managing on the Edge* (New York: Simon & Schuster, 1990), 73.
13. Paul Adler, "New Technologies, New Skills," *California Management Review* 29 (1986), 10.
14. "Management Discovers the Human Side of Automation, " *Business Week*, September 29, 1986, 70.

15. Ibid.

16. M. Hossein Safizadeh, "The Case of Workgroups in Manufacturing Operations," *California Management Review* 33 (1991), 61.

17. Allen Unsworth and Barbara N. McLennan, "Exports and the U.S. Economic Outlook," *U.S. Industrial Outlook 1990*, 16.

18. Stephen Woolcock, Jeffrey Hart, and Hans Van Der Ven, *Interdependence in the Post-Multilateral Era* (Cambridge, MA: Center for International Affairs, Harvard University, 1985), 73.

19. Ibid., 71.

20. Kenneth H. Bacon, "Foreign Banks Seek Help as Congress Begins Writing Some Checks on Them," *The Wall Street Journal*, June 6, 1991, A18.

21. George J. Stigler, "The Theory of Economic Regulation," *Bell Journal of Economics and Management Science* 2 (1971), 3–21.

22. John W. Rutter, "Recent Trends in International Direct Investment and the Implications for U.S. Business," *U.S. Industrial Outlook 1990*, 6.

23. Ibid., 7.

24. Robert Buzzell and Bradley T. Gale, *The PIMS Principles: Linking Strategy to Performance* (New York: Free Press, 1987).

25. Michael J. Piore and Charles E. Sabel, *The Second Industrial Divide* (New York: Basic Books, 1984).

26. John T. Dunlop and David Weil, "Human Resource Innovations in the Apparel Industry: An Industrial Relations System Perspective," unpublished ms. (Cambridge, MA: Harvard University, 1992).

27. Bridget O'Brian, "Southwest Airlines Is a Rare Air Carrier: It Still Makes Money," *The Wall Street Journal*, October 26, 1992, A1.

28. James Campbell Quick, "Crafting an Organizational Culture: Herb's Hand at Southwest Airlines," *Organizational Dynamics* 21 (Autumn 1992), 47.

29. O'Brian, "Southwest Airlines," A7.

30. Quick, "Crafting an Organizational Culture," 50.

31. O'Brian, "Southwest Airlines," A1.

32. Ibid., A7.

33. Anthony P. Carnevale and Harold Goldstein, "Schooling and Training for Work in America: An Overview," in Louis A. Ferman, Michele Hoyman, Joel Cutcher-Gershenfeld, and Ernest J. Savoie (eds.), *New Developments in Worker Training: A Legacy for the 1990s* (Madison, WI: Industrial Relations Research Association, 1990), 30.

34. Ibid., 27.

35. Keith Bradsher, "U.S. Lag in Phone Trade Seen," *New York Times*, August 17, 1990, C3.

36. Bank of America, "Human Resource Planning," *Perspectives* 11 (Winter 1990), 40.

37. Ibid., 43.

38. Paul E. Barton and Irwin S. Kirsch, *Workplace Competencies*, Policy Perspective Series (Washington, DC: Office of Educational Research and Development, U.S. Department of Education, 1990).

39. Ibid., 9.

40. Ibid., 8, 10.

41. Ina V. S. Mullis, John A. Dossey, Eugene H. Owens, and Gary W. Phillips, *The State of Mathematics Achievement* (Washington, DC: National Center for Education Statistics, U.S. Department of Education, 1991).

42. Ibid., 9.

43. Ibid., 7.

44. "Labor Letter," *The Wall Street Journal,* July 31, 1990, A1.

45. Gilbert Fuchsberg, "Many Businesses Responding Too Slowly to Rapid Work Force Shifts, Study Says," *The Wall Street Journal,* July 20, 1990, B1.

46. Bank of America, "Human Resource Planning," 49.

47. Carnevale and Goldstein, "Schooling and Training," 33.

48. "Where the Jobs Are Is Where the Skills Aren't," *Business Week,* September 19, 1988, 106.

49. Jeffrey Pfeffer and James N. Baron, "Taking the Workers Back Out: Recent Trends in the Structuring of Employment," in Barry M. Staw and L. L. Cummings (eds.), *Research in Organizational Behavior,* vol. 10 (Greenwich, CT: JAI Press, 1988), 257–303.

50. Rodger L. Dillon, "The Changing Labor Market: Contingent Workers and the Self-Employed in California," Special Report to Senator Dan McCorquodale and Senator Bill Greene, Office of Senate Research (Sacramento: Senate of California, 1987), 46.

51. Wayne J. Howe, "The Business Services Industry Sets Pace in Employment Growth," *Monthly Labor Review* 110 (1986), 29–36.

52. Peter T. Kilborn, "Part-Time Hirings Bring Deep Changes in U.S. Workplaces," *New York Times,* June 17, 1991, A1.

53. Dillon, "The Changing Labor Market," 33.

54. "Congressional Study Challenges Federal Use of Private Contractors," *New York Times,* September 16, 1991, A8.

55. Katherine G. Abraham, "Restructuring the Employment Relationship: The Growth of Market-Mediated Work Arrangements," in Katherine G. Abraham and Robert B. McKersie (eds.), *New Developments in the Labor Market* (Cambridge, MA: MIT Press, 1990), 106.

56. Ibid., 101–102.

57. James B. Rebitzer, "Short-Term Employment Relations and Labor Market Outcomes: Contract Workers in the U.S. Petrochemical Industry," unpublished ms. (Cambridge, MA: Sloan School of Management, MIT, 1991).

58. S. D. Nollen and V. H. Martin, *Alternative Work Schedules, Part 2: Permanent Part-Time Employment* (New York: Amacom, 1978).

59. Abraham, "Restructuring the Employment Relationship," 102.

60. Dillon, "The Changing Labor Market," 26.

61. L. Reibstein, "More Companies Use Free-Lancers to Avoid Cost, Trauma of Layoffs," *The Wall Street Journal,* April 18, 1986, 21.

62. Michael J. McCarthy, "Managers Face Dilemma with 'Temps,'" *The Wall Street Journal,* April 5, 1988, 31.

63. Ibid.

64. Keith Schneider, "Study Finds Link between Chemical Plant Accidents and Contract Workers," *New York Times,* July 30, 1991, A10.

65. Rebitzer, "Short-Term Employment Relations and Labor Market Outcomes," 3.

66. Walt Bogdanich, "Danger in White: The Shadowy World of 'Temp' Nurses," *The Wall Street Journal,* November 1, 1991, B1, B6.

Chapter 2

1. Masahiko Aoki, *Information, Incentives, and Bargaining in the Japanese Economy* (Cambridge, U.K.: Cambridge University Press, 1988), 8–9.

2. Harry C. Handlin, "The Company Built upon the Golden Rule: Lincoln Electric," in

Bill L. Hopkins and Thomas C. Mawhinney (eds.), *Pay for Performance: History, Controversy, and Evidence* (New York: Haworth Press, 1992), 154.

3. "The Lincoln Electric Company," Case 376–028 (Boston: Harvard Business School, 1975).

4. Handlin, "The Company Built upon the Golden Rule," 161.

5. Barbara Presley Noble, "An Approach with Staying Power," *New York Times*, March 8, 1992, F27.

6. Clair Brown, Michael Reich, and David Stern, "Becoming a High Performance Work Organization: The Role of Security, Employee Involvement, and Training," Working Paper 45, Institute of Industrial Relations (Berkeley: University of California, 1992), 3.

7. Susan N. Houseman, "The Equity and Efficiency of Job Security: Contrasting Perspectives on Collective Dismissal Laws in Western Europe," in Katherine G. Abraham and Robert B. McKersie (eds.), *New Developments in the Labor Market* (Cambridge, MA: MIT Press, 1990), 196–197.

8. Ibid., 202.

9. Christopher Buechtmann, "Employment Protection and 'De-Regulation': The West German Experience." Paper presented at the ILO/ILS/WZB Conference on Workers' Protection and Labor Market Dynamics, Berlin, May 16–18, 1990, 26.

10. Katherine G. Abraham and Susan N. Houseman, "Employment Security and Labor Adjustment: A Comparison of West Germany and the United States," unpublished ms. (College Park: University of Maryland, 1991).

11. Frank L. Schmidt and John E. Hunter, "Individual Differences in Productivity: An Empirical Test of Estimates Derived from Studies of Selection Procedure Utility," *Journal of Applied Psychology* 68 (1983), 407–414.

12. Handlin, "The Company Built upon the Golden Rule," 157.

13. "Nordstrom: Dissension in the Ranks?" Case 9–191–002 (Boston: Harvard Business School, 1990), 7.

14. George Akerlof, "Gift Exchange and Efficiency Wage Theory," *American Economic Review* 74 (1984), 79–83.

15. David I. Levine, "What Do Wages Buy?" unpublished ms. (Berkeley: Haas School of Business, University of California, 1992).

16. David I. Levine, "Can Wage Increases Pay for Themselves?" *Economic Journal* (in press).

17. Isadore Barmash, "A Flourishing Industry's Shining Star," *New York Times*, December 22, 1991, F7.

18. James W. Near, "Wendy's Successful 'Mop Bucket Attitude,'" *The Wall Street Journal*, April 27, 1992, A16.

19. Ibid.

20. Handlin, "The Company Built upon the Golden Rule," 159.

21. Andrea Gabor, "After the Pay Revolution, Job Titles Won't Matter," *New York Times*, May 17, 1992, F5.

22. Andrea Gabor, "Take This Job and Love It," *New York Times*, January 26, 1992, F1.

23. Roger T. Kaufman, "The Effects of IMPROSHARE on Productivity," *Industrial and Labor Relations Review* 45 (1992), 312.

24. Ibid.

25. Martin L. Weitzman and Douglas L. Kruse, "Profit Sharing and Productivity," in Alan S. Blinder (ed.), *Paying for Productivity: A Look at the Evidence* (Washington, DC: The Brookings Institution, 1990), 139.

26. "The Lincoln Electric Company," 16.

27. Ibid., 3.

28. Joseph R. Blasi and Douglas L. Kruse, *The New Owners* (New York: Harper Business, 1991), 257.

29. Corey M. Rosen, Katherine J. Klein, and Karen M. Young, *Employee Ownership in America* (Lexington, MA: Lexington Books, 1986).

30. Derek C. Jones and Takao Kato, "The Scope, Nature, and Effects of Employee Stock Ownership Plans in Japan," *Industrial and Labor Relations Review* 46 (1993), 352.

31. Ibid., 365.

32. Stuart Ogden, "The Limits to Employee Involvement: Profit Sharing and Disclosure of Information," *Journal of Management Studies* 29 (1992), 237.

33. Handlin, "The Company Built upon the Golden Rule," 156.

34. Presentation by Peter Thigpen at Stanford Graduate School of Business, February 26, 1991.

35. Richard T. Pascale, "Nordstrom, Inc.," unpublished case (San Francisco, 1991), Exhibits 7 and 8.

36. Handlin, "The Company Built upon the Golden Rule," 156.

37. David I. Levine and Laura D'Andrea Tyson, "Participation, Productivity, and the Firm's Environment," in Blinder (ed.), *Paying for Productivity*, 183–243.

38. J. Richard Hackman and Greg R. Oldham, *Work Redesign* (Reading, MA: Addison-Wesley, 1980).

39. Thomas F. O'Boyle, "Working Together: A Manufacturer Grows Efficient by Soliciting Ideas from Employees," *The Wall Street Journal*, June 5, 1992, A4.

40. Barnaby Feder, "At Monsanto, Teamwork Works," *New York Times*, June 25, 1991, C1.

41. Barbara Presley Noble, "An Approach with Staying Power," *New York Times*, March 8, 1992, 23.

42. Brian Dumaine, "Who Needs a Boss?" *Fortune*, May 7, 1990, 54.

43. Ibid., 55.

44. Paul S. Adler, "The 'Learning Bureaucracy': New United Motor Manufacturing, Inc.," in Barry M. Staw and Larry L. Cummings (eds.), *Research in Organizational Behavior* (Greenwich, CT: JAI Press, in press), 32.

45. Helene Cooper, "Carpet Firm Sets Up an In-House School to Stay Competitive," *The Wall Street Journal*, October 5, 1992, A1, A6.

46. Fox Butterfield, "Old Mill Pioneers Workers' Education," *New York Times*, January 18, 1993, A10.

47. Norm Alster, "What Flexible Workers Can Do," *Fortune*, February 13, 1989, 62.

48. Adler, "The 'Learning Bureaucracy,'" 35.

49. Ibid., 36.

50. Ibid., 17.

51. J. Patrick Wright, *On a Clear Day You Can See General Motors* (Grosse Point, MI: Wright Enterprises, 1979).

52. O'Boyle, "Working Together," A1, A4.

53. Edward P. Lazear, "Pay Equality and Industrial Politics," *Journal of Political Economy* 97 (1989), 561–580.

54. Paul Milgrom and John Roberts, "An Economic Approach to Influence Activities in Organizations," *American Journal of Sociology* 94 (1988), S154–S179.

55. Daryl J. Bem, "Self-Perception Theory," in Leonard Berkowitz (ed.), *Advances in Experimental Social Psychology*, vol. 6 (New York: Academic Press, 1972), 1–62.

56. Mark R. Lepper and David Greene, "Turning Play into Work: Effects of Adult Sur-

veillance and Extrinsic Rewards on Children's Intrinsic Motivation," *Journal of Personality and Social Psychology* 31 (1975), 479–486.

57. Jacqueline Mitchell, "Herman Miller Links Worker-CEO Pay," *The Wall Street Journal*, May 7, 1992, B1.

58. David Halberstam, *The Reckoning* (New York: William Morrow, 1986).

59. See, for example, Peter M. Blau, *The Dynamics of Bureaucracy* (Chicago: University of Chicago Press, 1955); and V. F. Ridgway, "Dysfunctional Consequences of Performance Measurement," *Administrative Science Quarterly* 1 (1956), 240–247.

60. Thigpen presentation.

61. Handlin, "The Company Built upon the Golden Rule," 154.

62. "The Lincoln Electric Company," 19.

63. James F. Lincoln, *Incentive Management* (Cleveland, OH: Lincoln Electric Company, 1951).

64. Pascale, "Nordstrom, Inc.," 5.

65. B. F. Skinner, *Science and Human Behavior* (New York: Macmillan, 1953).

66. Handlin, "The Company Built upon the Golden Rule," 153.

67. Douglas McGregor, *The Human Side of Enterprise* (New York: McGraw-Hill, 1960), 18.

68. Ibid., 33–34.

69. Ibid., 48–49.

70. Ibid., 23.

71. Notes from Thigpen presentation.

72. McGregor, *Human Side of Enterprise*, Ch. 8.

73. Paul Osterman, "How Common Is Workplace Transformation and How Can We Explain Who Adopts It? Results from a National Survey," unpublished ms. (Cambridge, MA: Sloan School of Management, MIT, 1992), 5.

74. Jeffrey B. Arthur, "The Link between Business Strategy and Industrial Relations Systems in American Steel Minimills," *Industrial and Labor Relations Review* 45 (1992), 490–491.

75. Ibid., 501.

Chapter 3

1. Interview with Jim Doran of Advanced Micro Devices, November 6, 1992.

2. Presentation by Peter Thigpen at Stanford Graduate School of Business, February 26, 1991.

3. "The Lincoln Electric Company," Case 376–028 (Boston: Harvard Business School, 1975), 18.

4. Richard T. Pascale, "Nordstrom, Inc.," unpublished case (San Francisco, 1991), 4.

5. Paul S. Adler, "The 'Learning Bureaucracy': New United Motor Manufacturing, Inc.," in Barry M. Staw and Larry L. Cummings (eds.), *Research in Organizational Behavior* (Greenwich, CT: JAI Press, in press), 11–12.

6. Ibid., 12.

7. Ibid.

8. Ibid.

9. Ibid., 14.

10. Ibid.

11. Ibid., 18.

12. Ibid.
13. Ibid., 19.
14. Ibid.
15. Ibid.
16. Ibid., 22.
17. Ibid., 29.
18. Ibid., 24.
19. Ibid.
20. Adler, "The 'Learning Bureaucracy,'" 24.
21. Harry C. Katz, Thomas A. Kochan, and Kenneth R. Gobeille, "Industrial Relations Performance, Economic Performance, and QWL Programs: An Interplant Analysis," *Industrial and Labor Relations Review* 37 (1983), 14.
22. Harry C. Katz, Thomas A. Kochan, and Mark R. Weber, "Assessing the Effects of Industrial Relations Systems and Efforts to Improve the Quality of Working Life on Organizational Effectiveness," *Academy of Management Journal* 28 (1985), 516.
23. Ibid.
24. Ibid., 519.
25. Ibid., 94.
26. Ibid.
27. Ibid., 98–99.
28. Ibid., 99.
29. John Paul McDuffie, "Beyond Mass Production: Organizational Flexibility and Manufacturing Performance in the World Auto Industry," unpublished ms. (Philadelphia: The Wharton School, University of Pennsylvania, 1992).
30. Ibid., 23.
31. John T. Dunlop and David Weil, "Human Resource Innovations in the Apparel Industry: An Industrial Relations System Perspective," unpublished ms. (Cambridge, MA: Harvard University, 1992), 3.
32. Ibid., 1.
33. Ibid., 2.
34. Ibid., 9.
35. Ibid., 12.
36. Ibid.
37. Ibid., 15.
38. Ibid., 17.
39. Ibid., 32.
40. Ibid., 40.
41. Richard E. Walton, *Innovating to Compete* (San Francisco: Jossey-Bass, 1987), 35.
42. Ibid., 38.
43. Ibid., 33.
44. Ibid., 49.
45. Ibid., 65.
46. Ibid.
47. Ibid., 61.
48. Ibid., 89.
49. Casey Ichniowski, "The Effects of Grievance Activity on Productivity," *Industrial and Labor Relations Review* 40 (1986), 75–89.
50. Agis Salpukas, "Warning on Airline Labor Relations," *New York Times*, June 5, 1992, C4.

51. Ibid.

52. Ibid.

53. Walter J. Gershenfeld, "Employee Participation in Firm Decisions," in Morris M. Kleiner, Richard N. Block, Myron Rooimkin, and Sidney W. Salsburg (eds.), *Human Resources and the Performance of the Firm* (Madison, WI: Industrial Relations Research Association, 1987), 155.

54. Dunlop and Weil, "Human Resource Innovations," 29.

55. Ibid., 16.

56. Ibid., 16–17.

57. Ibid., 36.

58. Richard T. Pascale, *Managing on the Edge* (New York: Simon & Schuster, 1990).

59. William C. Freund and Eugene Epstein, *People and Productivity* (Homewood, IL: Dow Jones–Irwin, 1984), 119.

60. Edward E. Lawler III, Susan Albers Mohrman, and Gerald E. Ledford, Jr., *Employee Involvement and Total Quality Management* (San Francisco: Jossey-Bass, 1992).

61. Ibid., 44.

62. Ibid., 16.

63. Paul Osterman, "How Common Is Workplace Transformation and How Can We Explain Who Adopts It? Results from a National Survey," unpublished ms. (Cambridge, MA: Sloan School of Management, MIT, 1992), 5.

64. Ibid., 12.

65. Gilbert Fuchsberg, "Quality Programs Show Shoddy Results," *The Wall Street Journal*, May 14, 1992, B1.

66. Albert R. Karr, "Work Skills Panel Urges Major Changes in School Education, Job Organization," *The Wall Street Journal*, June 19, 1990, A4.

67. Gershenfeld, "Employee Participation," 143.

68. Paul S. Goodman, "Realities of Improving the Quality of Work Life," *Labor Law Journal* 31 (1980), 487–494.

69. Courtlandt Cammann, Edward E. Lawler III, Gerald E. Ledford, and Stanley E. Seashore, *Management-Labor Cooperation in Quality of Worklife Experiments: Comparative Analysis of Eight Cases* (Ann Arbor: Survey Research Center, University of Michigan, Report to the U.S. Department of Labor, 1984).

70. Tom Rankin, "Integrating QWL and Collective Bargaining," *Work-Life Review* 5 (July 1986), 14–18.

Chapter 4

1. "Frank Lorenzo, High Flier," *Business Week*, March 10, 1986, 104.

2. "Frank Lorenzo: TWA's Rescuer Is a Street Fighter," *Business Week*, July 1, 1985, 21.

3. Agis Salpukas, "Lorenzo Is Said to Be Charting a New Flight Plan," *New York Times*, February 3, 1993, C5.

4. David Halberstam, *The Reckoning* (New York: William Morrow, 1986).

5. William J. Goode, *The Celebration of Heroes* (Berkeley: University of California Press, 1978).

6. Robert H. Frank, *Passions within Reason: The Strategic Role of the Emotions* (New York: W. W. Norton, 1988), 237.

7. James N. Baron, "The Employment Relation as a Social Relation," *Journal of the Japanese and International Economies* 2 (1988), 494.

8. Lex Donaldson, "The Ethereal Hand: Organizational Economics and Management Theory," *Academy of Management Review* 15 (1990), 369.

9. Kathleen M. Eisenhardt, "Agency Theory: An Assessment and Review," *Academy of Management Review* 14 (1989), 58.

10. Oliver E. Williamson, *The Economic Institutions of Capitalism* (New York: Free Press, 1985), 47.

11. Ibid., 221.

12. Ibid., 231.

13. Donaldson, "The Ethereal Hand," 371–372.

14. Louis Trager, "New Attendance Rules Irk Macy's Workers," *San Francisco Examiner*, April 16, 1991, B1.

15. Julie Amparano Lopez, "When 'Big Brother' Watches, Workers Face Health Risks," *The Wall Street Journal*, October 5, 1990, C9.

16. Ibid.

17. Tupper Hull, "State: Sears Defrauds on Auto Repairs," *San Francisco Examiner*, June 11, 1992, A1.

18. Lawrence M. Fisher, "Accusation of Fraud at Sears," *New York Times*, June 12, 1992, C1, C12.

19. Keith Bradley, Saul Estrin, and Simon Taylor, "Employee Ownership and Company Performance," *Industrial Relations* 29 (1990), 386.

20. Williamson, *Economic Institutions*, 38.

21. Ibid., 266.

22. Saul Estrin and Derek Jones, "Can Employee-Owned Firms Survive?" Discussion Paper 316 (London: Centre for Labour Economics, London School of Economics, 1988), 1.

23. Saul Estrin and Derek Jones, "The Viability of Employee-Owned Firms: Evidence from France," *Industrial and Labor Relations Review* 45 (1992), 331.

24. Ibid., 335.

25. Katrina V. Berman, "The Worker-Owned Plywood Cooperatives," in Frank Lindenfeld and Joyce Rothschild-Whitt (eds.), *Workplace Democracy and Social Change* (Boston: Porter Sargent, 1982), 164.

26. Ibid., 167–168.

27. Saul Estrin, Derek C. Jones, and Jan Svejnar, "The Productivity Effects of Worker Participation: Producer Cooperatives in Western Economies," *Journal of Comparative Economics* 11 (1987), 57.

28. Ana Gutierrez Johnson and William Foote Whyte, "The Mondragon System of Worker Production Cooperatives," in Lindenfeld and Rothschild-Whitt (eds.), *Workplace Democracy and Social Change*, 177–197.

29. Henry M. Levin, "Employment and Productivity of Producer Cooperatives," in Robert Jackall and Henry M. Levin (eds.), *Worker Cooperatives in America* (Berkeley: University of California Press, 1984), 16–31.

30. Bradley, Estrin, and Taylor, "Employee Ownership," 389.

31. Ibid.

32. Ibid., 396.

33. John Case, "Collective Effort," *Inc.*, January 1992, 33.

34. Ibid., 38.

35. Mark R. Lepper and David Greene, "Turning Play into Work: Effects of Adult Surveillance and Extrinsic Rewards on Children's Intrinsic Motivation," *Journal of Personality and Social Psychology* 28 (1975), 480.

36. Edward Deci, *Intrinsic Motivation* (New York: Plenum, 1975).

37. Lepper and Greene, "Turning Play into Work," 484.

38. Lloyd H. Strickland, "Surveillance and Trust," *Journal of Personality* 26 (1958), 201.

39. See also Arie W. Kruglanski, "Attributing Trustworthiness in Supervisor-Worker Relations," *Journal of Experimental Social Psychology* 6 (1970), 214–232.

40. John H. Lingle, Timothy C. Brock, and Robert B. Cialdini, "Surveillance Instigates Entrapment When Violations Are Observed, When Personal Involvement Is High, and When Sanctions Are Severe," *Journal of Personality and Social Psychology* 35 (1977), 423.

41. Ibid.

42. David Kipnis, "Does Power Corrupt?" *Journal of Personality and Social Psychology* 24 (1972), 37.

43. Ibid., 37–38.

44. Ibid., 38.

45. Ibid., 39.

46. James R. Larson, Jr., and Christine Callahan, "Performance Monitoring: How It Affects Work Productivity," *Journal of Applied Psychology* 75 (1990), 530–538.

47. See, for instance, W. Peter Archibald, "Alternative Explanations for Self-Fulfilling Prophecy," *Psychological Bulletin* 81 (1974), 74–84; Dov Eden, "Self-Fulfilling Prophecy as a Management Tool: Harnessing Pygmalion," *Academy of Management Review* 9 (1984), 64–73; and J. Sterling Livingston, "Pygmalion in Management," *Harvard Business Review* 47 (July–August 1969), 81–89.

48. Mark Snyder, "Self-Fulfilling Stereotypes," *Psychology Today* 16 (July 1982), 60–68.

49. Jack W. Brehm, *A Theory of Psychological Reactance* (New York: Academic Press, 1966).

50. Robert B. Cialdini, *Influence: Science and Practice* (Glenview, IL: Scott, Foresman, 1988), 232.

51. Peter T. Kilborn, "Workers Using Computers Find a Supervisor Inside," *New York Times*, December 23, 1990, 1.

52. Gary T. Marx and Sanford Sherizen, "Monitoring on the Job: How to Protect Privacy as Well as Property," *Technology Review*, 1986, 67.

53. See, for instance, Robert G. Eccles and Nitin Nohria, *Beyond the Hype* (Boston: Harvard Business School Press, 1992); C. W. Morris, *Signs, Language and Behavior* (New York: Prentice-Hall, 1949); Jeffrey Pfeffer, *Managing with Power* (Boston: Harvard Business School Press, 1992); and Karl E. Weick, "Cognitive Processes in Organizations," in Barry M. Staw and Larry L. Cummings (eds.), *Research in Organizational Behavior*, vol. 1 (Greenwich, CT: JAI Press, 1979), 41–74.

54. Michael C. Jensen and William H. Meckling, "Theory of the Firm: Managerial Behavior, Agency Costs and Ownership Structure," *Journal of Financial Economics* 3 (1976), 308.

55. Ibid., 310, emphasis in original.

56. Williamson, *Economic Institutions*, 20.

57. Ibid., 21.

58. Robert H. Frank, Thomas Gilovich, and Dennis T. Regan, "Does Studying Economics Inhibit Cooperation?" *Journal of Economic Perspectives* 7 (1993), 159.

59. Ibid.

60. Ibid., 167.

61. Weick, "Cognitive Processes in Organizations," 42.

62. "Singapore Airlines (A)," Case 9-687-022 (Boston: Harvard Business School, 1986), 1.

63. Ibid., 1–2.

64. Steve Evans, Keith Ewing, and Peter Nolan, "Industrial Relations and the British Economy in the 1990s: Mrs. Thatcher's Legacy," *Journal of Management Studies* 29 (1992), 571.

65. Ibid., 572.
66. Ibid., 574.
67. Ibid., 576.
68. Ibid., 577.

Chapter 5

1. "Boise to Hire Workers to Replace Strikers," *Lake Charles American Press*, October 19, 1983, 1.

2. "Maine Strikers Join Picketers at Boise Mill," *St. Albans Messenger*, July 24, 1986, 1.

3. "Strike Hits Lumber Mill in Emmett," *Idaho Statesman*, June 20, 1988, 1.

4. "Boise Protest Erupts into Riot," *The Daily Journal*, September 11, 1989, 1.

5. Transcript of speech by John B. Fery to American Paper Institute's Presidents Forum, November 8, 1986, 1.

6. Ibid.

7. Ibid., 4.

8. Christopher Hill, "Discussion," *Past and Present* 29 (1964), 63.

9. Dan Clawson, *Bureaucracy and the Labor Process: The Transformation of U.S. Industry, 1860–1920* (New York: Monthly Review Press, 1980).

10. Ibid., 30.

11. Ibid., 41.

12. Jens Christiansen and Peter Philips, "The Transition from Outwork to Factory Production in the Boot and Shoe Industry, 1830–1880," in Sanford M. Jacoby (ed.), *Masters to Managers: Historical and Comparative Perspectives on American Employers* (New York: Columbia University Press, 1991), 21–42.

13. Clawson, *Bureaucracy and the Labor Process*, 71.

14. Ibid., 76.

15. Jeffrey Pfeffer and James N. Baron, "Taking the Workers Back Out: Recent Trends in the Structuring of Employment," in Barry M. Staw and Larry L. Cummings (eds.), *Research in Organizational Behavior*, vol. 10 (Greenwich, CT: JAI Press, 1988), 257–303.

16. Harry Braverman, *Labor and Monopoly Capital* (New York: Monthly Review Press, 1974), 57, emphasis in original.

17. Ibid., 68.

18. Clawson, *Bureaucracy and the Labor Process*, 81.

19. Richard C. Edwards, *Contested Terrain: The Transformation of the Workplace in the Twentieth Century* (New York: Basic Books, 1979), 27.

20. Sanford M. Jacoby, *Employing Bureaucracy: Managers, Unions, and the Transformation of Work in American Industry, 1900–1945* (New York: Columbia University Press, 1985).

21. Ibid., 20.

22. Robert Lacey, *Ford: The Men and the Machine* (New York: Ballantine, 1986), 130.

23. Larry J. Griffin, Michael E. Wallace, and Beth A. Rubin, "Capitalist Resistance to the Organization of Labor before the New Deal: Why? How? Success?" *American Sociological Review* 51 (1986), 150.

24. Jacoby, *Employing Bureaucracy*, 41.

25. Ibid.

26. Quoted in Braverman, *Labor and Monopoly Capital*, 112.

27. Ibid., 113.

28. Ibid., 118.

29. Ibid., 107, emphasis in original.

30. Jacoby, *Employing Bureaucracy*, 18.
31. Lacey, *Ford*, 69.
32. Griffin, Wallace, and Rubin, "Capitalist Resistance to the Organization of Labor," 156.
33. Ibid.
34. Ibid., 159.
35. Edwards, *Contested Terrain*, 131.
36. Sanford M. Jacoby, "American Exceptionalism Revisited: The Importance of Management," in Sanford M. Jacoby (ed.), *Masters to Managers*, 183.
37. Lacey, *Ford*, 362.
38. Philip Taft and Philip Ross, "American Labor Violence: Its Causes, Character, and Outcome," in Hugh Davis Graham and Ted Robert Gurr (eds.), *Violence in America: Historical and Comparative Perspectives*, vol. 1 (Washington, DC: U.S. Government Printing Office, 1969), 288–289.
39. Jacoby, "American Exceptionalism," 183.
40. Quoted in Taft and Ross, "American Labor Violence," 243.
41. Jacoby, "American Exceptionalism," 183.
42. Barbara Kingsolver, *Holding the Line: Women in the Great Arizona Mine Strike of 1983* (Ithaca, New York: ILR Press, 1989).
43. Lacey, *Ford*, 360.
44. Jacoby, "American Exceptionalism," 180.
45. Ibid., 181.
46. Paul S. Adler, "The 'Learning Bureaucracy': New United Motor Manufacturing, Inc.," in Barry M. Staw and Larry L. Cummings (eds.), *Research in Organizational Behavior* (Greenwich, CT: JAI Press, in press), 38–39.
47. Ibid., 82.

Chapter 6

1. Michael C. Jensen and William H. Meckling, "Theory of the Firm: Managerial Behavior, Agency Costs and Ownership Structure," *Journal of Financial Economics* 3 (1976), 308.
2. "AB Volvo—The Lundby Truck Production Plant (M)," Case 9-676-191 (Boston: Harvard Business School, 1976).
3. Richard E. Walton, *Innovating to Compete* (San Francisco: Jossey-Bass, 1987), 300.
4. Benjamin Aaron, "Employee Voice: A Legal Perspective," *California Management Review* 34 (1992), 129.
5. Andrew D. Hill, *"Wrongful Discharge" and the Derogation of the At-Will Employment Doctrine*, Labor Relations and Public Policy Series 31 (Philadelphia: Industrial Research Unit, The Wharton School, University of Pennsylvania, 1987), 11–12.
6. Constance E. Bagley, *Managers and the Legal Environment* (St. Paul: West, 1991), 338.
7. Hill, *"Wrongful Discharge,"* 9.
8. James N. Dertouzos, Elaine Holland, and Patricia Ebener, *The Legal and Economic Consequences of Wrongful Termination* (Santa Monica, CA: RAND Corporation, 1988), 9.
9. Hill, *"Wrongful Discharge,"* 10.
10. Dertouzos, Holland, and Ebener, *Wrongful Termination*, 15.
11. Milo Geyelin, "Fired Managers Winning More," *The Wall Street Journal*, September 7, 1989, B1.
12. Dertouzos, Holland, and Ebener, *Wrongful Termination*, 25.

13. Ibid., 53.

14. Ibid., 38.

15. Ibid., 40.

16. Ibid., 39.

17. Ira Michael Shepard, Paul Heylman, and Robert L. Duston, *Without Just Cause: An Employer's Practical and Legal Guide on Wrongful Discharge* (Washington, DC: Bureau of National Affairs, 1989), 21–22.

18. "Labor Letter," *The Wall Street Journal*, May 12, 1992, A1.

19. Shepard, Heylman, and Duston, *Without Just Cause*, 280–281, emphasis in original.

20. Robert J. Flanagan, *Labor Relations and the Litigation Explosion* (Washington, DC: The Brookings Institution, 1987), 1.

21. Ibid., 22.

22. Ibid., 3, emphasis added.

23. "Putting a Damper on That Old Team Spirit," *Business Week*, May 4, 1992, 60.

24. Ibid.

25. Flanagan, *Labor Relations*, 42.

26. Ibid., 20–21.

27. Isabel Wilkerson, "AT&T Settles Bias Suit for $66 Million," *New York Times*, July 18, 1991, A12.

28. "Labor Letter," A1.

29. William B. Gould, *Japan's Reshaping of American Labor Law* (Cambridge, MA: MIT Press, 1984), 30–31.

30. Quoted in Douglas M. McCabe and David Lewin, "Employee Voice: A Human Resource Management Perspective," *California Management Review* 34 (1992), 118.

31. Douglas M. McCabe, *Corporate Nonunion Complaint Procedures and Systems* (New York: Praeger, 1988).

32. "The Portman Hotel Company," Case 9-489-104 (Boston: Harvard Business School, 1989), 3.

Chapter 7

1. Thomas Karier, "Unions and the U.S. Comparative Advantage," *Industrial Relations* 30 (1991), 1.

2. Jeffrey H. Keefe, "Do Unions Influence the Diffusion of Technology?" *Industrial and Labor Relations Review* 44 (1991), 261–274.

3. Robert Drago, "Quality Circle Survival: An Exploratory Analysis," *Industrial Relations* 27 (1988), 336–351.

4. Stephen Jarrell and T. D. Stanley, "A Meta-Analysis of the Union-Nonunion Wage Gap," *Industrial and Labor Relations Review* 44 (1990), 54–67.

5. Richard B. Freeman and James L. Medoff, *What Do Unions Do?* (New York: Basic Books, 1984), 57.

6. Steve G. Allen, "Unionization and Productivity in Office Building and School Construction," *Industrial and Labor Relations Review* 39 (1986), 187–201.

7. Steve G. Allen, "The Effect of Unionism on Productivity in Privately and Publicly Owned Hospitals and Nursing Homes," *Journal of Labor Research* 7 (1986), 59–68.

8. Steve G. Allen, "Further Evidence on Union Efficiency in Construction," *Industrial Relations* 27 (1988), 232–240.

9. William M. Boal, "Unionism and Productivity in West Virginia Coal Mining," *Industrial and Labor Relations Review* 43 (1990), 390–405.

10. M. Connerton, R. B. Freeman, and J. L. Medoff, "Productivity and Industrial Relations: The Case of U.S. Bituminous Coal," unpublished ms. (Cambridge, MA: Harvard University, 1979).

11. Edward Kalachek and Fredric Raines, "Trade Unions and Hiring Standards," *Journal of Labor Research* 1 (1980), 73.

12. Freeman and Medoff, *What Do Unions Do?*

13. Jeffrey Pfeffer and Alison Davis-Blake, "Unions and Job Satisfaction: An Alternative View," *Work and Occupations* 17 (1990), 259–283.

14. See, for example, Freeman and Medoff, *What Do Unions Do?*

15. Ibid., 181.

16. Such studies include Craig A. Olson and Brian R. Becker, "The Effects of the NLRA on Stockholder Wealth in the Late 1930s," *Industrial and Labor Relations Review* 44 (1990), 116–129; and Richard S. Ruback and Martin B. Zimmerman, "Unionization and Profitability: Evidence from the Capital Market," *Journal of Political Economy* 92 (1984), 1134–1157.

17. Freeman and Medoff, *What Do Unions Do?*, 183.

18. Ibid., 186.

19. John J. Lawler, *Unionization and Deunionization: Strategy, Tactics, and Outcomes* (Columbia: University of South Carolina Press, 1990).

20. Ibid., 93.

21. Barbara Kingsolver, *Holding the Line: Women in the Great Arizona Mine Strike of 1983* (Ithaca, NY: ILR Press, 1989), 124.

22. Richard B. Freeman and Morris M. Kleiner, "Employer Behavior in the Face of Union Organizing Drives," *Industrial and Labor Relations Review* 43 (1990), 363.

23. Lawler, *Unionization and Deunionization*, 90.

24. Masahiko Aoki, *Information, Incentives, and Bargaining in the Japanese Economy* (Cambridge, U.K.: Cambridge University Press, 1988), 147.

25. Ibid., 182.

26. Ibid., 155.

27. David I. Levine and Laura D'Andrea Tyson, "Participation, Productivity, and the Firm's Environment," in Alan S. Blinder (ed.), *Paying for Productivity* (Washington, DC: The Brookings Institution, 1990), 183–243.

28. Ibid., 205.

29. "United Parcel Service (A)," Case 9-448-016 (Boston: Harvard Business School, 1987), 3.

30. Ibid.

31. Dana Milbank, "National Steel Claims Strength in Its Labor-Management Alloy," *The Wall Street Journal*, April 20, 1992, B1.

32. Ibid.

33. Barry Bluestone and Irving Bluestone, *Negotiating the Future* (New York: Basic Books, 1992), 101.

34. Ibid., 102.

35. Richard E. Walton, *Innovating to Compete* (San Francisco: Jossey-Bass, 1987), 300.

36. Paul S. Adler, "The 'Learning Bureaucracy': New United Motor Manufacturing, Inc.," in Barry M. Staw and Larry L. Cummings (eds.), *Research in Organizational Behavior* (Greenwich, CT: JAI Press, in press), 53.

37. Ibid.

38. Ibid., 56.

39. Bluestone and Bluestone, *Negotiating the Future*.

40. Clair Brown and Michael Reich, "When Does Union-Management Cooperation

Work? A Look at NUMMI and GM–Van Nuys," *California Management Review* 31 (Summer 1989), 34.

41. Ibid., 39.

42. Ibid., 40–41.

43. Michael L. Dertouzos, Richard K. Lester, and Robert M. Solow, *Made in America: Regaining the Productive Edge* (Cambridge, MA: MIT Press, 1989), 98–99.

Chapter 8

1. M. M. Petty, Bart Singleton, and David W. Connell, "An Experimental Evaluation of an Organizational Incentive Plan in the Electric Utility Industry," *Journal of Applied Psychology* 77 (1992), 428.

2. Ibid., 430.

3. Ibid.

4. Gary Johns, "Constraints on the Adoption of Psychology-Based Personnel Practices: Lessons from Organizational Innovation," *Personnel Psychology* (in press).

5. Ibid., 6.

6. Janice A. Klein, "Why Supervisors Resist Employee Involvement," *Harvard Business Review* 62 (September–October 1984), 87–95.

7. David L. Bradford and Alan R. Cohen, *Managing for Excellence* (New York: John Wiley, 1984).

8. Andrea Gabor, "After the Pay Revolution, Job Titles Won't Matter," *New York Times*, May 17, 1992, F5.

9. Jan Carlzon, *Moments of Truth* (Cambridge, MA: Ballinger, 1987), 25.

10. Ibid., 66.

11. Charlotte Gold, *Labor-Management Committees: Confrontation, Cooptation or Cooperation?* (Ithaca, NY: ILR Press, 1986).

12. Niccolo Machiavelli, *The Prince* (Baltimore: Penguin, 1961), 51.

13. Daniel Kahneman and Amos Tversky, "Choices, Values, and Frames," *American Psychologist* 39 (1984), 341–350.

14. Carlzon, *Moments of Truth*, 75–76.

15. H. Thomas Johnson and Robert S. Kaplan, *Relevance Lost: The Rise and Fall of Management Accounting* (Boston: Harvard Business School Press, 1987).

16. "How the New Math of Productivity Adds Up," *Business Week*, June 6, 1988, 103.

17. Ibid., 104.

18. Aaron Bernstein, *Grounded: Frank Lorenzo and the Destruction of Eastern Airlines* (New York: Simon & Schuster, 1990), 60.

19. Rodney Clark, *The Japanese Company* (New Haven, CT: Yale University Press, 1979), 109.

20. William B. Gould, *Japan's Reshaping of American Labor Law* (Cambridge, MA: MIT Press, 1984), 4–5.

21. Ibid., 5.

Chapter 9

1. For material on sociotechnical systems, see William A. Pasmore, *Designing Effective Organizations: The Sociotechnical Systems Perspective* (New York: John Wiley, 1988); W.

Pasmore and J. Sherwood (eds.), *Sociotechnical Systems: A Sourcebook* (San Diego: University Associates, 1978); and the classic article by E. Trist and K. Bamforth, "Some Social and Psychological Consequences of the Longwall Method of Coal-Getting," *Human Relations* 1 (1951), 3–38.

2. Robert G. Eccles and Nitin Nohria, *Beyond the Hype: Rediscovering the Essence of Management* (Boston: Harvard Business School Press, 1992), 4.

3. Ibid., 26.

4. Ibid., 10.

5. Ibid.

6. Ibid., 29.

7. National Institute of Standards and Technology, *1991 Application Guidelines: Malcolm Baldrige National Quality Award* (Gaithersburg, MD: NIST, 1991), inside back cover.

8. Ibid., 5.

9. Ibid., 3.

10. Ibid., 10.

11. Andrea Gabor, *The Man Who Discovered Quality* (New York: Times Books, 1990), 13.

12. "A Note on Quality: The Views of Deming, Juran, and Crosby," Case 9-687-011 (Boston: Harvard Business School, 1986), 8.

13. Ibid., 13.

14. Gabor, *The Man Who Discovered Quality*, 7–8.

15. Neal Templin, "Team Spirit: A Decisive Response to Crisis Brought Ford Enhanced Productivity," *The Wall Street Journal*, December 15, 1992, A1.

16. Ibid.

17. David Halberstam, *The Reckoning* (New York: William Morrow, 1986).

18. Gabor, *The Man Who Discovered Quality*, 132.

19. Ibid., 133.

20. Templin, "Team Spirit," A6.

21. National Institute of Standards and Technology, *Malcolm Baldrige National Quality Award: 1989 Winner Milliken & Company* (Gaithersburg, MD: NIST, 1989), 1.

22. Milliken & Company, *Milliken: Quality Leadership through Research* (Spartanburg, SC: Milliken & Company, 1988), 6–7.

23. Robert C. Hill and Sara M. Freedman, "Managing the Quality Process: Lessons from a Baldrige Award Winner," *Academy of Management Executive* 6 (1992), 78.

24. NIST, *1991 Application Guidelines*, front cover.

25. Ibid., inside back cover.

26. Ibid., inside front cover.

27. Quoted in Gabor, *The Man Who Discovered Quality*, 10.

28. Ibid., 18.

29. Ibid., 7.

30. Ibid., 29.

31. Quoted in Gabor, *The Man Who Discovered Quality*, 25.

32. Ibid., 19.

33. Ibid., 107.

34. Ibid., 149.

35. David A. Garvin, "How the Baldrige Award Really Works," *Harvard Business Review* 69 (November–December 1991), 93.

36. Robert E. Cole, *Strategies for Learning* (Berkeley: University of California Press, 1989), 13–14.

37. Ibid., 134.

38. Ibid.
39. Ibid., 135.
40. Ibid., 305–306.
41. Richard E. Walton, *Innovating to Compete* (San Francisco: Jossey-Bass, 1987), 257.
42. Ibid.
43. Garvin, "How the Baldrige Award Really Works," 80.
44. Gilbert Fuchsberg, "Quality Programs Show Shoddy Results," *The Wall Street Journal*, May 14, 1992, B1.

Chapter 10

1. Andrea Gabor, *The Man Who Discovered Quality* (New York: Times Books, 1990), 215.
2. Michelle Levander, "GM's Hard Lessons," *San Jose Mercury News*, April 30, 1990, 7D.
3. Barry Bluestone and Irving Bluestone, *Negotiating the Future* (New York: Basic Books, 1992), 87.
4. Thomas A. Kochan, Harry C. Katz, and Robert B. McKersie, *The Transformation of American Industrial Relations* (New York: Basic Books, 1986).
5. Thomas A. Kochan and Robert B. McKersie, "Human Resources, Organizational Governance, and Public Policy: Lessons from a Decade of Experimentation," in Thomas A. Kochan and Michael Useem (eds.), *Transforming Organizations* (New York: Oxford University Press, 1992), 171.
6. Ibid., 176.
7. "The Portman Hotel Company," Case 9-489-104 (Boston: Harvard Business School, 1989).
8. "People Express (A)," Case 483-103 (Boston: Harvard Business School, 1983).
9. Peter M. Senge, *The Fifth Discipline: The Art and Practice of the Learning Organization* (New York: Doubleday/Currency, 1990).
10. "AB Volvo—The Lundby Truck Production Plant (M)," Case 9-676-191 (Boston: Harvard Business School, 1976), 4–5.
11. Interview with James Doran of Advanced Micro Devices, November 6, 1992.
12. Hard copy of electronic-mail message from the Solectron Corporation, March 18, 1993.
13. "AB Volvo," 6.
14. Alan G. Robinson and Dean M. Schroeder, "Training, Continuous Improvement, and Human Relations: The U.S. TWI Programs and the Japanese Management Style," *California Management Review* 35 (1993), 35.
15. Ibid., 38.
16. Ibid., 44.
17. Ibid., 35–36, emphasis added.
18. Ibid., 55.
19. John Paul MacDuffie and John F. Krafcik, "Integrating Technology and Human Resources for High-Performance Manufacturing: Evidence from the International Auto Industry," in Kochan and Useem (eds.), *Transforming Organizations*, 212.
20. See, for instance, Thomas J. Peters and Robert H. Waterman, Jr., *In Search of Excellence: Lessons from America's Best-Run Companies* (New York: Harper & Row, 1982); and William Ouchi, *Theory Z* (Reading, MA: Addison-Wesley, 1981).
21. Hewlett-Packard, "The Test of Time," brochure reprinted from the March–April 1989 issue of *Measure* magazine, 2.

22. Interview with Pete Peterson of Hewlett-Packard, April 14, 1993.

23. Amitai Etzioni, *The Moral Dimension: Toward a New Economics* (New York: Free Press, 1988), 1.

24. Ibid., 4–5.

25. Ronald Dore, "Japan's Version of Managerial Capitalism," in Kochan and Useem (eds.), *Transforming Organizations*, 18.

26. "A Secret Is Shared," *Manufacturing Engineering* 100 (February 1988), 15.

Index